DRAMA

AN INTRODUCTION

Macmillan International College Edition

Titles of related interest:

General Editor: Professor A. N. Jeffares, University of Stirling

Ian Milligan: *The Novel in English: An Introduction*
Charles Barber: *Poetry in English: An Introduction*
Richard Taylor: *Understanding the Elements of Literature*
M. M. Badawi: *Background to Shakespeare*
Bruce King: *The New English Literatures*
Bruce King: *West Indian Literature*
S. H. Burton and C. J. H. Chacksfield: *African Poetry in English*

DRAMA
AN INTRODUCTION

G. J. Watson

M

First published 1983 by
THE MACMILLAN PRESS LTD
London and Basingstoke
Companies and representatives throughout the world

Typeset by
Cambrian Typesetters, Farnborough, Hants
Printed in Hong Kong

ISBN 0 333 32452 8
ISBN 0 333 32453 6 (paper)

For my brothers and sisters
Mary, Nora, Margaret, Gerard,
Robert and Richard

Contents

Foreword   ix

Introduction   xi

Acknowledgements   xii

1. **The Nature of Drama**   1

   Definitions   1
   Origins and Universality   2
   Stage Conditions   4
   The Physicality of the Stage   7
   Plot and Action   11
   The Language of Drama   13
   Reading and Seeing   18

2. **Sophoclean Tragedy**   19

   Oedipus the King   19
   Antigone   30

3. **Religion and Tragedy**   39

   Marlowe's *Faustus*: Morality Play or Tragedy?   40

4. **Shakespearean Tragedy**   49

   Character   49
   The Tragic Effect   50
   Hamlet: 'The Tragedy of a Man Who Could
      Not Make Up His Mind'?   50
   King Lear: Optimism, Pessimism and the
      Tragic Experience   62
   Macbeth: Shakespeare's Imagery   72

5. Comedy and Satire: *A Midsummer Night's
    Dream* and *Volpone* and Later
    Developments in Comedy   80

    Comedy as a Form   80
    Shakespeare: *A Midsummer Night's Dream*   81
    Ben Jonson: Non-Romantic Comedy   92
    Later Developments in Comedy   102

6. Ibsen and Miller: The Individual and Society   112

    Ibsen: Towards Modern Tragedy   112
    Hedda Gabler   116
    Miller's *Death of a Salesman*   125

7. Chekhov and the Drama of Social Change:
    The Cherry Orchard   132

8. Shaw and Brecht: 'Making Us Think'   147

    Shaw   147
    Brecht   157

9. Beckett and Pinter: Empty Spaces and
    Closed Rooms   171

    Beckett: Life Is Illusion   171
    Pinter: 'Stalking Round a Jungle'   186

    References   198

    Select Bibliography   204

    Index   215

Foreword

This *Introduction* rightly reminds us that drama is a communal act, the representation of crucial actions by living people on a stage in front of an audience. The history of drama goes back to remote origins: it is related to the myths and legends of a people; it has to do with such things as fertility cults; and it can be a powerful expression of religious worship. Such a history is inevitably complex. There have been periods of intense activity, impressive achievement, such as those when the great Greek dramatists, the tragedians Aeschylus, Sophocles and Euripides, and the comic writer Aristophanes, enriched the life of the Athenians and subsequent audiences up to those of our time, or when the Elizabethan and Jacobean dramatists, nobly headed by Marlowe, Shakespeare and Jonson, gave the English language memorable expression in a vast variety of plays. Ben Jonson's remark that Shakespeare was not of an age but for all time is a test to apply to all other dramatists as well: do they last the course? Have they still an impact upon a modern audience; does their presentation of human action — and inaction — at crucial moments in the lives of the characters they create still excite us, move us, enrich us, cause us to reflect? The answers to such questions are, perhaps, surprisingly often, yes — surprisingly to those who have not realised the power of literature to make specific situations and responses to them universal.

Great drama, as Dr Watson shows us so effectively in this book, has its lasting immediacy. He has selected plays from different periods of history, from different cultures, to illustrate the nature of dramatic art in the English language, and so he considers the Greeks, the Elizabethans, the comic dramatists of the seventeenth and eighteenth centuries, while also examining the treatment of society in more recent authors such as the Norwegian Ibsen, the American Arthur Miller, the Russian Chekhov. He comments on contemporary writers — the Nigerian authors Soyinka and John Pepper Clark, for instance, and various Australian dramatists as well as on the dramatists of the earlier part of this century who, in Yeats's case, cast the Irish legends and, in Synge's and O'Casey's, the life and language of the Irish countryside and city, into an exuberant vitality of language. And Dr Watson also shows us the techniques of the theatre employed by the Anglo-Irish dramatist Shaw and the German Brecht in compelling audiences to think for themselves, to look at contemporary conventions critically. More than this, he turns our attention to the new and often apparently difficult plays of Samuel Beckett and Harold Pinter, explaining some of the reasons why they write their particular kinds of play.

This *Introduction*, then, is one that shows us the vast scope of drama, that suggests ways of studying it, that stimulates us by conveying the author's sense of enjoyment in considering the power of drama to move all of us, however different our backgrounds and interests, to express — by concentrating upon particular situations — the variety and yet the universality of human experience.

Stirling, 1982   *A. N. Jeffares*

Introduction

This book is aimed at students working for 'A' level examin-
ations, and should also be useful for first-year university
students of English.

The book attempts to sharpen the student's sense of the
special nature of drama as a genre, and of its variety and
power. It offers detailed critical appreciation of the nature
and effectiveness of dramatic methods within a number of
great plays, selected from a range of different cultures and
historical periods. It proceeds on the principle that the
student will derive a livelier critical understanding of major
terms — tragedy, comedy, poetic drama, naturalist theatre,
and so on — by working outwards towards them from individual plays, rather than by working inwards from the
abstractions of general theory. The plays have not been
chosen at random, but to invite comparison and contrast of
different theatrical methods and dramatic strategies. At the
same time, each dramatist is seen in relation to his social and
cultural context.

A brief bibliography is appended.

Acknowledgements

The author and publishers wish to thank the following who have kindly given permission for the use of copyright material:

Associated Book Publishers Ltd and Pantheon Books (a Division of Random House, Inc.) for extracts from Bertolt Brecht's 'Mother Courage and Her Children' translated by Eric Bentley, and in the U.S. by Ralph Manheim, and 'The Good Person of Szechwan' translated by John Willett, in *Plays*, Volume II, published by Methuen & Co., London; extracts from *Pinter: A Study of His Plays* by Martin Esslin, and *The Birthday Party* by Harold Pinter, both published by Methuen & Co., London.

Faber & Faber Ltd and Grove Press Inc., for extracts from *Waiting for Godot* by Samuel Beckett (U.S. Copyright © 1954 by Grove Press Inc., renewed 1982 by Samuel Beckett).

Elaine Greene Ltd on behalf of Arthur Miller for an extract from the Introduction to the *Collected Plays* published by Secker & Warburg, copyright © 1958 by Arthur Miller, and a speech from *Death of a Salesman*, copyright © 1949 by Arthur Miller.

David Higham Associates Ltd on behalf of Michael Meyer for extracts from his translation of *Hedda Gabler* by Henrik Ibsen.

Oxford University Press for extracts from Wole Soyinka's *Collected Plays* Vols I & II. Copyright © Wole Soyinka 1963.

Penguin Books Ltd for extracts from *King Oedipus* and from *Antigone* in *Sophocles: The Theban Plays* translated by E F Watling (Penguin Classics 1947) Copyright © E F Watling 1947, and renewed 1974.

The Society of Authors on behalf of the Bernard Shaw Estate for extracts from *Man and Superman*.

1 *The Nature of Drama*

Definitions

There are almost as many definitions of drama as there are
critics of it, but from some representative remarks we can
establish the essential elements of the form. G. B. Tennyson
says: 'Drama is a story that people act out on a stage before
spectators.' Eric Bentley remarks: 'The theatrical situation,
reduced to a minimum, is that A impersonates B while C
looks on.' For Marjorie Boulton, a play 'is not really a piece
of literature for reading. A true play is three-dimensional; it
is literature that walks and talks before our eyes'.[1] The crucial
stresses are, again and again, on the *theatricality* of drama,
that it is an art which requires performance on a stage for its
full effect; that it involves real-life people pretending to be
imagined people; and that it places particular emphasis on
action, of a concentrated, often intense, kind. The primacy
of action in drama is a product of the peculiarly physical
nature of the form:

> When we ask what it is that drama can do better than any-
> thing else, we find that plot and character can be done
> nearly as well in most respects, and in point of fulness and
> detail much better, by the novel or other narrative forms
> of writing, but that the drama being a visible show is
> incomparable for crises, for those sudden turns of action
> which the eye takes in at a glance before a word is spoken,
> with the double advantage of a thrill for the audience and
> a saving of space for the dramatist. These critical moments
> are its moments of triumph, and a born dramatist so
> contrives his plot that a number of these follow one another
> in an ascending scale of excitement.[2]

Drama, then, is representation of carefully selected actions by living people on a stage in front of an audience.

Origins and Universality

Drama is a communal art involving a group of performers and a larger group who watch the performance. This communal aspect of drama is rooted in its remote origins, in primitive fertility rites and in religious observances. Drama's relationship to the myths, legends and folk observances of a culture is the major source of its power. The plays of Wole Soyinka (b. 1934), for example, are firmly rooted in aspects of the religion and myths of the Yoruba people of Nigeria. *The Road* (1965) is based on the Egungun ceremony in which a human is ritually possessed by the god Ogun, who created the bridge between men and gods. The title refers to his courageous journey across the original chaos. Murano, the Professor's servant, though mute because of an accident, is a symbolic character who is arrested between the divine and human worlds. Possessed by Ogun, he is in touch with a spiritual mystery which defies rational comprehension. The Professor's quest for illumination — his 'road' — fails because of his attempts to comprehend rationally the incomprehensible. Another Nigerian dramatist, J. P. Clark (b. 1935) bases his *Ozidi* (1977) on a week-long ceremonial ritual performed by the Ijaw people of the Niger Delta. The play is vitalised by its use of African imagery, drums and masks. Robert Serumaga (b. 1939) in his play *Renga Moi* (1975) similarly uses traditional art forms in an exciting and exhilarating assertion of African cultural vitality. Though Malawian drama in English, in the works of writers such as James Ng'ombe (b. 1949), Joe Mosiwa (b. 1950) and Chris F. Kamlongera (b. 1949), has been written mainly for schools and radio broadcasts, the possibilities of an exciting cross-fertilisation with the traditional *nyau* of the area are evident. *Nyau* is a form of spirit worship among the Mang'anja, originating in a myth which relates how the primal unity of man, animal and spirit was broken by man's invention of fire. The masks, dances and symbolism of *nyau* ceremonial comprise the basis for a fruitful indigenous dramatic tradition.

At the beginning of this century, English drama was revitalised by the use of Irish legend, folk-tale and symbolism, and by the use of Irish idioms, in the plays of W. B. Yeats (1865–1939) and J. M. Synge (1871–1909). Synge's *The Shadow of the Glen* (1903) and *Riders to the Sea* (1904) deal with elemental situations which cross cultural boundaries. Indeed, the Ugandan dramatist Erisa Kironde (b. 1940) in *The Trick* (1966) has effectively transposed *The Shadow of the Glen* into an African setting. Another Ugandan, Tom Omara (b. 1946), in his short play *The Exodus* (1965) uses a mythic story of quarrelling triplets to illuminate the 'divisions between brothers who live east, west and south of the mighty river Nile'. K. Das (b. 1929) did much to give confidence to the fledgling Malaysian theatre with his *Lela Mayang* (1968), an effectively tragic dramatisation of a traditional tale.

Both Greek and British drama were originally closely connected with religious worship, and although in each case the drama was secularised quite rapidly, it can still call upon powerful ritualised effects when necessary. The theatrical effect is to *involve* the audience (in a way a reader cannot be involved) in celebration of the fertility of life, as in the multiple marriages that end the comedies of Shakespeare (1564–1616), *As You Like It* (1599) and *A Midsummer Night's Dream* (1595?). The choric song at the end of a Greek tragedy strikes the note of solemn wonder and fear at life's mysteriousness and terror; and the brilliantly stylised chanting of the horrors of war in the second Act of *The Silver Tassie* (1928) by Sean O'Casey (1890–1964) has a similar ritualised power. The ritualistic aspects of a play such as Wole Soyinka's *A Dance of the Forests* (1960) are noticeable, because this is a drama of our time which springs from a culture where gods and men are still felt to be in communication. And even in the industrialised modern Western world, some part of the ancient, ritual power of drama can be glimpsed in plays such as *Royal Hunt of the Sun* (1964) and *Equus* (1973) by Peter Shaffer (1926–82), and the ironically titled *Savages* (1973) by Christopher Hampton (b. 1946).

The universal appeal of drama, however, is not based on the longevity of the form, but on its *naturalness*. The impulse to act and to imitate can be observed quite easily in any young child in any part of the world: it seems instinctive, and psychologists point out that it is one of the most educative processes for the child. Delight in impersonation, mimicry and dressing up does not fade with childhood — witness the popularity of certain television mimics, the festive masks of the carnival and fancy-dress party, even the robes, uniforms, gowns and wigs worn by members of various professions, garb chosen often not so much for utility as for an outward sign of a public role being performed by the individual. Drama works through many artificial conventions, such as the chorus and soliloquy, but all of us share, to a greater or lesser extent, the histrionic impulse drawn on and shaped by the dramatist.

Stage Conditions

It is not profitable to speculate on whether the vision and structure of a play demanded a certain kind of stage, or whether the physical nature of the stage at any given time in the history of the drama conditioned the kind of drama produced. It was — and is — probably a reciprocal process. What is crucial, since drama is at least as much a thing of the stage as of the page, is the need to develop and exercise our theatrical imaginations, and this requires some knowledge of stage conditions and techniques.

Greek drama was presented in huge amphitheatres, which could accommodate as many as fifteen thousand spectators. The audience sat in tiers almost completely around the stage, which was about sixty or seventy feet across. Scenery was non-existent or minimal, and in the plays of Sophocles there were only three actors apart from the chorus, a group who spoke, sang and danced in unison. The size of both stage and audience area encouraged the actors to wear stylised masks, indicative of either their status or the emotions they experienced. Movement was very formalised, and obviously speech had to be declaimed formally. Greek drama, then, and especially Greek tragedy, exists on an austere, uncluttered stage that is well suited to the gravity and amplitude of the plays, which do not pretend in the dignified eloquence of their larger-than-life characters to give us a 'slice of life', any more than the Greek stage aims at realistic effects. The Elizabethan playhouse was also circular, though much smaller and partly enclosed. The greatest difference between it and the Greek theatre consisted in its platform stage, which projected out into an audience who surrounded it on three sides, while other (usually wealthier) spectators sat around the stage higher up in covered galleries. Though still basically declamatory, as witness the soaring grandeur of what Ben Jonson, in his elegy on Shakespeare, called 'Marlowe's mighty line' and the great set-piece verse speeches of Shakespeare's tragic heroes, Elizabethan acting styles could be more intimate than Greek styles, because of the relative proximity of the audience. This encouraged the wonderfully flexible tone of much Elizabethan drama: it can accommodate both the stately formality of the 'love-contest' that opens *King Lear* and the impudent colloquial informality of Edmund's prose soliloquy shortly afterwards. Further, the action could take place on this platform stage, but also on an inner stage, and on balconies and galleries over the stage. There was a 'tiring house' back stage for costuming and retiral, so the plays were not, as Greek plays were, bound by the extra intensities of unity of action, place and time. Indeed, as Muriel Bradbrook says, the chief characteristic of Shakespeare's stage is its neutrality and its corresponding virtue, flexibility: 'the un-localised drama . . . allowed Shakespeare to indulge in loose flowing construction, episodic plots, and complex action'.[3] The austere, single-scene focus of the *Antigone* (*c*. 442 BC) of Sophocles (*c*. 496—406 BC) gives the play *its* power; the multitude of short bustling scenes in Shakespeare's *Antony and Cleopatra* (1607) contributes greatly to our sense of the fate of the then known world being at issue.

Neither Greek nor Elizabethan drama is naturalistic, though the Elizabethan is less formal. From the late seventeenth century, however, the proscenium, or picture-frame, stage became ever more popular, and this led to a much greater emphasis on 'realism', both in terms of acting styles and in settings. Elaborately detailed dispositions for the inclusion and placing of furniture in, for example, many of the plays of Ibsen (1828—1906), Chekhov (1860—1904) and O'Casey are designed to convey to an audience a strong sense of the reality of the illusion before it. Indeed, sometimes this kind of staging is called 'fourth-wall theatre': the audience constitutes the fourth wall of an imaginary room, the actors perform before them in the space of the other three walls, and studiously ignore — or pretend to ignore — all the people watching them. This is, of course, just as artificial a convention — in fact, in some ways even more extraordinary — than the more obvious non-naturalistic conventions of older theatres, such as the Greek chorus or the Elizabethan soliloquy, which frankly acknowledge the presence of the audience. Though dramatists such as Pirandello (1867–1936) and Brecht (1898–1956) and, in different ways, Shaw (1856–1950) and Beckett (b. 1906), have objected to fourth-wall theatre on the grounds that it tends to encourage verisimilitude (the illusion of reality) for its own sake, and that it lacks the flexibility of older theatrical modes, it does have its own strengths. It encourages the depiction of character in intensely intimate psychological terms, for example; and the realism of setting can, in skilled hands, make powerful dramatic points. The claustrophobia which Ibsen's Hedda Gabler feels in her constricted life, for instance, is economically suggested by the room in which she is first presented to us; and the grim poverty of the exploited lives of South African blacks in *The Blood Knot* (1961) by Athol Fugard (b. 1932) is conveyed not only by the sad ritual of poor Zach's nightly foot-washing, but by the fact that the action never moves outside the one-room shack in which the play opens:

> *The walls are a patchwork of scraps of corrugated iron, packing-case wood, flattened cardboard boxes, and old hessian bags. There is one door, one window (no curtains), two beds, a table, and two chairs. Also in evidence is a cupboard of sorts with an oil-stove, a kettle, and a few pots. The shack is tidy and swept, but this only enhances the poverty of its furnishings.*

A similar authenticity gives *Boesman and Lena*, a later play (1969) by Fugard, its power, and the shocking brutality of the white man's bulldozing of the blacks' temporary shack is captured equally well in the realistic dialogue appropriate to this kind of theatre, as in Lena's bleak phrase, 'Put your life on your head and walk, sister.' The naturalistic style of *The Need to Be* (1970) by Patrick Yeoh (b. 1941) likewise does much to convey the realities of the appalling poverty of life in the squatter areas of Kuala Lumpur, where 'happiness' is a better-quality cigarette. Sarif Easmon (b. 1930) of Sierra Leone in his *The New Patriots* (1966) also uses the naturalistic method to dramatise the problems of tribalism and corruption. Clearly, naturalism is especially appropriate for plays of social comment. There is a direct link between the so-called 'problem' plays of the middle-period Ibsen and a work such as *Sons and Daughters* (1964) by the Ghanaian J. C. de Graft (b. 1932), which focuses on the clash between traditional ways of life and new middle-class attitudes.

The Physicality of the Stage

Though stage conditions have altered over the centuries and in different cultural contexts, the physical nature of a stage performance is pre-eminently what distinguishes drama from the other literary arts. The novel can do certain things which are impossible to portray on the stage, but, by the same token, the combination of actor, set, words and movement gives to drama its special power, enabling it to work simultaneously on many aspects of an audience's sensibilities. Even the reader of a play-text, to experience it in all its fullness, must, as it were, perform the whole play in his imagination. In Wole Soyinka's *Kongi's Harvest* (1967) the dictator Kongi's attempt to usurp the authority of the traditional rulers by eating the first yam at the harvest festival is frustrated in the horrific moment when he is served, instead of the symbolic yam, the head of a victim he has executed. On the stage this is intensely exciting and evidences the marvellous theatricality of Soyinka's imagination:

> *The rhythm of pounding emerges triumphant, the dance grows frenzied. Above it all on the dais, Kongi, getting progressively inspired, harangues his audience in words*

drowned in the bacchanal. He exhorts, declaims, reviles, cajoles, damns, curses, vilifies, excommunicates, execrates until he is a demonic mass of sweat and foam at the lips. Segi returns, disappears into the area of pestles. A copper salver is raised suddenly high; it passes from hands to hands above the women's heads, they dance with it on their heads; it is thrown from one to the other until at last it reaches Kongi's table and Segi throws open the lid. In it, the head of an old man.
In the ensuing scramble, no one is left but Kongi and the head, Kongi's mouth wide open in speechless terror.
A sudden blackout on both.

Stripped of the dancing and chanting, of the sudden arrest of motion and the plunge into darkness, the moment clearly loses much. In certain ways, this *coup de théâtre* is reminiscent of the dumb Kattrin's frenzied drumming in an attempt to waken the sleeping town at the end of Brecht's *Mother Courage and her Children* (1947). The sudden physical shock which drama conveys so well is not, of course, dependent on noise — witness the powerful moment in *King Lear*:

Albany. The gods defend her! Bear him hence awhile.
[Edmund is borne off.]
[Enter Lear, with Cordelia in his arms.]

In fact, many dramatists have exploited the effects of silence on the stage, evidence of drama's ability to work through non-verbal means. Iago's tight-lipped refusal to explain himself, at the end of Shakespeare's *Othello* (1604), adds the final touch of horror to a superb portrait of malevolence. In its different way, the silent exit of Thiono at the end of *The Black Hermit* (1968) by Ngugi wa Thiong'o (b. 1938) says much more than words could. Beckett and Pinter (b. 1930) are especially expert in the use of dramatic silence for effects of poetry or menace. And one of the finest dramatic examples of all is the agonised silence of Brecht's Mother Courage when brutally presented with the body of her dead son, Swiss Cheese, whom she dare not admit to recognising.
Other aspects of the immediate physicality of drama,

equally important, include the use of the physical grouping of the actors, the use of colour for visual impact, and the ability to juxtapose, for effects of immediate contrast or comparison, differing dramatic voices and contexts. In Sophocles's *Antigone*, for example, the main conflict — that between private and public viewpoints — is brought home at once by the simple device of presenting the two sisters of the doomed family, Ismene and Antigone, alone and quarrelling then separating in the middle of the huge amphitheatre, which is followed by the chorus of Theban elders singing an ode to the civic glory of their city. There is, too, an extreme poignancy in the solitary appearance of the old servant, Firs, at the end of Chekhov's *The Cherry Orchard* (1904) immediately after the crowded bustle of the departure of the family he has served for so long and who have now forgotten him. Likewise, nobody can fail to notice Hamlet's silence and distance from the rest of the court on his first appearance in Shakespeare's tragedy (1601) while Claudius deals at some length with his recent marriage, the military threat from Norway, and the request from young Laertes to return to France.

Hamlet's solitariness is emphasised by his clothes of mourning, his 'inky cloak', in marked contrast to the gaudiness of dress worn by the rest of the court in honour of the marriage of Gertrude and Claudius. The comedy of Malvolio's simpering appearance before Olivia, in Shakespeare's *Twelfth Night* (1600?) — 'Sweet lady, ho ho!' — is enhanced enormously by his ridiculous dress, in yellow stockings and cross-gartered. The comic dramatists of the Restoration period similarly employ ridiculously gaudy costume to emphasise the affectation of the silly fops who strut on their stage. In *The Cherry Orchard* Chekhov uses the mute white purity of the orchard for a number of strong symbolic effects: for Mrs Ranevsky especially, it stands for the innocence of a way of life now irrevocably lost. The dramatic impact of the powerfully anti-colonialist play *Sergeant Musgrave's Dance* (1959), by John Arden (b. 1930), is largely bound up with its use of colour. Four deserters from the British Army, who have been engaged in punitive colonial action, bring back the skeleton of a dead comrade to the mining town in England in which he was born. At the play's climax, they hoist the skeleton, draped in its red army tunic, before the townspeople in an attempt to bring home to them the realities of war. The white of the skeleton's bones and the white of a freezing winter, the black of the coal which the miners produce and the black of death, the red of the soldiers' uniforms and of blood, the gold of girls' hair and of money, the green of growth and fertility — all these emphasise how the play's effects are gained by a use of primary colour; they culminate in the white bones showing grotesquely through the red uniform.

Many of these effects are achieved through drama's suitability for and tendency towards striking juxtapositions. Put most simply, drama can show many different things happening at once. Sean O'Casey's plays about Ireland's turbulent history in the early part of this century do this very successfully. For instance, in the second act of *Juno and the Paycock* (1924), the bibulous party in the Boyles' tenement flat is cut across by the grief-stricken mother setting out for her murdered son's funeral; the act ends with yet another violent clash of contexts as young Boyle encounters harsh political fanaticism while the crowd's prayers at the funeral provide an ironic counterpoint:

> *The Young Man:* Boyle, no man can do enough for Ireland!
> *[He goes. Faintly in the distance the crowd is heard saying:]*
> Hail Mary, full of grace, the Lord is with Thee;
> Blessed art Thou amongst women . . .

The last act of *The Plough and the Stars* (1926) brings the ironic tragi-comedy of life to an even sharper point, simultaneously dramatising the immediacy of death and the incorrigible mundanity of the living. Dublin is burning at the height of the Easter Rising. The setting again is a tenement, containing the coffin of a consumptive girl and a still-born child:

> *The dusk has well fallen, and the glare of the burning buildings in the town can be seen through the windows, in the distant sky. The Covey and Fluther have been playing*

cards, sitting on the floor by the light of the candles on the stool near the coffin. When the curtain rises the Covey is shuffling the cards, Peter is sitting in a stiff, dignified way beside him, and Fluther is kneeling beside the window, cautiously looking out.
Fluther [furtively peeping out of the window]. Give them a good shuffling . . . Th' sky's getting reddher and reddher.

This form of contrast, though relatively simple, is undeniably powerful; equally powerful and more complex aspects of dramatic simultaneity can be found in the plays-within-the-play in Shakespeare's *Midsummer Night's Dream* and *Hamlet*.

Plot and Action

These physical aspects of the stage, and the presence of an audience, impose certain limitations on the dramatic form. The plot and action must, of necessity, be highly selective and relatively bold and clear to accommodate what Shakespeare calls 'the two hours' traffic of our stage'. The dramatist must forgo some of the effects exploited by the novelist —his form cannot encompass the lovingly detailed descriptions of landscape given us by Hardy (1840–1928) for example, or the robust authorial interventions so common in the works of Fielding (1707–54), Dickens (1812–70) and Thackeray (1811–63), or the refined subtleties and nuances of the later novels of Henry James (1843–1916). The limitations of drama are also, however, its virtues. The selectivity of the plot, the brevity of the action, make for economy and intensity and a satisfying sense of interconnectedness and causality. A large part of the impact of *Othello*, for example, is due to the speed with which it hurtles towards its catastrophe. An audience watching Iago's machinations unfold on the stage is not given time to speculate on the unlikelihood of Othello's words about Desdemona's stolen hours of lust having — even for him — the remotest basis in fact. The sheer concentration of effects in drama suits well with its natural tendency to deal with human beings in conflict and crisis of a passionate kind. The theatre is a place of excitement. Beginning with

Aristotle, the great Greek philosopher (384–322 BC) who wrote an important treatise on tragedy called *The Poetics*, critics have stressed the primacy of action in drama, and rightly, since what it deals with is people *doing* things to others and to themselves. The general shape of dramatic action — a formula which works for most plays — is five-fold. There is an introduction or exposition, which gives the audience necessary basic information. Some complication then produces the second stage of 'rising action', where the tempo of events increases; then there is a crisis or turning point (as, for example, when Othello and Iago solemnly pledge themselves to vengeance on Desdemona and Cassio); the next phase is a 'falling action', usually involving some slackening of the tension; and finally the climax or catastrophe.

This is, of course, only a formula. Part of the satisfaction offered by drama is the way in which different dramatists create variations on this basic structure of action. Ibsen's *The Wild Duck* (1884), for example, has a leisurely and 'traditional' exposition in which two servants, in discussing the family they work for, put us in possession of vital information. The first scene of Shakespeare's *Othello* also gives us necessary information, but the tone is feverishly excited as Roderigo and Iago disturb the peace of Brabantio's sleeping household with their shouted crudities about Othello — all is bustle and confusion and urgency. Shakespeare's *Macbeth* ends with a note of order restored after cataclysmic upheaval; this is very different from the ending of *Dr Faustus* (1592) by Marlowe (1564–93), where the hero's terror is caught brilliantly in the powerful imagery and broken rhythms of his last soliloquy. Indeed, certain dramatists create the particular and individual quality of their plays by deliberately flouting expectations based on the usual shape of a dramatic action. Brecht invites *us* to create a satisfactory ending for his *Good Woman of Setzuan* (1943); and the ending of Beckett's *Waiting for Godot* (1952) is clearly in one sense a *non-ending*:

    Vladimir: Well? Shall we go?
    Estragon: Yes. Let's go.
    [They do not move.]

Indeed, the plays of both Chekhov and Beckett are dramatic paradoxically to the extent that in the apparently random inconsequentiality of the characters' speech and actions they seem to abandon drama's ancient stress on 'tight' plotting and concentrated action. Nevertheless, works such as *The Cherry Orchard* and *Waiting for Godot* could not achieve their strange and haunting effects were it not for every audience's automatic connection of a play with action.

The Language of Drama

It is necessary to stress the theatrical, physical aspects of any play since so many of us have only limited or occasional access to a theatre, and may tend to regard a play as merely an animated novel. However, to say this is not to undervalue the verbal, 'literary' aspects of a play. The text is clearly the basis on which everything rests. The actor must begin his interpretation of a character from the dramatist's words; the director's vision of the whole work will equally be dependent on those words.

We realise the crucial role of the words when we make the simple reflection that every single idea, fact or viewpoint in a play has to be spoken aloud. The dialogue is all the language of a play: the author cannot intrude with explanatory, evaluative or descriptive passages of comment as the novelist may. His dialogue must further the plot, illuminate character, create an appropriate atmosphere or tone and enable the audience to grasp the underlying theme or moral idea of the play, and do all these things simultaneously. As with other features of the dramatist's art, this requires a high degree of selectivity and concentration, as much in prose as in verse.

It will readily be seen that even 'realistic' prose on the stage is, in fact, highly shaped and polished to create the required dramatic effect, while preserving an appearance of naturalness. Harold Pinter, for example, is much praised for the authenticity of his dialogue, and it is true that in a play like *The Caretaker* (1960) he does show a wonderful ear for the cadences and syntax of uneducated English speech. But the dialogue of the tramp Davies is constructed around a series of repeated and interwoven motifs, such as his racial prejudice, his fixation with his shoes, and his image of his own fastidiousness. Thus in the opening sequence of the play he curses 'all them Greeks . . . Poles, Greeks, Blacks, the lot of them, all them aliens', abuses the 'Scotch git' at his work-place, and a little later reveals in his story of the trip to the monastery at Luton to pick up some shoes that one of the 'bastard monks' was an 'Irish hooligan'. At the start he mentions that he left his wife because she washed her underclothes in the vegetable pan, whereas *he* has 'eaten [his] dinner off the best of plates'. This motif is repeated most amusingly later when Davies boasts proudly of his mate in Shepherd's Bush who runs the best public lavatory, and who always slips Davies the best soap. The point is that each of Davies's remarks taken on its own has the *apparent* inconsequentiality of ordinary speech, but has actually been used by the dramatist in a deliberate artistic pattern which helps to unify the character and the play, and creates subtle comic effects. A similar 'poetry' arising out of a sense of the vigour of the colloquial and vernacular, even of slang, enriches the dramas of the Australians Jack Hibberd (b. 1940) and Alexander Buso (b. 1944): the former's *A Stretch of the Imagination* (1971) and the latter's *The Front-Room Boys* (1969) and *Coralie Lansdowne Says 'No'* (1974) illustrate the comedy, the cruelty and the occasional elegance of 'vulgar' speech. Athol Fugard in *Sizwe Bansi Is Dead* (1972) wonderfully exploits the gap between the threatening pomposity of the Afrikaans speech of the Ford plant managers and the humorous obscenity of the black workers ('Big-shot cunt from America coming to visit you . . . Mr Ford is the grandmother baas of them all').

Witty or comic dramatists positively delight in stressing the artificiality of their dialogue. They make a feature, as it were, of the necessary stylisation of dramatic language. The elegant polish of such dialogue is a pleasure in itself, but it is also an appropriate means of suggesting the modish artificiality of a whole group of society, or of a prevailing code of manners, as in Restoration comedy and in *The Importance of Being Earnest* (1895) by Oscar Wilde (1854—1900). These dramatists are more than half in love with the butterfly worlds they create; and the very explicitness with which their dialogue measures and creates their artificial worlds is disarming, and makes us fall half in love with them too.

Dramatic language is nearly always far more energetic than 'ordinary speech', a difference caused by the concentration and intensity of the mode. The dynamism of the language is itself intimately connected with the 'doing' aspect of drama, its stress on action. In Soyinka's *A Dance of the Forests*, for instance, the tree-imp Murete addresses Eshuoro, a wayward spirit, in superbly dynamic vituperation: 'Why . . . you . . . mucus off a crab's carbuncle. You stream of fig pus from the duct of a stumbling bat . . . You are only the greasy recesses of a rodent's nest.' Vituperation can be expected to be vigorous. But notice how, in the following, J. M. Synge's dramatic language turns even a funeral into a kind of comic—heroic epic encounter, where the coffin is launched, as it were, on seas of alcohol. The passage is from *The Playboy of the Western World* (1907):

> wasn't it a shame I didn't bear you along with me to Kate Cassidy's wake, a fine, stout lad, the like of you, for you'd never see the match of it for flows of drink, the way when we sunk her bones at noonday in her narrow grave, there were five men, aye, and six men, stretched out retching speechless on the holy stones.

A marked feature of Synge's dramatic language is its poetic quality — 'stretched' and 'retching', to take one small point from that passage, have obviously been carefully chosen to chime. There is no reason why dramatic prose should not be poetic, and it is perhaps useful to be reminded that there need be no fundamental antagonism between prose and poetry in the language of drama. Many Elizabethan plays juxtapose them to great effect: Marlowe brings out the humanity and frailty of Faustus, for instance, by giving him a prose scene with his fellow scholars in between the splendid verses of the invocation to Helen of Troy and the last soliloquy. In Soyinka's *Kongi's Harvest*, the contrast between a highly ritualised verse, suggesting the traditionalism of the old ways, and the new prose of a ruthless bureaucracy, is very much the main dramatic point. As one of Kongi's faceless servants puts it:

I think I see something of the Leader's vision of this harmony. To replace the old superstitious festival by a state ceremony governed by the principle of Enlightened Ritualism . . . The period of isolated saws and wisdoms is over, superseded by a more systematic formulation of comprehensive philosophies.

The 'isolated saws and wisdoms' are, of course, expressed in verse.

Prose can be poetic, and the theatre through other means — setting, grouping, lighting, costume, colour — can create its own poetry. It is not a self-evident fact, in other words, that, as T. S. Eliot (1888–1965) and other distinguished theorists have argued, verse drama is the highest kind of drama. Nevertheless, poetic language can do certain things in drama especially well and clearly.

Through the range of reference in its imagery, for instance, dramatic poetry can greatly broaden the scope or scale of a play, overcoming, as Una Ellis-Fermor has pointed out, 'the disadvantage of that brevity which is essential to the concentration and immediacy of drama'.[4] In Shakespeare's *King Lear* (1606?) Lear's speeches in the storm scene give what is essentially a family quarrel a cosmic dimension, his words conjuring up a universe of injustice and exploitation. In Shakespeare's *Antony and Cleopatra* (1607?) Antony says to Cleopatra on his first appearance:

> Let Rome in Tiber melt, and the wide arch
> Of the ranged empire fall! Here is my space.

The words, as with many of Antony's images, make real for us the public world and Antony's role as one of its 'triple pillars', hence increasing the drama of the clash between his public duty and his private feelings for his Egyptian queen. The imagery here also, however, does something that is so pervasive through all of Shakespearean drama that it needs little further illustration: its own eloquence, even magniloquence, is more than anything else responsible for creating the effect of largeness and grandeur of character which Lear and Antony, Othello and Macbeth and the other tragic heroes have in common. As a critic says of the Shakespearean tragic hero:

> His individual accent will vary with his personality, but there is always a residue of hyperbole. This, it would seem, is for Shakespeare the authentic tragic music, mark of a world where a man's reach must always exceed his grasp and everything costs not less than everything.[5]

The economy with which verse can reveal details of personality and motivation indicates its ability to force the audience back into the intensities of the immediate on-stage situation, as well as to transport it imaginatively to wider realms. Othello's simple but intensely moving words as he comes to murder Desdemona reveal his soldier's wish to believe he is doing judicial execution, not murder, while his repetitions show the strain he is under in preserving a judicial calm:

> It is the cause, it is the cause, my soul.
> Let me not name it to you, you chaste stars.
> It is the cause.

The economy of verse also enables a dramatist to focus with great clarity the essential issue or ideas of his play. This is so of Sophocles's treatment of the imagery of sight and blindness in *Oedipus* (*c.* 427 BC); and in contemporary times Wole Soyinka generates a genuinely powerful poetry from one of his major themes, the complicated issue of the relation of progress to traditionalism. Baroka in *The Lion and the Jewel* (1958) is not necessarily speaking for his creator, but his words focus precisely the dramatic conflict:

> I do not hate progress, only its nature
> Which makes all roofs and faces look the same.
> And the wish of one old man is
> That here and there,
> Among the bridges and the murderous roads,
> Below the humming birds which
> Smoke the face of Sango, dispenser of

The snake-tongue lightning; between this moment
And the reckless broom that will be wielded
In these years to come, we must leave
Virgin plots of lives, rich decay
And the tang of vapour rising from
Forgotten heaps of compost, lying
Undisturbed . . .

And finally, poetic imagery in drama can create, almost tangibly, the atmosphere or moral tone of a play — the imagery of blood and darkness in Shakespeare's *Macbeth* (1606?) is perhaps the clearest example.

Reading and Seeing

A play, then, is something which exists in a study or a library, and something which achieves its fullest life on a stage. But there is no reason why the play-reader should not be able to activate his theatrical imagination, just as the director or actor must realise the play theatrically on the basis of many careful readings. Good reading will help good seeing; good seeing will help good reading. The crucial point is to realise that drama is a hybrid art form. Its longevity through human history suggests it is also a healthy one.

2 Sophoclean Tragedy

Oedipus the King

Intensity

The most notable feature of *Oedipus the King*, even on a first viewing or perusal, is its matchless and terrifying intensity, an intensity which is inseparable from its economy as a work of art. Its plot is single and of determined bounds: it tells how Oedipus discovers the secret of his birth, and the effect of this discovery on himself, his wife/mother, and the appalled citizenry. Nothing extraneous is permitted, and the relentless logic of Oedipus's step-by-step progression towards the awful truth gives the play an ever-increasing tension and excitement, which — since his story was known to his audience — is itself a mark of Sophocles's dramatic artistry. It has often been said that *Oedipus* is the first detective story, and in the sense that a man quests for the answer to a riddle (the riddle of himself), the point of the remark is clear; but Sophocles, quite apart from the grandeur of his conception, rigidly eschews the digressions, the false trails and the unfocused naturalism that are regular features of the detective story.

'Knowing the Story': Irony

The modern audience or reader is asked implicitly again and again in contemporary plays, and especially novels, to put a high value on the new, the surprising, so that to understand the artistic advantages of treating a familiar story may require some effort. In the first place, it enables the audience to appreciate more fully and in an appropriate mood of receptivity the details of the artist's treatment of his theme, without any irritable reaching after 'what happens next'. Thus, for example, a master-stroke in *Oedipus* is that when, relatively early in the play, Oedipus is told the awful truth about himself by Teiresias, circumstances conspire to ensure that he does not, cannot and will not, believe it. The ironic contrast stands out the more clearly precisely because the audience knows the truth: the old man, literally blind, 'sees' more than the vigorous king who prides himself on his knowledge and intelligence, yet is metaphorically completely blind. Again, another example of supreme Sophoclean artistry is seen in his handling of the Corinthian messenger, whose blithe assumption that he can allay any lingering fears in the mind of Oedipus by revealing that Polybus and Merope were not, in fact, his parents, serves only to precipitate the ultimate catastrophe. Here, and elsewhere in *Oedipus*, Sophocles shows himself a master of *peripeteia* (literally, a reversal of circumstances), of what happens when a man's actions are found to have consequences the direct opposite of what the agent meant or expected. Aristotle argued that such reversals were a marked feature of good tragedies, and for the Greek audience (and even for a modern one) there is a special pleasure in observing how deftly Sophocles contrives such moments.

An overwhelming sense of irony permeates the play. The priest's supplication to Oedipus 'the first of men' to save Thebes now as he had before, is directed precisely at the man who is unwittingly the cause of the plague and pestilence which are ravaging the city; Oedipus's curse on the killer of Laius is an elaborate if unconscious cursing of himself; Jocasta's efforts to still her husband's fears actually give him one of his first concrete intimations of his role in Laius's death, when she mentions 'the place where three roads meet'; the Corinthian messenger's well-meant attempt to show the falseness of the fatal oracle only proves its truth; and, subsuming all the incidental ironies, there is the audience's experience of the grim process by which Oedipus comes to see how, in attempting to avoid his fate, he has ensured its coming to pass.

Sophocles's use of irony in the play matters for reasons that go well beyond mere locally effective dramatic touches, though these are indeed always extremely effective. It is also quite clear that it does not operate simply to create a feeling of smug superiority in the audience *vis-à-vis* Oedipus (*we* know more than *you* do): he is too much to be pitied and admired to allow any room for the reductive kind of irony that operates against, say, Malvolio in *Twelfth Night*, who is equally wrong about the realities of *his* situation. Rather, irony is Sophocles's way of saying something about the human condition: it organises the details of his way of telling the story because it lies at the heart of his vision of the frightening insecurity of human life. Despite the apparently very special nature of Oedipus's fate, he represents mankind which, as Sophocles sees it, is always at the mercy of the tragic gap between appearance and reality, and can never be assured of prosperity or happiness in his mysterious universe. The great and wise ruler of the play's opening is revealed, by a remorseless irony, to be accursed above all men and the Chorus comments at the end of the play on the *general* significance of what has happened: it does not suggest that Oedipus has been an unusually unlucky victim of an unusually malevolent scheme of the gods:

Sons and daughters of Thebes, behold: this was Oedipus,
Greatest of men; he held the key to the deepest mysteries;
Was envied by all his fellow-men for his great prosperity;
Behold, what a full tide of misfortune swept over his head.
Then learn that mortal man must always look to his ending,
And none can be called happy until that day when he carries
His happiness down to the grave in peace.

A final point can be made about Sophocles's intensive use of irony. This dictates the detailed organisation of the plot; it expresses a special awareness of the nature of human life; but it also suggests the presence of some logic or some design in the universe, a pattern which exists although the human being may not realise it is there until he comes into painful contact with it. When Jocasta hears from the Corinthian messenger the news of the death of Oedipus's supposed father, Polybus, she exults in this apparent proof of the irrelevance of the chilling oracle:

Where are you now, divine prognostications!

She goes on to urge her sceptical views on Oedipus:

Chance rules our lives, and the future is all unknown.
Best live as we may, from day to day.

This notion of a random universe is a doctrine which would deny the very basis of all serious Greek thought, which believed that the universe was not chaotic and 'irrational', but was based on a logical order. The pervasive dramatic irony in the play is a product of the gap between this order, harsh and frightening though it may be, and the imperfect human understanding of it. Jocasta is wrong: there is an order; and indeed the very perfection of the form of *Oedipus* suggests Sophocles's intuition of that order. Irony, then, is for Sophocles a mode of dramatic organisation but also a mode of vision, a way of understanding and expressing the world. As in all great art, content and form are indissolubly linked.

The Tragic Hero and the Tragic Flaw: 'Hamartia'

Despite — or because of — its economy of construction and formal perfection, *Oedipus the King* is a play which has provoked endless critical disagreements. The first, and perhaps most intensely debated, issue has been the question of Oedipus's responsibility for what happens to him: how far can he be said to be guilty, or is he entirely innocent? The relationship between character and fate has always, of course, been of consuming interest to tragic artists and to those interested in tragedy; in the case of *Oedipus*, the interest has been sharpened by a famous passage in Aristotle's *Poetics*, where he states that the cause of a tragic hero's downfall must lie 'not in any depravity, but in some great error on his part' — and he mentions Oedipus as a good example. Aristotle's word for this 'serious error' is *hamartia*, often explained as the flaw in the character of the tragic hero that brings about his downfall. Clearly this formulation, and indeed the whole notion of a 'tragic flaw', invites scrutiny of the moral nature of the hero.

Oedipus could be arraigned morally on several counts. He is guilty of impiety in trying to evade Apollo's oracle (just as his parents were similarly guilty) by various puny stratagems; he is guilty of the murder of Laius — that he does not know the identity of the old man whom he strikes down at the crossroads does not materially affect the moral charge; he is guilty of amazing rashness and lack of prudence: given his knowledge of the oracle, why does he marry a woman old enough to be his mother? or get into any kind of dangerous quarrel with an older man? He shows himself to be hasty and hot-tempered in his treatment of the revered prophet Teiresias and of his honest brother-in-law Creon; and also to be over-confident in his own abilities, especially in self-esteem for his knowledge and intelligence. Finally, he himself seems to accept his own guilt in punishing himself so savagely in the horrible mutilation of self-blinding, which, he explicitly proclaims, is a voluntary act, his own judgement of himself. None of this is to argue that he is a *bad* man, of course; but if it can be felt that he is a good man with a tragic moral flaw (or flaws), then his fate might seem more comprehensible, more in line with a sense of justice in the order of things. It is rarely the case in tragedy that 'the punishment fits the crime', since the punishment always seems disproportionately severe in relation to the hero's faults, but such a reading of the character of Oedipus at least suggests some connection between what he is and what happens to him.

This view of Oedipus, however, seems wrong. First, it must be remembered that Aristotle is not a *prescriptive* critic — that is, he does not presume to say that the tragic hero *must* have a flaw. Aristotle was merely describing the plays that he knew, but such is his immense intellectual prestige, and so avidly were his words taken as laws by later critics (especially those of Renaissance Italy), that a misleading and undue emphasis has been given to the idea of *hamartia* as a *necessary* component of the tragic hero's make-up. Secondly, as E. R. Dodds has pointed out in a most stimulating essay,[1] *hamartia* is an ambiguous word, which might be applied to false moral judgements (indicating moral flaws) but equally to purely intellectual error, to being simply mistaken (with no moral overtones). Perhaps the reason why so many students of

Oedipus have looked for *hamartia* in the moral sense in the hero is due to an anachronistic importation of Christian value-systems into the Greek world. The Christian emphasis on individual moral responsibility and on the connection between guilt and retribution is very marked, even in relatively secular contexts. Shakespearean tragedy lends itself easily to the idea of moral flaws in the heroes producing inevitable consequences – we need think only of Macbeth and Lear. But it may seriously distort a Greek tragedy to look at it through Shakespearean spectacles.

The Innocence of Oedipus

Clearly, Oedipus is in error in the sense that, when the play opens, he does not know that he has killed his father and has married his mother. In this sense, the idea of *hamartia* is applicable to him. But his behaviour largely escapes the moral strictures advanced above. Oedipus does not seem impious: his flight from Corinth and his beloved foster-parents when he hears the dire oracle shows how seriously he regards it. The oracle, too, is a divine prediction, not a divine command: Oedipus does not attempt to flout the orders of the god. His actions in the play show his piety: he sends Creon to Apollo's temple to learn what he should do to help his suffering city, and on receipt of the god's message immediately sets in train the quest for the killer of Laius. Similarly, it is an act of wisdom and piety to send for help to Teiresias, who, as the Chorus say, 'stands nearest' to the god. His attitude to Teiresias, at least initially, is reverent; he approaches him as a suppliant, and his anger at the seer's riddling uncommunicativeness originates not out of a sense of outraged egotism but rather out of concern for his people:

> Something you know, and will not tell? You mean
> To fail us and to see your city perish?

His piety seems the more evident when put alongside some of the speeches of the more sceptical Jocasta.

Sophocles has not dramatised the incident of the killing of Laius in such a way as to show up Oedipus in a bad light. It is reported (by Oedipus himself), not seen; and although the reporting rather than the direct dramatisation of violent actions was a convention of the Greek theatre (in this play, for example, Jocasta's suicide and Oedipus's self-blinding occur off-stage), the ultimate effect is to weaken any sense of moral outrage. (Shakespeare, whose stage *did* permit violent deeds to be shown, is careful to preserve sympathy for his heroes by having Duncan murdered off-stage in *Macbeth*, and by avoiding showing us directly the fate of Rosencrantz and Guildenstern in *Hamlet*.) It is quite clear that Laius was the aggressor:

The leader roughly ordered me out of the way:
And his venerable master joined in with a surly command.
It was the driver that thrust me aside, and him I struck,
For I was angry. The old man saw it, leaning from the carriage,
Waited until I passed, then, seizing for weapon
The driver's two-pronged goad, struck me on the head.

It is difficult, too, to feel that his treatment of Teiresias and Creon constitutes a major moral flaw in Oedipus. Sophocles is not asking us to see him as a wholly perfect man, and the hot temper he displays here and his suspicion of Creon's motives only serve to make him a more credible character. When we compare the emotional brutality of King Lear to his favourite daughter, or Macbeth's full awareness of the enormity of his deed in murdering his king who is also his guest, these spurts of anger in Oedipus seem minor indeed. Further, as Professor Dodds points out, 'Years before the action of the play begins, Oedipus was already an incestuous parricide; if that was a punishment for his unkind treatment of Creon, then the punishment preceded the crime — which is surely an odd kind of justice.'[2]

There seems at first more substance to the charge of a highly culpable rashness and lack of prudence in Oedipus. True, he thought he had left his parents safely behind him in Corinth, but as a pious Greek should he not have steered clear of all contexts which in the slightest degree impinged on the matter of the oracle? But the play as Sophocles has presented it does not press at all on this point: when the catastrophe bursts on

Oedipus, neither he nor anyone else stresses or laments his imprudence. Rather, the Chorus immediately strikes the tone which dominates the closing passages of the play:

All the generations of mortal men add up to nothing!
Show me the man whose happiness was anything more than
illusion
Followed by disillusion.
Here is the instance, here is Oedipus, here is the reason
Why I will call no mortal creature happy.

What has happened to Oedipus illustrates a general law of life: no finger of accusation is pointed at him. He was given no way out: the oracle was unconditional, and greater prudence would not have saved him from his fate. His punishment of himself in self-mutilation is not to be understood as an admission of personal moral corruption and guilt: he may be innocent, his intentions may have been entirely praiseworthy, but for the Greeks — and the play brings this out most power-fully — actions such as those of Oedipus are objectively horrible, irrespective of his motives: they bring pollution on the city. Oedipus himself, when he knows the truth, does not appeal to the innocence of his motives and his personal un-consciousness of sin. Rather, he sees himself as an unclean thing which must be banished.

To sum up, Oedipus seems a genuinely good and admirable man. His intelligence and knowledge has saved Thebes once, in the encounter with the Sphinx, and his courage in pursuing the truth, however devastating the personal cost, saves Thebes again by removing from her the cause of the plague — himself. Sophocles emphasises that courage and that regard for the truth by showing how strenuously others try to dissuade Oedipus from his quest for the answer — Teiresias, Jocasta and the Theban Shepherd all try to stop him. The priest's praise of him in the opening scene seems entirely justified:

If we come to you now, sir, as your suppliants,
I and these children, it is not as holding you
The equal of gods, but as the first of men,
Whether in the ordinary business of mortal life,
Or in the encounters of man with more than man.

Oedipus seems not just admirable, but innocent, and it is hard to make out a convincing case for a moral flaw in him which precipitates his tragedy.

Determinism and Freedom

Is the play then a determinist tragedy which in showing an innocent man victimised by fate denies the notion of free will and indeed the very idea of human freedom or responsibility? If it were so, it would not be such a great play; and from a certain angle it might not be considered truly tragic. Man seen as a totally hapless puppet or plaything of the gods (or fate, or society) lacks the power of arousing admiration, which the great tragic heroes so signally possess. In being deprived of choice, he must perforce lack dignity. Determinism will make the tragic protagonist seem entirely *passive*, a mere plaything of forces which lie beyond his control or even his understanding. But Oedipus strikes the audience as vigorous and *active*, controlling the development of the plot, making all the vital decisions, unremitting in his pursuit of the identity of the killer of Laius. The sense of Oedipus as a free agent is vividly alive before us on the stage.

How is this compatible with the overwhelming determinism that seems built in to the oracle's ghastly prediction? Has Sophocles merely worked some dramatic sleight of hand which deludes the audience? If we consider the difference between Oedipus at the beginning of the play and Oedipus at the end, the answer to these problems becomes clearer. Before a word is spoken in the drama Oedipus is an incestuous parricide: the only difference is that at the end of the play he *knows* he is one. The oracle did not say: You will kill your father, sleep with your mother, *and then find out that you have done these things*. Had it done so, the sense of determinism would indeed have been overwhelming. As it is, Sophocles has constructed his play in such a way as to highlight the special kind of freedom Oedipus has — the freedom to know, the freedom to pursue the truth. This is surely why Sophocles uses the marked pattern of what may be called incremental repetition in the play, whereby Teiresias, Jocasta and the Theban Shepherd all try, with increasing desperation, to stop

Oedipus in his quest for the truth. This is why Oedipus seems, and is, active, since knowing, and the pursuit of knowing, is a powerful mode of action; and in this case, the essence of the tragedy. 'The immediate cause of Oedipus's ruin is not "Fate" or "the gods" . . . and still less does it lie in his own weakness; what causes his ruin is his own strength and courage, his loyalty to Thebes, and his loyalty to the truth. In all this we are to see him as a free agent.'[3]

It would be wrong to overstress this line of the argument at the expense of minimising the sense of the mysterious awfulness of the fate of Oedipus. Great tragedy does not enforce the idea that a man's fate is entirely in his own hands: such is too cheeringly moral a view. Rather, it seems to hold a balance between the sense of determinism and the sense of freedom. How should we regard the gods in the play? If we say that the gods here predict but do not compel, we must also say that the predictions of the gods invariably come true, and that in the case of Oedipus, the oracle was unconditional: he was left with no way out, except in terms of the ignorance discussed above. A. J. A. Waldock remarks brusquely of these malevolent enemies of Oedipus (as he sees them): '*Nothing can excuse the gods, and Sophocles knew it perfectly well.*'[4] But if this is so, and if the play is designed primarily as an indictment of the injustice of the powers that order the universe, it is surely rather odd that nobody in the play — not even Jocasta, who sometimes seems to doubt that anything other than chance rules life — is given a speech embodying such an indictment, even after the catastrophe has burst upon the king. Neither the Chorus nor (much more significantly) Oedipus abuse the gods for the injustice of his fate. The Greek scholar H. D. F. Kitto has suggested that Sophocles believed the universe to be essentially logical — 'the pattern may harshly cut across the life of the individual, but at least we know that it exists . . . Whether or not it [the order of the universe] is beneficent, Sophocles does not say.'[5] But at least this order, it is implied, is preferable to the chaos and chance referred to by Jocasta ('Chance rules our lives . . . Best live as we may'). The justly admired logic of the plot 'is the reflection of the logic that Sophocles sees in the universe'.[6]

The student of drama is entitled to ask, when all historical

explanations have been made, questions of the dramatic
effect on him of a given play. And surely here we can see the
dramatic point of the gods and the oracle, especially given
the way in which *Oedipus* concentrates attention on the status
of the hero's intellect and knowledge. It is the application of
these in the case of the solution of the riddle of the Sphinx
which draws forth the admiration of the suppliant priest and
of the Chorus; it is the application of these to his own personal
— and fatal — quest for the killer of Laius that draws forth
any audience's admiration. There is a gap between the best
qualities — and best intentions — of Oedipus and the objective
reality which, despite these, makes him what he is. What this
gap dramatises most powerfully is the inscrutability of man's
fate in a universe whose laws he can never fully comprehend.

The Tragic Effect

Oedipus the King, therefore, is a play which shows the unmerited suffering of a good and upright man. To search for
the 'cause' in the malevolence of the gods is not only to go
beyond the evidence supplied by Sophocles, but also to
simplify the play by reducing its universality. There is more
to it than a divine vendetta against a man who is too clever
by half; similarly, it is difficult to accept the argument that
the gods are simply giving a salutary lesson, through the hapless Oedipus, of the need for all men to be modest and humble.
The play cannot be moralised thus. It asks us to *experience*
simultaneously the terror and the dignity of existence. The
gods function essentially as a metaphor for the inscrutability
of man's condition, for his frequent feeling of being controlled
by a process he does not understand; as a sign of the instability
of life, as a constant reminder to man that he is not the
measure of all things. Whether we believe in the gods literally
or take them thus metaphorically, the imaginative effect and
impact is similar; and of a kind which inspires sufficient fear
on its own, without requiring the addition of malevolence.

Yet, curiously, the play is not depressing. In part, this is
because we recognise the *truth* of its observation by reference
to general experience: the innocent *do* suffer, the thunderbolt
does come from the clear blue sky. We respond with admir-

ation to the clear-eyed and formally perfect way in which
Sophocles has embodied the idea. Further, perhaps there is
something therapeutic in the spectacle of unmerited suffering.
Thomas Gould puts it like this:

> Justice — in the sense that punishments fit crimes or that
> all catastrophes stem from serious flaws of character or
> understanding — is something we suspect is true but wish
> were not. Proof that we need *not* accept this constant
> burden of self-condemnation because there really is such
> a thing as . . . entirely unmerited misery — that is the
> interesting thing.[7]

But, above all, and offsetting the terror, is the sense of man's
dignity embodied in Oedipus's courage and uprightness in his
unravelling of his last terrible riddle, and in the strength with
which he accepts and endures his fate. If the inexorable and
uncomprehended logic which confronts Oedipus seems to
point towards men's puniness, the king's behaviour as he
seeks out, confronts and endures his destiny conveys an at
least equally strong sense of human nobility.

Antigone

Although the play deals with events after the death of Oedipus,
it was written earlier, probably about 442 BC. It is a simpler,
less teasing play than *Oedipus the King*, and its central theme
is much easier to pinpoint. This involves a very clear conflict
between differing conceptions of law, between human law
and a higher, more fundamental law. It is a vital and recurrent
problem. Athol Fugard, for instance, in a searing indictment
of the evils of apartheid in South Africa, uses Sophocles's
work in his play *The Island* (1974). Two prisoners on Robben
Island stage an impromptu version of *Antigone* with a full
sense of its relevance as an assertion, in the teeth of unjust
laws, of the inalienable rights of the individual. In Sophocles's
play, there is the heroine's passionate conviction that though
Creon may be head of state, his edict about the non-burial of
Polynices is simply wrong:

> I did not think your edicts strong enough
> To overrule the unwritten unalterable laws
> Of God and heaven, you being only a man.

On the other hand, there is Creon's principle:

> He whom the State appoints must be obeyed
> To the smallest matter.

Thus the play may be seen as a 'contest between two passion-ately held convictions of right',[8] between individual conscience and State policy, where as the Chorus puts it 'there is much to be said on both sides'. For the German philosopher, Hegel (1770–1831), *Antigone* is a supreme tragedy, because it presents so clearly what he sees as the essential tragic impasse, where equally valid claims collide, where principles with equal ethical justifications clash. On this view, Antigone and Creon each have right on their side, or — putting it the other way round — in so far as each is wrong, the mistake comes from failing to see the merits of the opposite case. Stated thus, it is a theme of perennial and absorbing interest, importance and relevance — these are the kinds of conflict which exercise us all as we face the complexities of political, military, moral and even medical ethics in our societies, where choices are not easy.

However, though the play does indeed engage with these issues, we must be careful not to extrapolate themes from it in the teeth of the dramatic evidence supplied by Sophocles. It is a great tragedy, but close examination does not support the notion of a delicate balance held between equally valid principles: the tragic emphasis is placed elsewhere. It is easiest to see this by considering the presentation of the two central characters.

Antigone: Egotist or Tragic Heroine?

An initial experience of the play leaves an overwhelming feeling of sympathy for Antigone: she is young, helpless but courageous, burdened with the sadness and the horror of the curse on the family, bereft of the support of her sister Ismene, wrenched away from her fiancé, Haemon, and doomed to die a horrible death. Critics impressed by the Hegelian idea of the tragedy have therefore tried hard to find flaws in her which would balance the more obvious flaws to be perceived in her antagonist Creon. It is argued, for example, that she is weary of the world and wants to die a romantic death,[9] rather in the manner of a Greek version of Ibsen's Hedda Gabler. This would explain her refusal to contemplate her sister dying with her, which would in a way tarnish the isolated purity of her self-conceived role of solitary victim. Indeed, her whole treatment of Ismene might be considered to be coldly self-righteous:

> *Ismene:* How can I bear to live, if you must die?
> *Antigone:* Ask Creon. Is not he the one you care for?

Perhaps, too, she chooses the course she does not out of any high principle, but uses the cloak of high principle to mask a deep-rooted personal hatred of Creon, who has taken over the place once filled by her beloved father. Though Haemon seems to be deeply in love with her, he hardly seems present to her consciousness and she refers to him only occasionally. This, it has been suggested, may be due to the fact that she feels a powerful, if unacknowledged, incestuous love for her dead brother, Polynices, attested by the intensity with which she speaks of him. Finally, apart from these psychological points, there is the criticism of her actual deed in contravening Creon's edict, that it shows stubbornness, self-will and an overweening anti-social pride. This is the view of the Chorus in the last encounter with Antigone:

> My child, you have gone your way
> To the outermost limit of daring
> And have stumbled against Law enthroned.

Such criticism need not be refuted in detail, point by point; what matters is to see that this sort of psychological — indeed, psychoanalytic — probing of character is wrong-headed in that it shows a fundamental misunderstanding of the nature of Sophoclean drama. Sophocles is not a naturalistic dramatist.

It is not his aim to present fully rounded portraits of people who can be considered 'real', and whose inner motives and concealed and unspoken thoughts we must elicit. Such critical procedures may yield dividends with Shakespeare's characters, and are even more appropriate to the drama of, say, Ibsen and Chekhov. But for Sophocles, Antigone's character is only of interest in so far as it embodies an idea or principle — individual conscience, say, or piety or compassion — central to the dramatic conflict in his play. The stage-experience of the play would make this even clearer. The masks on the actors; the formal groupings — especially those scenes where Creon and Antigone confront one another with the Chorus anxiously standing by; the very explicitness of the arguments which proceed on a level of general principle; the elaborate and beautiful Choric odes which regularly punctuate the action — all this is as far removed as it is possible to be from the naturalistic theatre where the characters, as W. B. Yeats put it, 'when they are deeply moved . . . look silently into the fireplace',[10] and where, as a result, the audience is positively invited to the kind of speculative psychologising which has often been misapplied to Antigone.

It is easy enough to demonstrate that Sophocles does not invite the naturalistic, psychological approach to the character of Antigone from the evidence the play itself provides. In the role of the Sentry, who first reveals to Creon that his orders have been contravened and later returns with the culprit, there is a marvellously 'realistic' and humorous vignette of a down-to-earth, common-sense character, where sympathy for Antigone, fear of Creon, and the urge to save his own skin are commingled in the most natural of ways; and where — even in translation — an earthy, colloquial quality is embodied in his words. What this shows is that Sophocles could create naturalistic characters when he wanted to; it then follows that he did not *wish* to focus on quirks and idiosyncracies of character in creating his central figures. The creation of great drama does not depend solely on the characters being wholly three-dimensional. The opening scenes of *Antigone* are intensely dramatic, and the characters are extremely well drawn, but it is what they stand for, what they represent in the play's larger terms that matters, not any irrelevant minutiae of psychological shading. There is Antigone's passionate and intransigent commitment to her course, there is the timidity of the obedient and cowed Ismene; and then, in a larger and even more poignant contrast, after the departure of the sisters under the weight of their differing but related misery, the Choric song of joy for the deliverance of the city.

On this argument, Antigone stands out as a tragic heroine, and her relations with Ismene and the Chorus serve to emphasise this: they are dramatic foils to her greatness of spirit and belief in principle, not means by which to measure her egotism, cold-heartedness or hypothetical incestuous feelings. The tragic hero — or in this case, heroine — is rarely moderate in either belief or statement having an absolute and rigorous commitment to the truth of a personal vision. Against this are placed the voices of moderation, realism, accommodation, of the timidity of ordinariness — Ismene's:

> I can do no other
> But as I am commanded; to do more is madness.

and the Chorus:

> She shows her father's stubborn spirit: foolish
> Not to give way when everything's against her.

In a way, this clash — between the attitudes of what might be called the community and the stance of the heroic individual — is as fascinating as the more obvious clash between Antigone and Creon. It illustrates a seemingly perennial aspect of tragic drama.

Creon

It is only by an over-generalised extrapolation from *Antigone* that it is possible to see it as a clash between two equally valid principles of *right*. Creon is not a bad man but the dramatic evidence suggests fairly overwhelmingly that he is *wrong*, and therefore the 'principle' that in Hegel's view he allegedly embodies — the rights of the State — is hollow, dramatically unsubstantiated. The crucial decision is to forbid the burial of Polynices. Consider the various ways in which this is spoken of in the play by a variety of characters, including Creon himself:

(1) To be left unburied, unwept, a feast of flesh
    For keen-eyed carrion birds. [Antigone]
(2) He is to be left unburied, left to be eaten
    By dogs and vultures, a horror for all to see. [Creon]
(3) We swept off all the earth that covered the body,
    And left it a sodden naked corpse again;
    Then sat up on the hill, on the windward side,
    Keeping clear of the stench of him, as far as we could. [Sentry]
(4)   [do not] leave him naked
    For dogs to maul and carrion birds to peck at. [Haemon]
(5) The blood that stains our altars and our shrines,
    The blood that dogs and vultures have licked up,
    It is none other than the blood of Oedipus
    Spilled from the veins of his illfated son. [Teiresias]

By using words such as these, Sophocles intends his audience to be aware of the sheer brutality of Creon's edict — the emphasis on the mangling of the body needs, for its impact, no special reference to or knowledge of Greek customs but arouses rather 'the sheer physical horror, the sense of indecent outrage, that we all feel at the idea of a loved body being eaten'.[11] In giving it this emphasis, Sophocles contrives our assent to Antigone's claim that she is 'convicted of reverence', and to the view that Creon has broken the 'unwritten, unalterable laws' of the gods. The Chorus may well be right in their surmise that the first mysterious covering of Polynices's body is an act of the gods, which gives ironic force to Creon's intemperate riposte — 'Blasphemy, to say the gods could give a thought to carrion flesh!' Certainly he blasphemes directly in angrily rejecting the advice of Teiresias, and demonstrates his overweening self-will:

> Let the eagles
> Carry his carcase up to the throne of Zeus;
> Even that would not be sacrilege enough
> To frighten me from my determination
> Not to allow this burial.

Creon, as he is presented in the play, is not a good ruler. He himself claims that one of the marks of a wise king is readiness to listen to good advice — and he then proceeds to reject all other advice, from the Chorus, from his son Haemon, from Teiresias. The Chorus's great ode, near the beginning of the play, on the achievement of man, has sometimes been understood as a criticism of the law-breaker, Antigone, and perhaps this is how the Chorus intends it:

> O wondrous subtlety of man, that draws
> To good or evil ways! Great honour is given
> And power to him who upholdeth his country's laws
> And the justice of heaven.
> But he that, too rashly daring, walks in sin
> In solitary pride to his life's end,
> At door of mine shall never enter in
> To call me friend.

But, most ironically, the words apply much more accurately to Creon who, in making his law, breaks more fundamental laws and, in the light of his bitter experience, admits it:

> Now I believe
> It is by the laws of heaven that man must live . . .
> O the curse of my stubborn will!

Haemon warns him to listen to good advice, and points out the tyrannical aspect of Creon's conception of rule, which asserts that he must be obeyed 'right — or wrong'. Haemon tells Creon of the admiration of the people of Thebes for Antigone's honourable action, and the following exchange reveals clearly how far Creon has, in his stubborn self-will, moved from the practice of good government:

Creon: Since when do I take my orders from the people of Thebes?
Haemon: Isn't that rather a childish thing to say?
Creon: No. I am king, and responsible only to myself.
Haemon: A one-man state? What sort of a state is that?
Creon: Why, does not every state belong to its ruler?
Haemon: You'd be an excellent king — on a desert island.

Indeed, Haemon wins every argument in this great scene in the middle of the play, and Creon stands as a peculiarly bankrupt advocate of the principle of the rule of law. Haemon is no mere author's spokesman, but vital to the tragic effect of the play. Sophocles chooses to play down the love-relationship between Antigone and Haemon (this does *not* mean that Antigone can only love her brother) because he wishes to emphasise something else, the father–son relationship. As one critic puts it, 'Creon might have been punished in some general way for his sins, but only through a Haemon can the truth be brought home to him in personal anguish.'[12]

Is it Antigone's tragedy or Creon's tragedy? One easy way out of this would be to say that we have two tragedies encompassed in the single play, but such an answer would not satisfy those who feel that there is, during the play, a dramatic change of emphasis. It begins as a play about a conflict of law and ends as a play about a man whose *hamartia* is stubborn self-will; another way of putting this would be to say that it begins by concentrating on Antigone and ends by concentrating on Creon. But such criticism is not justified. If we ask of the tragedy that it cohere only on the level of character, then perhaps we would feel a diffusion of concentration as between Antigone and Creon. But the play coheres superbly on the level of general idea or theme: it embodies the idea of the power of those 'unwritten, unalterable laws' to which Antigone commits herself and which Creon contravenes. Within the framework of that single unifying idea the various individual sections mesh and interact: Antigone's deed focuses and releases all Creon's obstinacy, and her action is the ultimate catalyst of all the other actions including the deaths of Haemon and Eurydice and the breaking of Creon.

Such an interpretation might be felt to reduce the play to a simple religious, pious or moral tract: obey the gods, or else. This might be powerful, but not necessarily tragic: the certainties of religious belief and the uncertainties of tragedy are not easily reconciled or even compatible. However, *Antigone* does not resolve the tangled problem of the relationship between 'divine' law and human justice simplistically. Creon is not a bad man, though a stubborn one, and his punishment, as always in tragedy, far outweighs his sin –

both wife and son dead and, in dying, cursing him. As for Antigone, apart from the tragic spectacle of innocence crushed, Sophocles also introduces the crucial idea that her fate is part of the curse on her family. The Chorus tells her that 'this is the expiation you must make for the sin of your father', and she seems to accept the grim idea as she goes to her death:

> My father — the thought that sears my soul —
> The unending burden of the house of Labdacus.

She may be morally right, in other words, but still condemned to act a role in a drama she did not make and does not control. Thus, here too, the world retains, in the vision of a great tragic artist, its mystery. As in *Oedipus the King*, so here: there are no easy answers.

3   Religion and Tragedy

Greek drama and, after it, English drama both have their roots in religious ritual; and the gods have a crucial if unseen role to play in both *Oedipus* and *Antigone*. The general problem of the nature of the relationship between religion and tragedy merits some attention here. It is probably true that religious and tragic views of life are incompatible, if the religious view of life is doctrinal or didactic — if that is, it suggests that there is an answer to the riddle of the universe, that there is a comprehensible scheme of rewards and punishments for human kind, that there is an easily discernible moral code which solves the dilemma of how to live. Tragedy insists on the mysteriousness of man's fate, it presents his situation as a predicament, and enforces the notion that suffering is immitigable and, on occasion, unjustified. Above all, it teaches no easy moral lessons. In the tragedies of Sophocles, for instance, there is no real strain between the religious view of life implied by the presence of the gods and their unalterable laws, and the tragic emphasis on the instability and frailty of man's life because, though Sophocles in no way indicts the divine powers, he presents them as remote, inscrutable, not necessarily benevolent. Thus he is able to deal, as great tragedians must, with man's cosmic situation, without any anti-tragic importation of the comforting feeling that all is for the best in the best of all possible worlds.

With Christianity, an acute edge is given to the problem. Here is a religious view of life which is totally anti-tragic, in its emphasis on the redemptive power of Christ's sacrifice, in its stress on the benevolence of God, in its confident optimistic belief in an afterlife where things will be put right, and in the completeness of the moral code which grows out of such beliefs. What then is to be said of tragedies written in a

Christian age? There is, of course, an extra dimension of 'innerness' added to the conception of man by Christianity, its interest in processes and movements hidden in the depths of the soul, which is reflected with great power in the drama, especially the drama of Shakespeare. As Hamlet says:

> But I have that within which passeth show,
> These but the trappings and the suits of woe.

But the basic conflict between Christianity and tragedy remains. What happens characteristically in tragedy written inside a Christian world view is that the dramatist simply suppresses the note of hope and optimism built into major Christian doctrines, especially those of the Redemption and the Resurrection. To adapt the famous words of Coleridge, the dramatist procures for the moment that willing suspension of faith which constitutes the tragic sense of life. There is, however, one great play which raises directly the problem of the relationship between tragedy and religion, or tragic and moral views of life: Marlowe's *Dr Faustus*.

Marlowe's *Faustus*: Morality Play or Tragedy?

The play tells the story of a man who sells his soul to the devil in return for twenty-four years of power and pleasure, and is consequently damned to eternal punishment. Obviously such a story will not have the note of hope and optimism associated with the concept of heavenly bliss, but in the explicitness of its invocation of Christian views of life after death and in a tendency to present the protagonist's fate as a cautionary tale, *Dr Faustus* may seem to replace the tragic with the merely didactic.

Some external factors could be used to buttress this view. Marlowe was the first great dramatic celebrant of the aspiring mind of Renaissance man, with its hungry and compulsive urge to comprehend and dominate the universe:

> Nature that framed us of four elements
> Warring within our breasts for regiment,

Doth teach us all to have aspiring minds.
Our souls, whose faculties can comprehend
The wondrous architecture of the world
And measure every wandering planet's course,
Still climbing after knowledge infinite,
And always moving as the restless spheres,
Will us to wear ourselves and never rest . . .

The lines are from *Tamburlaine* (1587), a flamboyant and defiant challenge to the orthodox piety of Marlowe's generation in its glorification of ruthless and triumphant individualism. *Dr Faustus* could be seen as Marlowe's recantation, or, if that is going too far, as an expression of deeply felt orthodox convictions which the earlier play had extravagantly flouted. Certainly Marlowe's source for *Dr Faustus*, an English translation of a German 'biography' of one Georg or Johannes Faustus, suggests in its title the moralistic attitude of an orthodox age: 'The Historie of the damnable life, and deserved death of *Doctor John Faustus*'.

Such is the precise note of the words of the Chorus which conclude the play. Faustus is held up as a solemn warning:

Faustus is gone: regard his hellish fall,
Whose fiendful fortune may exhort the wise
Only to wonder at unlawful things:
Whose deepness doth entice such forward wits,
To practise more than heavenly power permits.

Marlowe's play is greatly influenced in overall conception and in certain structural details by the English morality play tradition. The morality play was an allegory about the Christian way of life in which the characters were personifications of virtues and vices, engaged in a struggle for the soul of a representative man. (The best-known of these plays is *Everyman*, written in the fifteenth century.) Thus in Marlowe's play, the Old Man who in Act 5 pleads with Faustus to repent might well be called, in the manner of *Everyman*, Good Counsel; the parade of the seven deadly sins is a little morality pageant within the play; and the Good and Bad Angels who contest over Faustus's soul are directly imported from the morality tradition.

All this imparts a certain didactic flavour. The general pattern of the action seems to reinforce the moralistic shaping of the drama. A creature in origin bright and good has been deformed: 'at the beginning Faustus wished to rise above his humanity; at the close he would sink below it, be transformed into a beast or into "little water drops" '.[1] Marlowe puts considerable stress on the baseness of Faustus's motivation for signing away his immortal soul. Though some critics, who seem to be creating their own myth of Faustian aspiration, see him as a heroic Promethean seeker for knowledge, the play emphasises his desire to 'live in all voluptuousness'. He has a lust for riches, pleasure and power — these lines are reasonably representative:

> I'll have them fly to India for gold;
> Ransack the ocean for orient pearl,
> And search all corners of the new-found-world
> For pleasant fruits and princely delicates.

The imagery of surfeiting is frequently found in his language: he is 'glutted', 'cloyed', 'ravished' with his sweet magic.

The text of *Faustus* is notoriously complicated, and Marlowe may not be responsible for much of the detail in the exceedingly tedious middle scenes, where Faustus plays tricks on the Pope, puts on conjuring shows at the court of Charles, and procures out-of-season grapes for the pregnant Duchess of Vanholt. But the conception, the idea, of the scenes may well be his, in which case the morality play element is intensified. On this view, what Marlowe shows is the triviality of Faustus, and the emptiness of his bargain, the betrayal of ideals and 'the lapse into luxury and buffoonery':[2] the middle, however flawed in literary and dramatic execution, illustrates the deterioration in Faustus's character which morally justifies the ending.

These elements in the play do not, of course, prevent it from working in theatrical and literary terms with considerable power. But they do work against the sense of tragedy. If Faustus is a weak and trivial man, and if we are asked to see his 'hellish fall' as an exhortation to go and not do likewise, it is difficult to feel sympathy for the hero or terror at the mystery of his doom. The divine rules were clear; Faustus broke them knowing full well what he was about; he got what he deserved, and he was not even magnificent in his badness. Such didacticism, and the vision of tragedy, are deeply at odds. Further, the prominence of Christian doctrines in the play poses problems for believer and non-believer. The non-believer may be antagonised by the rigidities of orthodoxy; the believer, ironically, may be unable to respond to the drama *as a drama* because of the very power with which Marlowe dramatises the ideas of hell and eternal punishment, especially in Faustus's magnificent last soliloquy:

> Now hast thou but one bare hour to live,
> And then thou must be damned perpetually . . .
> O God,
> If thou wilt not have mercy on my soul,
> Yet for Christ's sake, whose blood hath ransomed me,
> Impose some end to my incessant pain . . .

As Dr Johnson (1709—84) said of *Paradise Lost* (1667) by John Milton (1608—74) in words that may express what some might feel about *Faustus*, 'the good and evil of Eternity are too ponderous for the wings of wit; the mind sinks under them in passive helplessness.'[3]

Faustus as a Renaissance Man

Marlowe has, however, dramatised feelings in the play which greatly complicate the simple morality structure outlined above.

> All things that move between the quiet poles
> Shall be at my command: emperors and kings
> Are but obeyed in their several provinces,
> Nor can they raise the wind, or rend the clouds;
> But his domain that exceeds in this,
> Stretcheth as far as doth the mind of man.

The verse here gives authentic embodiment to the ennobling dynamism of Renaissance humanism. Marlowe's conception of Faustus as the quester after knowledge, as one who remains, despite his great achievements, restlessly dissatisfied, who would seek heroically to confront and transcend human limitations, is a huge advance in dignity and imaginative grandeur on the tawdry conjurer of his source-book. This Faustus is no mere voluptuary (though he may be that as well). He seeks knowledge of the nature of heaven and hell, of the motions of the stars and of ultimate physical and meta-physical questions. He is not content with received knowledge, he would risk everything — even damnation — to find out for himself. The beauty of the surging verse — Marlowe's 'mighty line' — which he is given to speak invests even his more commonplace desires for pleasure and power with a glamorous poetic appeal:

> Have not I made blind Homer sing to me
> Of Alexander's love, and Oenon's death?
> And hath not he, that built the walls of Thebes
> With ravishing sound of his melodious harp,
> Made music with my Mephostophilis?

This kind of verse registers the appeal to Marlowe of his pro-tagonist, a man aflame with that liberating sense of the beauty, dignity and capacities of mankind which the Renaissance brought to Europe. The most famous lines in the play — Faustus's invocation of Helen of Troy — may well suggest his dalliance with the ultimate sin of demoniality (bodily intercourse with spirits), but to respond thus to them is wilfully to shut one's ears to the nobility and grandeur of the verse, which — at least temporarily — gags moral criticism:

> Was this the face that launched a thousand ships,
> And burnt the topless towers of Ilium? . . .
> O, thou art fairer than the evening's air,
> Clad in the beauty of a thousand stars . . .
> More lovely than the monarch of the sky
> In wanton Arethusa's azured arms . . .

There is nothing of gross sensuality here: 'all the glory that was Greece was embodied, for the Renaissance, in this woman;

her story was the story in brief of another world, superhuman and immortal'.[4] Marlowe presents this humanist side of Faustus with great power and — as the verse indicates so superbly — with complete imaginative understanding, from the inside.

'Yet art thou still but Faustus, and a man.' This is the truly tragic conflict in the play, indeed its central theme, the clash between Renaissance aspirations and the older orthodox Christian tradition with its insistence on the limitations and imperfections of man's estate. What is truly impressive is that each of these mighty opposites conflict *in the soul of the hero*, and that each is given full poetic and dramatic weight. For if Faustus is convincing in, say, his address to Helen, so is he when riven by the religious consciousness he has abjured but from which he cannot free himself:

> What art thou, Faustus, but a man condemned to die?
> Thy fatal time draws to a final end;
> Despair doth drive distrust into my thoughts.

Thus there is an intense inner drama which is the prototype for Shakespeare's greatest tragedies, and which forbids us to take a simple didactic view of the play as a cautionary tale.

The Development of Faustus

If the play is seen as a tragedy, one aspect of Faustus's development needs some further comment. It is usually assumed that Faustus is a better man at the beginning than at the end of the play. Here is another area where theology and tragedy conflict with confusing results. Whatever a theologian might say, Faustus is actually a better man at the moment when he is carried off to damnation. This is clearly doctrinal heresy, but dramatic and tragic good sense. For all of his intellectual and academic attainments, Faustus does not really *know* (in the sense of realise, feel on his pulses) what he is doing when he makes the contract with hell. The sense of a precociously brilliant adolescent suffering from moral myopia is dramatised superbly by Marlowe in the great scenes between Faustus and Mephostophilis.

Faustus: How comes it then that thou art out of hell?
Mephostophilis: Why this is hell, nor am I out of it.
                   Think'st thou that I, who saw the face of God,
                   And tasted the eternal joys of heaven,
                   Am not tormented with ten thousand hells,
                   In being deprived of everlasting bliss? . . .
Faustus: What, is great Mephostophilis so passionate
                   For being deprived of the joys of heaven?
                   Learn thou of Faustus manly fortitude.

There is a horrible jauntiness here which goes along with the
terrible, flippant use of Christ's dying words, '*Consummatum
est*', as Faustus signs the fatal bond. Consider, too:

Faustus: I think hell's a fable.
Mephostophilis: Ay, think so still, till experience change thy
                   mind.

In short Faustus is a moral child whose crucial act — the signing of the bond — invites his damnation while simultaneously
— a supreme touch of irony — it begins the painful process
of his moral and emotional education. The distance that
Faustus has travelled is illustrated by a comparison of the
early scene with Valdes and Cornelius, where Faustus is all
vaunting boastfulness and sonorously self-regarding, with the
very late scene — in marvellously intimate prose — with the
scholars, where Faustus is humanised, concerned for his
fellows, now fully aware of the significance of his deed, that
he is cut off not just from God but from humanity:

Ah, gentlemen, hear with patience, and tremble not at my
speeches; though my heart pants and quivers to remember
that I have been a student here these thirty years — O would
I had never seen Wittenberg, never read book — and what
wonders I have done, all Germany can witness, yea, all the
world — for which Faustus hath lost both Germany and
the world — yea, heaven itself — heaven, the seat of God,
the throne of the blessed, the kingdom of joy, and must
remain in hell for ever. Hell, ah hell, for ever! Sweet
friends, what shall become of Faustus, being in hell for
ever?

Marlowe's play and Shakespeare's *Macbeth* are frequently compared, as 'tragedies of damnation'. Surely the contrasts are as striking as any similarity. Both plays focus on the inner nature, the moral core of the protagonists, but the development of each is different. Macbeth's conscience and sensitivity are fully active before the murder of Duncan — all the great early soliloquies show a mind agonised by its knowledge of the fullness of evil in its will. By contrast, Faustus seems so unaware, so ignorant of what he is doing that he might almost be called innocent: in theological terms, his conscience is not informed. However, if we compare the two at the end of their respective plays, we find that Macbeth is 'supped so full of horrors' that he is coarsened and degraded, whereas Faustus has come morally alive, intensely and quiveringly aware of good and evil. This is one of the reasons why it should be impossible (though it has been done) to hear the last great soliloquy as the snivellings of a craven wretch who has merited his punishment. As R. B. Sewall says in an eloquent essay:

> If to the orthodox it is more a sinner's fate than a hero's, there is something of the classic apotheosis in Faustus's final moments. He transcends the man he was. He goes out no craven sinner but violently, speaking the rage and despair of all mankind who would undo the past and stop the clock against the inevitable reckoning.[5]

It is hard to feel that justice has been done; and if Faustus is in certain major ways a better man at the end than he was at the beginning, Marlowe's play is not only tragic, but deeply subversive of orthodoxy, in the suggestion that moral growth might cost damnation.

A Flawed Masterpiece

Dr Faustus, however, remains a flawed masterpiece. This is not so much because of the undoubted weakness of the middle scenes: it is more a matter of a central incoherence in Marlowe's own vision. The great central clash between religious orthodoxy and Renaissance individualism is not so much something which Marlowe dramatises, as something inside which he is himself caught. The problems of Faustus lay so close to Marlowe's heart that he could not state them objectively, in the formal terms of art. After the terrible splendours of Faustus's last speech comes the alliterative moralising of the Choric conclusion. 'Tragedy' and 'morality' are in desperate incompatibility: the case for and against Faustus can be argued with equal convincingness, because his creator has left the jagged edges of his own uncertainty so visible in the drama. And yet the intensity of Marlowe's scrutiny of his protagonist's divided mind gave powerful impetus to the greatest tragedies of the Elizabethan period. 'This, above all other dramas, is the foundation of Shakespeare's tragedy.'[6]

4 *Shakespearean Tragedy*

Character

In Shakespeare's tragedies, as in *Dr Faustus*, there is a concentration on the inner moral life of the protagonist, its
growth or debasement, which is a feature of tragedy created
inside a Christian world view. This did not matter so much
to the Greeks, who felt that a man's nature is completely
expressed in what he does. While there is a great deal of crucial
action in Shakespeare's plays, this action does not tell the
whole story about a man — 'one may smile and smile, and be
a villain' as Hamlet discovers, and the intensity with which
Shakespeare presents Macbeth's seared conscience throughout
the play makes it impossible to accept the phrase 'this dead
butcher' as a wholly adequate epitaph on the man.

But while giving definitive shape and emphasis to the inner
life of his protagonists, a characteristically Christian emphasis
in which motive matters at least as much as deed, Shakespeare
mostly suppresses — to the benefit of his tragedies — explicit
theological references. There is neither comforting nor com-
pensating heaven — for the other tragic heroes, as for Hamlet,
'the rest is silence'; and though Shakespeare embodies most
powerfully in the plays a conception of moral order in the
universe (seen most clearly perhaps in *Macbeth* and *King
Lear*), it is a moral order which depends less on supernatural
sanctions and backing than on 'Nature'. Similarly, evil is
more 'humanised' in Shakespeare than in Marlowe's *Faustus*,
being diffused through and embodied in more naturalistically
conceived characters.

Characterisation is Shakespeare's greatest strength, though
there has been a tendency in our century to deny the importance of character in his work. This is in part a reaction against

the undoubted excesses of Romantic and Victorian critics, who treated Shakespeare's characters rather too much as if they were real people, and inquired into their 'lives' both before and after the period covered by the play. Instead, many twentieth-century critics prefer to see the plays as 'visionary statements' which embody some impersonal generalisation on human life (the criticism of G. Wilson Knight has been influential here), or as dramatic poems creating meaning through densely interlocking verbal patterns. Thus L. C. Knights says, '*Macbeth* has greater affinity with *The Waste Land* than with *The Doll's House*'[1] — it is more like Eliot's poem than Ibsen's play because, for Knights, *Macbeth* is a dramatic poem, and he speaks dismissively of the idea of the poetry 'illustrating character'.

However, though verbal patterns in Shakespeare's plays can create atmosphere, establish thematically relevant clusters of images, and so on, above all what the poetry communicates is the unmistakable ring of the highly individualised voice. It is Shakespeare's special genius thus to make his characters come to life and to make audiences or readers care intensely about what happens to them.

The Tragic Effect

The Shakespearean tragic effect has two related aspects: first, we witness the destruction or waste of human fineness, distinction or greatness; secondly, this loss is directly connected with the spread of evil, spilling outwards like a deadly poison or infection from some single act of folly or brutality, and feeding on everything that comes in its way. This evil is in the end usually destroyed or extirpated, but this is no cause for untempered rejoicing since the good and the innocent have been destroyed too. Goodness has no aces up its sleeve in a corrupt world: it has only its own integrity. *Hamlet* is the great example.

Hamlet: 'The Tragedy of a Man Who Could Not Make Up His Mind'?

Hamlet has probably aroused more critical discussion than

any other play in the history of the stage. In part this is a tribute to the sheer excitement of the dramatic story — rather like *Oedipus*, this is a great thriller. But mainly it is the character of the young prince himself which has provoked all the interest. Why does Hamlet, who promises the ghost that he will sweep to his revenge 'with wings as swift as meditation', delay that revenge? The question of Hamlet's delay involves consideration of all the other problems which have teased readers and spectators of the play. How is one to regard the ghost? Is Hamlet a neurotic, morbidly obsessed with sex? Is he mad? What is his attitude to revenge? How may one explain his behaviour in the last Act? and so on. In other words the examination of the reasons for Hamlet's delay turns out to be something larger — an examination of the dark and mysterious world in which he lives and moves. This is a mark of the artistic integrity of the drama, that it is very difficult to isolate any one theme or motif from the whole work.

Problems of the Situation

Some would deny that Hamlet delays at all, arguing that once he has tested the truth of the ghost's story by means of the mouse-trap (the play within the play), he kills Claudius at the first real opportunity he gets. The trouble with this view is that it can offer only over-ingenious reasons to explain away the fact that Hamlet himself twice bitterly berates himself for his delay. In Act 2, scene 2, he upbraids himself for cowardice:

> it cannot be
> But I am pigeon-livered, and lack gall
> To make oppression bitter, or ere this
> I should ha' fatted all the region kites
> With this slave's offal.

And in the other great soliloquy, which has an equal accent of sincerity, in Act 4, scene 4, he exclaims:

> How all occasions do inform against me,
> And spur my dull revenge!

It seems perverse to fly in the face of this evidence.

The Ghost

Shakespeare stresses the fact that Hamlet faces a real problem in his dealings with the ghost. Current Elizabethan attitudes were that a ghost could be an illusion, or a phantom portending some danger to the State, or a dead man's spirit come from the grave because of something left undone, or from purgatory by divine permission, or a devil in the shape of a dead person come to lure the living to damnation. These attitudes are powerfully and explicitly dramatised in the play. In the first scene, Horatio tells Bernardo and Marcellus that it is but their 'fantasy', and speaks to it himself thus, 'Stay, illusion!' Later Horatio sees it as a portent which 'bodes some strange eruption to our state', and when it appears a second time his words suggest something more sinister — 'I'll cross it though it blast me', he says, and remarks that on the cock-crow 'it started like a guilty thing upon a fearful summons'. But these impressions of something evil are qualified by the awe-struck words of Marcellus:

> We do it wrong, being so majestical,
> To offer it the show of violence.

Hamlet's reaction when he first hears of it suggests that he thinks it may be a diabolic manifestation:

> If it assume my noble father's person,
> I'll speak to it though hell itself should gape.

But when he sees it he does not know whether it is a 'spirit of health' or 'goblin damned'. While he very understandably accepts, as he stands in its presence, that the ghost (who speaks, most movingly, like a purgatorial spirit) is his father's spirit, he is later to feel that 'the spirit that I have seen/May be a devil'; and he plans the mouse-trap specifically to test the truth of the ghost's story. And though Claudius's reaction to the play does seem to confirm the truth of that story, the ghost remains an enigma since, as Shakespeare shows with the witches in *Macbeth*, spirits may tell the truth and yet be evil.

Appearance and Reality

The artistic point of these deliberate ambiguities is clear: they establish a major element in Hamlet's dilemma and, further, represent in the most powerful way an aspect of a major theme of the play: the difficulty of distinguishing appearances from reality. In his first scene Hamlet retorts bitterly to his mother, 'Seems, madam! nay it is, I know not "seems".' But the real and haunting difficulty of his situation as it is borne in on him is that it is not so easy to distinguish what 'seems' from what 'is'. A ghost has 'assumed' his noble father's person. And the burden of his story is that he was deceived by 'my most seeming-virtuous queen', and that Claudius may smile and smile and yet be a villain. Polonius tells his son that 'the apparel oft proclaims the man', but the play everywhere gives the lie to the foolish Polonius: outward appearance and inner reality rarely coincide in Elsinore, men are rarely as they seem.

Shakespeare stresses the confusion of appearance and reality in the language of the play with the pervasive use of terms like 'apparition', 'assume', 'put on', 'shape' and 'seems', and by imagery of clothing, painting, and acting — activities which disguise or mask truth. All this combines to create an overwhelming impression of a nightmarish world where no simple action seems possible, where a man may strike at his own shadow. The play within the play, where Hamlet attempts to make a fiction reveal the truth, is a fine symbol of the complexity of the relation between appearance and reality. What it also brings home again is the difficulty of Hamlet's position: he lives in a world of 'seeming', yet for him, correct judgement of deceitful appearances and hidden truths is literally a matter of life or death.

Claudius

Considerations of Hamlet's delay should also take account of the nature of his adversary, and of the practical difficulties that face him. Shakespeare's characterisation of Claudius establishes him as no bloated buffoon, but a shrewd and dangerous enemy, as Act 1, scene 2 economically demonstrates. He has the regal manner to perfection — witness the stately formality of the verse in his first speech. After appropriate expressions of grief for the death of King Hamlet, he cleverly emphasises the concurrence of all his councillors with his marriage to Gertrude, at once subtly flattering their 'better wisdoms' and disarming any potential protest at his haste by making his marriage seem the fruit of many weighty policy meetings. He goes on immediately to discuss at some length the Norwegian threat and commands the immediate dispatch of ambassadors. The image he conveys here is of a man of decision (which he indeed shows himself to be), with perhaps the implication that the Danes are lucky to have a statesman at the helm in this crisis — rather than a young untried student. Then the majesty of Denmark shows himself in another guise, as a kind of genial uncle to Laertes, his tone to the youth ingratiating Claudius further with his chief councillor, Polonius. At last Claudius addresses Hamlet. By leaving him until now, Claudius manages to suggest his magnanimity in overlooking Hamlet's deep mourning clothes, an ostentatious insult in the context of the wedding festivities. He then shows himself capable of giving Hamlet wholly admirable philosophic consolations for the fact of mortality. In short, on his first appearance Claudius creates a strong impression of competence, confident security and magnanimous reasonableness.

Hamlet's difficulties in establishing the reliability of the ghost and in attempting to out-guess a shrewd and powerful antagonist certainly help to explain something of his delay in 'sweeping' to his revenge. These are difficulties of the situation rather than of personal temperament, and when the action of the play is seen in this light, as in some way it must be, as a kind of deadly chess-game, Hamlet seems far from inactive or indecisive.

Hamlet's Temperament

There are, however, more complex factors in the situation. In Hamlet's very first soliloquy he dwells with painful particularity on his mother's behaviour:

A little month or ere those shoes were old
With which she followed my poor father's body

Like Niobe, all tears, why she, even she —
O God, a beast that wants discourse of reason
Would have mourned longer — married with my uncle . . .
(Act 1, scene 2)

The intensity of Hamlet's reaction to what he sees as his
mother's sexual rapacity is a powerful and continuous feature
of his personality, and is dramatised with special and horrifying force in Act 3, scene 4, where he confronts her in her
bedchamber. The bitter images are expressive of an intense
revulsion —

Nay, but to live
In the rank sweat of an enseamed bed
Stewed in corruption, honeying, and making love
Over the nasty sty . . .

Hamlet's treatment of Ophelia is surely connected with his
revulsion from the evidence of his mother's sexuality:
Gertrude's behaviour has led him to generalise 'Frailty, thy
name is woman'. He has loved Ophelia with a young man's
idealising love (as his letter to her, quoted in Act 2, scene 1,
makes clear), but his idealisation has been given a severe shock
by his mother's 'o'er-hasty' marriage, by the ghost's revelation
of her adultery and, following hard upon this, Ophelia's
rejection of him on the orders of Polonius. The sudden change
in Ophelia's behaviour cannot but remind him of his mother's
falling-off; some sense of this added shock to his being is
communicated in Ophelia's description of how he came to
her in silence, and after a long perusal of her face,

rais'd a sigh so piteous and profound
As it did seem to shatter all his bulk.
(Act 2, scene 1)

He suspects that all women share the corruption that he has
discovered in his mother; his mind is tainted with gross images
of human sensuality and beastliness. Hence his cruelty to
Ophelia in the nunnery scene ('You jig, you amble, and you
lisp . . . and make your wantonness your ignorance'), and in

the play-scene, where Gertrude's proximity lends an added bitterness to his bawdy jesting with Ophelia.

Some critics explain Hamlet's delay as due to an obsessive concern with his mother's behaviour. This 'neurosis', as they see it, leads him to neglect his main business — avenging his father. But the destruction of Hamlet's idealism, his belief in love and goodness, his trust in nobility and his faith in humanity, by a shattering revelation of evil and treachery constitute the very essence of his tragedy. Life has become meaningless to him:

> How weary, stale, flat and unprofitable
> Seem to me all the uses of this world!
>
> (Act 1, scene 2)

The play is full of a profound sense of loss and waste, and nowhere is it felt so painfully and poignantly as in the contrast between what Hamlet was and what his awareness of corruption has done to him. As Ophelia says of him:

> O, what a noble mind is here o'erthrown!
> The courtier's, soldier's, scholar's, eye, tongue, sword,
> Th' expectancy and rose of the fair state,
> The glass of fashion, and the mould of form,
> Th' observed of all observers, quite quite down . . .
>
> (Act 3, scene 1)

The poetic power with which Shakespeare presents Hamlet's disillusion makes the critical attitude that would blame him for allowing his painful reflections on his mother to impede a swift, no-nonsense revenge seem crass.

The Moral Question: Revenge

The difficulties of his situation, and his sensitive and individual temperament, are not the only factors which cause Hamlet to hesitate. There is left the great moral problem examined by the play: even if Claudius and Gertrude are guilty of all the ghost's charges, is Hamlet justified in seeking revenge? There are two wrong ways of answering this question. One is to refer all that happens in *Hamlet* to the many revenge plays of the period, which constituted an extremely popular genre or sub-genre. The revenge theme on the stage, in works such as *The Spanish Tragedy* by Kyd (1557—95) and the missing *Hamlet* play which Shakespeare would have known, quickly acquired certain conventions — the ghost of the murdered person urging revenge, a hesitation or delay on the avenger's part, and his feigned or acted madness. Further, 'the revenge is accomplished terribly, fittingly, with irony and deceit. Once his resolution is screwed to the point, the revenger becomes exceedingly cunning, dissembles with the murderers, and adroitly plans their downfall'.[2] So, according to this view, moral questions do not arise: Shakespeare's play simply works according to a successful and proven stock formula. But it is not legitimate to judge the exceptional on the basis of expectations aroused by the average: *Hamlet* indeed uses, but it also examines and probes, the conventions of the revenge play.

Another unfruitful critical strategy is to relate *Hamlet* to the ethical debate on revenge. The Elizabethans were familiar with the uncompromising biblical text: 'Avenge not yourselves . . . Vengeance is mine; I will repay, saith the Lord' (Romans, 12:19). They had also, however, considerable sympathy for some kinds of private revenge. But *Hamlet* is a play, not a debate on ethical or doctrinal problems.

If we respond to the play, rather than to extraneous matters of convention and doctrine, we observe that Hamlet seems to think of his revenge as an unquestionable duty when under the stress of great emotion. It is not surprising that he should wish to 'sweep' to his revenge in the actual presence of his father's spirit, in Act 1, scene 5, when natural perturbation is aggravated by the spirit's account of his pains in purgatorial fires and by his direct appeal to Hamlet's love. The same is true of Hamlet's words in Act 3, scene 4 ('Do you not come your tardy son to chide'): again he is in the presence of the ghost, and in the middle of an intensely emotional scene with his mother.

Likewise, the vengeful statements in the great soliloquy at the end of Act 2, scene 2 ('I should ha' fatted all the region kites/With this slave's offal') come after the 'passionate' player's speech that Hamlet had requested, almost as if he wished to be worked to a passion. The two most unequivocally vengeful speeches, that beginning 'Tis now the very witching time of night' (Act 3, scene 2), and that over the praying Claudius (Act 3, scene 3) which Dr Johnson found 'too horrible to be read or uttered', must be seen in the context of Hamlet's violent excitement at the success of the mouse-trap. There is a suggestive pattern here: where Hamlet sees himself most clearly as an avenger, Shakespeare has placed him in a situation of great emotional stress of one kind or another.

There is much evidence that in less heated moments Hamlet has scruples about revenge, despite the almost intolerable pressure put on him by the ghost's command. The scene where he has promised to sweep to his revenge ends with the much more reflective and rueful couplet:

> The time is out of joint. O cursèd spite,
> That ever I was born to set it right!
>
> (Act 1, scene 5)

This suggests at very least no great enthusiasm for the task laid on him. Again, only twenty lines after he has been speaking about fatting the region kites with this slave's offal, he is musing that the spirit he has seen may be a devil and that he must have 'more relative' grounds for proceeding against Claudius. Nevertheless, the impression is left at the end of Act 2, scene 2 that Hamlet is prepared to take his revenge if the play proves Claudius's guilt; yet, when we next see him he is pondering (Act 3, scene 1):

> Whether 'tis nobler in the mind to suffer
> The slings and arrows of outrageous fortune

and alluding to that conscience which makes cowards of us all. Later, he asks himself explicitly whether his failure to carry out the revenge is due to 'some craven scruple/Of thinking too precisely on th' event'; and even in Act 5, when Hamlet has direct evidence of Claudius's attempt on his life to add to the other crimes, he is still asking questions of his conscience:

> is't not perfect conscience
> To quit him with this arm?

There is no contradiction between these facts and the fact that at other times Hamlet expresses himself vengefully. What it shows is how thoroughly Shakespeare has dramatised the problem of revenge, building it into the very fabric of his hero's mind. Hamlet does not see his scruple clearly for what it is — to the dramatic advantage of the play, the absence of a full-scale explicit debate on the rights and wrongs of revenge preserving *Hamlet* from the simplicities of the morality play. When he is conscious of his scruple he considers it to be 'craven', that his conscience makes him a coward, that he is 'a dull and muddy-mettled rascal', that he is 'pigeon-livered'. In fact, it is this 'thinking too precisely on th' event', this unwillingness to be or become the bloody and resolute avenger, that gives him most of his nobility and moral heroism.

The implication of the question 'Why does Hamlet delay?' is frequently that there is something weak and disabling in that delay. But the play itself suggests that Shakespeare means us to sympathise with — and even admire — Hamlet's scruples about revenge and his consequent delay. For our reactions to Hamlet are connected with our reactions to an avenger who *is* bloody, bold and resolute, who scorns any thought of delay — Laertes.

Hamlet and Laertes

The situations of the two young men are deliberately paralleled: as Hamlet says, 'by the image of my cause I see/The portraiture of his' (Act 5, scene 2). But Hamlet is overgenerous here, for Laertes, though originally honourable, has become corrupt. He shows a brutal readiness 'to cut Hamlet's throat i' th' church' but it is not so much the brutality that alienates the audience — Hamlet is occasionally brutal — as his willing acceptance, at Claudius's prompting, of devious and dishonourable methods to encompass his revenge (Act 4, scene 7). Not content with the suggestion that in a rigged fencing match he may 'with ease,/Or with a little shuffling' kill Hamlet with an unbated sword, he refines on the idea with a touch worthy of Claudius himself — he will poison the tip of the sword with the 'unction of a mountebank'. He even accepts the final villainous trick, the poisoned chalice which will be ready for Hamlet should the other stratagems fail. We cannot miss the irony or the force of the contrast with the truly honourable man when in Act 5, scene 2, Laertes says that Hamlet's generous apology to him does not satisfy his 'terms of honour'. In the conventional revenge play, such as Kyd's *Spanish Tragedy* or *The Revenger's Tragedy* (1607) of Tourneur (1575—1626), the avenger rapidly becomes as cunning, deceitful and bloody as those who have wronged him. Laertes slides easily into treachery and villainy; quite clearly Shakespeare conceives of Hamlet as a departure from type, and his reflective brooding on the event seems all the more sympathetic by contrast with the unthinking revenger.

Hamlet's Heroic End

Every audience is led to expect that somehow or other, Hamlet will punish Claudius's crime. How will Shakespeare contrive this without contradicting the emotional responses aroused in the audience by his unflattering implications about mind-less revenge? He must retain sympathy for Hamlet's scrupulous-ness — the quality that differentiates him from Laertes and for that matter from Claudius — while at the same time enabling him to end in a truly heroic manner.

The solution of this difficult dramatic problem is a brilliant one. Towards the end of Act 4, the responsibility for sustain-ing the impetus of the plot shifts from Hamlet to Claudius and Laertes, with their evil designs on Hamlet's life. We are thus prepared for the more passive Hamlet of the first part of Act 5, whose meditations on the grave and on Providence fit the more easily into the dramatic framework. In the grave-yard scene, Hamlet displays an acceptance of men's mortality and a sense of the pettiness of human action when viewed in the context of eternity. This attitude is not fatalistic, since Hamlet stresses the necessity of 'readiness' for anything that may come; nor does it mark a radical and disfiguring break with the Hamlet seen up to now. His readiness to leave his affairs in the hands of Providence may be seen as a logical — even inevitable — extension of that scruple about the justice of blood-revenge, a deeply embedded scruple but one of which he has never been fully aware in the torments of his situation. The scruple has been a powerful *feeling*, not an explicit moral policy.

Shakespeare does not want to leave us with an impression of a prince who is too passive — hence the excellent dramatic device of the duel. The decision of Claudius and Laertes to use the fencing match as a vehicle for their treachery, and Hamlet's discovery of that treachery, enable him to execute justice on Claudius at last, and in a heroic context. The last memories of *Hamlet* will be of the prince with sword in hand, so that it is entirely appropriate that Fortinbras should order, to accompany his funeral procession, 'The soldiers' music and the rite of war'. Finally, such a setting for Hamlet's decisive act adds to our sympathy and admiration of him in a special way. In the context of 'shuffling', of poisoned swords and challenges, the truth of his treacherous adversary's tribute to him, that he is 'Most generous, and free from all contriving', acquires a special force and poignancy. To the last, Hamlet has refused to descend to the moral level of his opponent.

The Tragic Effect

Part of the sense of tragedy in *Hamlet* comes from the power of Shakespeare's presentation of a corrupt world. It has frequently been pointed out how often the play's imagery refers to poison, a poison of evil infecting the heart of the state and seeping outwards to infect almost everyone. It is fitting that in the end all the major characters (save Ophelia, whose innocence is preserved only by her madness) should die of that poison in a literal as well as a figurative sense. If the Danish court stands as a symbol of human life, Shakespeare's vision of the condition of man takes one to the heart of darkness.

How is the good man to act in such a world without himself becoming tainted? It is virtually impossible. At very least, he must suffer, as Hamlet does, a knowledge of evil which tests to destruction his capacity for idealism, love, and faith in humanity. Life itself becomes 'an unweeded garden/That grows to seed'. But more, to live in this world is occasionally to have to use its weapons. Hamlet has to 'seem', he kills Polonius, he is partly responsible for Ophelia's madness, he sends two friends of his youth to death. As Maynard Mack says: 'He had never meant to dirty himself with these things, but from the moment of the ghost's challenge to act, this dirtying was inevitable. It is the condition of living at all in such a world. To quote Polonius, who knew that world so well, men become "a little soil'd i' th' working".'³ *Hamlet* is a powerful tragedy of loss and waste and disillusion.

Most ironically — and painfully — Hamlet's catastrophe is not due to his failings but to his admirable qualities. We are not to see his 'delay' as evidence of dithering immaturity or disabling neurosis, but as at least partly due to the very fineness of his nature. Had he been more brutal, had he been less scrupulous, had he descended to the level of Claudius, had he had less capacity for insight into and reflection upon his situation, he might have been a successful 'doer' in the world of corruption. The concept that a man's goodness may help to make catastrophe inevitable is a deeply disturbing and tragic idea, producing in audiences what Willard Farnham aptly calls 'moral vertigo'.⁴

This, however, is not the whole story. Hamlet's 'noble mind' is (*pace* Ophelia) *not* 'o'erthrown'. He cannot live in his rotten world without some of its grime rubbing off on him, yet we are left with an overwhelming impression of how successfully Hamlet has retained his nobility of spirit, despite everything. Placed in a horrible situation, not of his own making, he emerges as perhaps the most sympathetic of Shakespeare's tragic heroes. The characteristic balance of great tragedy is maintained: *Hamlet* arouses fear for the mystery of man's fate, and admiration for the greatness of his soul.

King Lear: Optimism, Pessimism, and the Tragic Experience

A paradoxical feature of tragedy is that, generally speaking, the viewing or reading of a tragic drama is not necessarily depressing. This is, at first sight, surprising, since tragedy deals with the bleaker sides of human experience and takes full account of suffering and death. Yet tragedy is often enjoyable (otherwise why should we go to the theatre?), and the reasons for this are not far to seek. Tragic drama may affirm the nobility of man's nature, or simply face with clear-eyed vision the worst possible aspects of life, or embody its perceptions in the dignity and beauty of aesthetic perfection. And we find these 'compensations' in plays as different, and as widely separated in time, as *Oedipus* and *Hamlet*.

Concentration on these 'compensations' produces what may be called the optimistic view of tragedy. 'Hamlet and Lear are gay', as W. B. Yeats writes in his poem 'Lapis Lazuli', and so too should we be. We should not, however, over-rationalise tragedy, domesticate it by shutting our eyes to its power to disturb, to terrify. If we can see reasons for 'optimism' in our experiencing of the tragic situation, we must not simply blink away the darker implications in that situation. *King Lear*, often seen as the grimmest and most profound of Shakespeare's tragedies, is a good example of the comprehensiveness of great tragedy, and therefore a living dramatic proof of the inadequacy of one-sided critical perspectives.

Cruelty

King Lear asks the great tragic questions — what sort of moral universe do we live in? where is justice to be found? — with especial intensity. Much of the action in the play has a cruelty rarely equalled elsewhere in Shakespeare, or indeed in any drama. Drama is — because of its physicality — especially effective in depictions of cruelty. In Soyinka's *The Strong Breed* (1963), for instance, a young school-teacher becomes a sacrifical scapegoat for a corrupt society. He is whipped before being killed, and the action is dramatised with merci-less and terrifying power. Soyinka is extremely aware of man's inhumanity to man — nearly the whole of his later play *Madmen and Specialists* (1970) is drenched in the cruelty of that faceless, bureaucratic kind which makes our modern world so frightening. The Malaysian play, *A Tiger is Loose in our Community* (1967) by Edward Dorall (b. 1936), ends with four neighbours systematically kicking to death a young man who has been stabbed. The blinding of the aged Gloucester in *King Lear* is, however, a supreme example of cruelty. He is host to the merciless Cornwall and Regan, but this does not save him:

Cornwall:	See't shalt thou never. Fellows, hold the chair.
	Upon these eyes of thine I'll set my foot . . .
	Out, vile jelly!
	Where is thy lustre now? . . .
Regan:	Go thrust him out at gates, and let him smell
	His way to Dover.

(Act 3, scene 7)

Lear does not encounter quite such physical savagery, but the famous parallelism of the two plots, where old men are rejected and treated cruelly by their children, contrives to link Gloucester's physical anguish to Lear's mental torture, as he stands defenceless in the storm. Further, the parallelism suggests that this is the way of the world — as A. C. Bradley puts it, it 'terrifies by suggesting that the folly of Lear and the ingratitude of his daughters are no accidents or merely individual aberrations, but that in that dark cold world some fateful malignant influence is abroad, turning the hearts of the fathers against their children and of the children against their fathers, smiting the earth with a curse.'[5] That so much cruelty should be generated from family contexts sharpens the horror.

Animal Imagery

It is not surprising, therefore, that so many of the images of the play should see human nature as bestial and predatory: evil is seen as animalism. Goneril and Regan are 'dog-hearted daughters', 'tigers', 'she-foxes'; Goneril is a 'detested kite' with a 'wolvish visage'; she strikes her father with her tongue 'Most serpent-like upon the very heart' and would 'in his anointed flesh rash boarish fangs'. Edgar as poor Tom describes himself as 'hog in sloth, fox in stealth, wolf in greediness, dog in madness, lion in prey'. Oswald is a 'whoreson dog . . . a cur'. Contemplating this bestial world, where behaviour fully justifies description, Albany remarks:

> If that the heavens do not their visible spirits
> Send quickly down to tame these vile offences,
> It will come
> Humanity must perforce prey on itself
> Like monsters of the deep.
>
> (Act 4, scene 2)

A Universe of Evil

King Lear also has a more sweeping range of reference than the other tragedies, in the sense that his experience turns Lear's eyes not only intensely on his own particular griefs, but outwards on a corrupted and blasted world. Shakespeare's bleak vision in the play is thus given a resonant universality:

> See how yond justice rails upon yond simple thief.
> Hark in thine ear: change places and, handy-dandy,
> which is the justice, which is the thief? . . .
> Thou rascal beadle, hold thy bloody hand!
> Why dost thou lash that whore? Strip thy own back;
> Thou hotly lusts to use her in that kind
> For which thou whipp'st her. The usurer hangs
> the cozener.
> Through tattered clothes great vices do appear;
> Robes and furred gowns hide all. Plate sin with gold,
> And the strong lance of justice hurtless breaks:
> Arm it in rags, a pigmy's straw does pierce it.
>
> (Act 4, scene 6)

This is only one of many speeches which are not strictly necessary for the advancement of the action, but which are vital constituent elements in our sense of the moral darkness of the dramatic universe of the play.

Suffering as Redemptive

These are among the aspects of *King Lear* which caused critics to suggest that Shakespeare may have here yielded to the 'infirmity of misanthropy and despair'.[6] Another view of the play, however, which does not in any way minimise the imaginative impact of its cruelty and beastliness, advances a far more positive interpretation, arguing that the suffering of Lear and Gloucester, though appalling, is educative and, ultimately, redemptive. Cordelia, Kent and the Fool all attempt to instruct Lear in the ways of wisdom, but, says G. I. Duthie in his excellent edition of the play, 'his most effective teacher is Suffering . . . He learns to be patient under affliction. He learns repentance, humility and charitable fellow-feeling with even the lowest of distressed humanity.'[7] The mental and physical anguish that Lear undergoes do indeed lead him to a deeper and truer perception of life. The change in him can be observed first in the storm scene:

> Poor naked wretches, whereso'er you are,
> That bide the pelting of this pitiless storm,
> How shall your houseless heads and unfed sides,
> Your looped and windowed raggedness, defend you
> From seasons such as these? O' I have ta'en
> Too little care of this! Take physic, pomp;
> Expose thyself to feel what wretches feel,
> That thou mayst shake the superflux to them
> And show the heavens more just.
>
> (Act 3, scene 4)

The educative or redemptive function of suffering for Lear is emphasised by the essentially similar pattern in the Gloucester sub-plot. Gloucester, too, learns from his agony:

> Let the superfluous and lust-dieted man
> That slaves your ordinance, that will not see
> Because he does not feel, feel your power quickly;
> So distribution should undo excess,
> And each man have enough.
>
> (Act 4, scene 1)

It is not just a matter of their suffering bringing Lear and Gloucester to a more general understanding of the world: it leads them to the fullest and most moving reconciliation with the children they have wronged, and in doing so initiates them into what is close to being a paradisaical fullness of life. Lear's words to Cordelia in Act 5, scene 3, suggest this most explicitly:

> When thou dost ask me blessing, I'll kneel down
> And ask of thee forgiveness. So we'll live,
> And pray, and sing, and tell old tales, and laugh . . .
> And take upon's the mystery of things,
> As if we were God's spies . . .

The progress of a foolish man (for Lear, unlike Oedipus or Hamlet, can certainly be accused of serious moral flaws) towards wisdom and spiritual regeneration through suffering, is 'optimistic' on two main counts. First, it means that the suffering is not pointless — compare the very different account of suffering, grotesque and horrible because never understood, in such modern 'absurdist' classics as the novels of Franz Kafka (1883–1924) and Samuel Beckett's work. Secondly, such an arrangement of the action is strongly suggestive of some of the central beliefs of Christianity, a religion of its nature basically optimistic. Christ's life and death provide the ultimate example of redemptive suffering, and his teaching stresses that a man must lose his life to find it. Other features of the play have been seen as markedly Christian, especially the characterisation of Edgar and Cordelia. Edgar returns good for evil, and counsels his father repeatedly against despair; and Cordelia is conceived as a Christ-like figure. She is thus described weeping over her father's sufferings:

> There she shook
> The holy water from her heavenly eyes
> (Act 4, scene 3)

and she speaks of going about her father's business, in Act 4, scene 4, in words that seem to echo directly Christ's own.[8] In Act 4, scene 6, a gentleman says of Lear:

> Thou hast one daughter
> Who redeems nature from the general curse
> Which twain have brought her to.

The climactic image comes in the great reconciliation scene
(Act 4, scene 7), when the father in his disorientation cries
out to his daughter:

> You do me wrong to take me out o' th' grave:
> Thou art a soul in bliss; but I am bound
> Upon a wheel of fire . . .

The play is set in a pagan world, of course, and therefore
we would not expect more explicit allusions to or drawing on
Christian doctrine. But it is significant that within the non-
Christian context which his source-story imposed on him,
Shakespeare should utilise these markedly Christian views of
suffering and of goodness. And occasionally 'good' characters
imply that there is a fundamental principle of justice at work
in the moral universe. For instance, when Albany hears of the
killing of the vicious Cornwall by the servant outraged at
Cornwall's treatment of old Gloucester, he exclaims:

> This shows you are above,
> You justicers, that these our nether crimes
> So speedily can venge.
> (Act 4, scene 2)

To sum up, the 'optimistic' view of *King Lear* sees the play as
an expression of a profoundly religious view of life: the
universe has a purpose, love and goodness are the balm of
hurt minds, suffering can lead to moral salvation.

'The Gods' and the Death of Cordelia

This approach is based on evidence in the drama, but the
trouble is that it is rather selective in its choice of evidence.
For example, the concept of 'just gods' is challenged at many
points in the play. Gloucester gives utterance to the bleakest
alternative view, that the gods are malevolent:

As flies to wanton boys are we to th' gods;
They kill us for their sport.

(Act 4, scene 1)

Another point of view is the determinist position, that human destiny is governed by remote and indifferent astrological influences, by what Lear calls in the opening scene 'the operation of the orbs/From whom we do exist and cease to be'. Kent expresses this view most concisely as he broods on the difference between Cordelia and her tigerish sisters:

It is the stars,
The stars above us, govern our conditions.

(Act 4, scene 3)

But perhaps the very ideas of the gods, just or unjust, or of the governing stars, are nonsense. Human life is entirely in human hands, and human nature is corrupt. This is Edmund's position. As he gives orders to the captain to murder Lear and Cordelia he remarks curtly (Act 5, scene 3), 'Know thou this, that men/Are as the time is'. Earlier, with sturdy atheism he contemptuously dismisses any notion of higher powers:

An admirable evasion of whoremaster man, to lay his goatish disposition to the charge of a star! My father compounded with my mother under the Dragon's tail, and my nativity was under Ursa Major, so that it follows I am rough and lecherous. Fut, I should have been that I am, had the maidenliest star in the firmament twinkled on my bastardizing.

(Act 1, scene 2)

And Goneril and Regan abide unconsciously by Edmund's conscious code. 'Nature' is their 'goddess', and nature is amoral. The general significance of all these contradictory references in the play, for any of which supporting evidence could be marshalled from the action, is to make the whole question of the nature of justice a key issue. It would be very difficult to argue that Shakespeare means us to give our full assent to any one of these views and to discount the others.

Rather, the dramatic effect is to bring home in a powerful way to us how very precarious and fragile the mere concept of cosmic justice is in the world of *King Lear*.

The greatest problem for those who wish to argue for a positive vision of life in the play is the death of Cordelia. It is not just that Cordelia is wholly good and innocent, but that her murder is in a sense purely fortuitous – Edmund, who ordered it, countermands the order, but too late. And, as if to shock us the more into a full apprehension of the injustice of this death, immediately before the entrance of the anguished father with the limp, dead body of his daughter in his arms, Albany has called out in supplication 'The gods defend her!' Only in Shakespeare's play does the aged king have to bear this agony: in three of the source versions of the story Lear dies first, and in the other, neither dies. The appalling stroke is then a deliberate artistic choice. The great eighteenth-century editor of Shakespeare, Dr Johnson, speaks for generations of readers and audiences:

> Shakespeare has suffered the virtue of Cordelia to perish in a just cause, contrary to the natural ideas of justice, to the hope of the reader, and, what is yet more strange, to the faith of chronicles . . . And if my sensations could add anything to the general suffrage, I might relate, that I was many years ago so shocked by Cordelia's death, that I know not whether I ever endured to read again the last scenes of the play till I undertook to revise them as an editor.[9]

Cordelia's death cannot be subsumed into the idea that for Lear, suffering is redemptive, because when it happens he has already attained to the fulness of spiritual regeneration. The last scene had opened with his ecstatic vision of the future:

> We two alone will sing like birds i' th' cage;
> When thou dost ask me blessing, I'll kneel down
> And ask of thee forgiveness.

It closes with his cry of anguish which seems to arraign the evil chance, injustice and misery of all human life:

Why should a dog, a horse, a rat have life,
And thou no breath at all? Thou'lt come no more,
Never, never, never, never, never!

The only appropriate response to Lear's final anguish is
Kent's:

Vex not his ghost: O let him pass; he hates him
That would upon the rack of this tough world
Stretch him out longer.

The metaphor, appropriately enough, is drawn from the
torture chamber; and the wan sense of restoration of order
right at the end, so different from the positive sense of the
cleansed state of the body politic that we get in *Macbeth* and
Hamlet, does little to offset the gloom of the final moments
of *King Lear*.

None of these remarks is intended to deny the existence of
any uplifting or encouraging perceptions in the play, but
rather to question the validity of any view of the play which
would leave us with the essentially anti-tragic feeling expressed
by Milton at the end of his *Samson Agonistes*:

Nothing is here for tears, nothing to wail
Or knock the breast . . .

There is plenty 'for tears' in *King Lear*, and for more than
tears. The play makes us feel a sense of dread at the human
condition itself. Tragedy can, but does not necessarily, comfort us. Some words of Kafka apply very well to the effect of
a work like *King Lear*:

If the book we are reading does not wake us, as with a fist
hammering on our skull, why then do we read it? So that
it shall make us happy? Good God, we would also be happy
if we had no books, and such books as make us happy we
could, if need be, write ourselves. But what we must have
are those books which come upon us like ill-fortune, and
distress us deeply, like the death of one we love better
than ourselves, like suicide. A book must be an ice-axe to
break the sea frozen inside us.[10]

Macbeth: Shakespeare's Imagery

While an over-concentration on a Shakespearean play as a
poem or an exclusive attention to the symbolic patterns of
the imagery leads to a neglect of the 'dramatic reality' (Wolf-
gang Clemen's phrase)[11] of the play — its dramatic technique,
plot, manipulation of character, and so on — nevertheless it is
in Shakespeare's tragedy that we see the most impressive
illustration of the advantages of poetic drama. Shakespeare's
imagery is never merely decorative, but functional, embodying character, creating moral meaning, and directing attention
towards the central theme of the play. *Macbeth* provides a
particularly clear example of the artistic and dramatic effectiveness of Shakespeare's use of imagery.

Sleep

It is largely through the imagery which he puts in Macbeth's
mouth, for example, that Shakespeare retains sympathy for
his hero, despite his bloody and premeditated crime. He has
killed Duncan in his sleep, a fact which strikes his imagination,
in the immediate aftermath, with special horror:

> Methought I heard a voice cry 'Sleep no more!
> Macbeth does murder sleep', the innocent sleep,
> Sleep that knits up the ravell'd sleave of care,
> The death of each day's life, sore labour's bath,
> Balm of hurt minds, great nature's second course,
> Chief nourisher in life's feast . . .
>
>   (Act 2, scene 2)

The heaped-up phrases are not merely decorative embellish-
ments of a single, simple idea: they register most fully not
just the yearning for a peace which his brutal deed has
destroyed for ever, but also the *intensity* of Macbeth's awareness of the beauty of the natural order which he has disrupted.
The idea of sleep becomes a powerful motif in the play, as
Macbeth experiences the hollowness of his kingship and,
more ironically, envy of his victim:

But let the frame of things disjoint, both the worlds suffer,
Ere we will eat our meal in fear, and sleep
In the affliction of these terrible dreams,
That shake us nightly. Better be with the dead,
Whom we, to gain our peace, have sent to peace,
Than on the torture of the mind to lie
In restless ecstacy. Duncan is in his grave;
After life's fitful fever he sleeps well . . .

(Act 3, scene 2)

The 'terrible dreams that shake us nightly' are projected outwards, in dramatic terms, in Lady Macbeth's sleepwalking
scene — the Lady Macbeth whose reaction to Macbeth's
initial apostrophe of sleep was a puzzled 'What do you mean?'
— and Macbeth is forced to pray on her behalf, not for the
'innocent sleep', the 'balm of hurt minds' (that is no longer
possible), but for the drug of oblivion:

Canst thou not minister to a mind diseas'd,
Pluck from the memory a rooted sorrow,
Raze out the written troubles of the brain,
And with some sweet oblivious antidote
Cleanse the stuff'd bosom of that perilous stuff
Which weighs upon the heart?

(Act 5, scene 3)

Macbeth *has* murdered sleep; but it is the intensity of his
imaginative grasp of the fact, conveyed through this imagery,
in which bath and balm, nourishment and cleansing, are
opposed by torture and fever, restlessness and disease, that
makes us retain our sympathy for him. He is a man whose
imagination will not leave him alone. Thus imagery (and that
associated with sleep is of course only one example) performs
an important dramatic function in deepening the apprehension
of character. Macbeth's haunted imagery-laden language is his
inner self. Bradley puts it eloquently: 'Macbeth's better nature
. . . instead of speaking to him in the overt language of moral
ideas, commands and prohibitions, incorporates itself in
images which alarm and horrify. His imagination is thus the
best of him.'[12]

Blood

Macbeth is a play which is drenched in blood — the word is used over one hundred times in the play. The bloody sergeant at the beginning speaks of Macbeth and Banquo meaning 'to bathe in reeking wounds'; Duncan's 'silver skin' is 'lac'd with his golden blood'; Scotland weeps and bleeds under the tyrant. The most powerful reference is Macbeth's appalled reaction to his hands after the murder:

> What hands are here? Ha! they pluck out mine eyes.
> Will all great Neptune's ocean wash this blood
> Clean from my hand? No, this my hand will rather
> The multitudinous seas incarnadine,
> Making the green one red.
>
> (Act 2, scene 2)

This horrifying image of the sea turning blood-red is taken further later, where Macbeth sees himself not as one trying to cleanse himself with water but as one wading in blood:

> I am in blood
> Stepped in so far, that, should I wade no more,
> Returning were as tedious as go o'er.
>
> (Act 3, scene 4)

Lady Macbeth ripostes impatiently to Macbeth immediately after the murder 'A little water clears us of this deed'; but blood is not so easily cleansed, as the audience sees in the sleepwalking scene where she ineffectually attempts to 'wash' her hands: 'Here's the smell of the blood still: all the perfumes of Arabia will not sweeten this little hand'.

Darkness

As powerful as the many references to blood — of which the above are only a few — is a constant harping on darkness and night in *Macbeth*. The murder of Duncan is something that can only be contemplated in the absence of light; it is some-

thing that is too terrible to be looked upon. Macbeth says in
Act 1, scene 4:

> Stars, hide your fires!
> Let not light see my black and deep desires;
> The eye wink at the hand; yet let that be,
> Which the eye fears, when it is done, to see.

And Lady Macbeth, also in the first Act, similarly makes the
link between darkness and the fear of vision:

> Come, thick Night,
> And pall thee in the dunnest smoke of Hell,
> That my keen knife see not the wound it makes,
> Nor Heaven peep through the blanket of the dark,
> To cry, 'Hold, hold!'
>   (Act 1, scene 5)

The homeliness of the word 'peep', as of a frightened child in
a darkened bedroom, immeasurably increases the horror of
the words, as do Macbeth's references to the sport of falconry
and his observation of the natural world in the following,
when he contemplates the murder of Banquo and Fleance:

> Come, seeling Night,
> Scarf up the tender eye of pitiful day,
> And, with thy bloody and invisible hand,
> Cancel, and tear to pieces, that great bond
> Which keeps me pale! — Light thickens; and the crow
> Makes wing to th' rooky wood,
> Good things of day begin to droop and drowse . . .
>   (Act 3, scene 2)

(The last line here, of course, connects with the ideas of the
naturalness of innocent sleep from which the guilty Macbeth
is excluded.) Towards the end, Lady Macbeth cannot be
without light 'by her continually; 'tis her command'; and
Macbeth himself can only see life as a brief candle which
must be quenched. Their prayers for darkness to replace light
have been duly heard.

The imagery of blood and darkness does more than any-thing else to establish the atmosphere of the play. By 'atmos-phere' is meant not the general emotional feeling, the sense of an ominous physical setting, but the moral atmosphere of the drama. References to blood and darkness, like the poison imagery in *Hamlet* or the animal imagery in *King Lear*, connect organically with the thematic core of the play, with Shake-speare's vision of the nature of evil, and give that vision powerful imaginative reverberation.

Nature

Shakespeare's imagery, then, creates character and establishes thematic keynotes. It does far more than eke out the imper-fections of a bare or primitive stage, lacking in scenery, by painting verbal pictures which establish locality for the audience. Consider, for example, the exchange between Duncan and Banquo in front of Macbeth's castle.

> *Duncan:* This castle hath a pleasant seat; the air
> Nimbly and sweetly recommends itself
> Unto our gentle senses.
> *Banquo:*   This guest of summer,
> The temple-haunting martlet, does approve,
> By his loved mansionry, that the heaven's breath
> Smells wooingly here: no jutty, frieze,
> Buttress, nor coign of vantage, but this bird
> Hath made her pendent bed, and procreant cradle:
> Where they most breed and haunt, I have observ'd
> The air is delicate.
>   (Act 1, scene 6)

Shakespeare's poetry does set the scene here, and does so with a nice irony, the 'pleasant seat' being where Duncan will meet his death, and it is also exceedingly lyrical. But the lines embody a key image in a complex interrelated series of images which establishes the contrast between beneficent nature and the unnatural distortion which Macbeth's deeds unleash in the moral world. These harmless and beautiful birds of day contrast with the birds of prey who behave so strangely after Duncan's murder:

> 'Tis unnatural,
> Even like the deed that's done . . .
> A falcon, towering in her pride of place,
> Was by a mousing owl hawk'd at, and kill'd.
>
> (Act 2, scene 4)

'Temple-haunting' assumes a poignant and ironic contrast when Macduff later cries out:

> Most sacrilegious Murther hath broke ope
> The Lord's anointed Temple.
>
> (Act 2, scene 3)

The chief impression left by Banquo's words is of the grace and beauty of natural fertility — 'loved', 'wooingly', 'bed', 'procreant', 'breed' all suggest the bounty and order of nature. Human relationships share in this healthy natural and organic order: as Duncan says to Macbeth:

> I have begun to plant thee, and will labour
> To make thee full of growing.
>
> (Act 1, scene 4)

And Lady Macbeth admits that Macbeth's nature is 'too full o' th' milk of human kindness' (where 'kindness' means 'nature').

The deeds of Macbeth and his wife are wholly unnatural, and the language serves to keep alive before us an image of the natural order even when it is being grossly contravened. The point could be illustrated at great length, but one brief example will suffice. It arises from all the associations of milk with fertility and maternity and nourishment. People are *naturally* imbued with the milk of human kindness: to lose it, they must 'de-nature' themselves — as Lady Macbeth does (in Act 1, scene 5):

> Come, you spirits
> That tend on mortal thoughts, unsex me here,
> And fill me, from the crown to the toe, top-full
> Of direst cruelty! . . .
> Come to my woman's breasts,
> And take my milk for gall, you murth'ring ministers . . .

And yet more horribly, she indicates how far she is prepared to go in perverting the natural as she urges Macbeth to the 'sticking-place':

> I have given suck, and know
> How tender 'tis to love the babe that milks me:
> I would, while it was smiling in my face,
> Have plucked my nipple from his boneless gums,
> And dash'd the brains out, had I so sworn
> As you have done to this.
> (Act 1 scene 7)

The words evoke powerfully the deepest maternal instincts and simultaneously an appalling readiness to subordinate them to more ruthless claims. In fact (though the superb phrase is used by Malcolm of himself), both Macbeth and his wife

> Pour the sweet milk of concord into Hell.

Much more could be said of Shakespeare's imagery in *Macbeth* — Caroline Spurgeon, for example, drew attention[13] to what she feels is Shakespeare's essential visual image of Macbeth, by discussing the pervasive use of imagery to do with clothes, which culminates in the striking lines in Act 5, scene 2:

> now does he feel his title
> Hang loose about him, like a giant's robe
> Upon a dwarfish thief.

Shakespeare's images, then, do not merely cloak the thought or decorate or prettify it. They are dramatically functional, creating and shaping our view of character and theme, establishing atmosphere and evaluative touchstones and — of course — enhancing the expression of feeling. The interconnectedness of Shakespearean imagery in a work like *Macbeth* is at once conducive to, and ultimate evidence of, the unity of the drama.

5 Comedy and Satire: 'A Midsummer Night's Dream' and 'Volpone', and Later Developments in Comedy

Comedy as a Form

There are two main problems which face the student and lover of comedy right at the outset. The first is that there has been over the centuries a steady tone in the statements of critical theorists — frequently accompanied by an unspoken agreement in the minds of their readers — implying that dramatic comedy is tragedy's poor sister, an inferior, unserious and essentially trivial form.

Apart from this question of relative status, the second immediate difficulty consists in the dispute over the definition — or even the possibility of definition — of comedy as a form. There have been psychological theories of comedy which have attempted to explain how it works by explaining laughter, there have been 'mythic' or 'ritualistic' theories of comedy which concentrate on its connections with ancient fertility customs; there is a moralistic theory of comedy which sees its essential business as the correction of folly; there have been more strictly literary theories of comedy which attempt to trace its traditional lineaments from what are called Greek 'Old' and 'New' Comedy, and there are many other theories besides. Under the weight of such formidable abstractions, the hapless individual comic text may well disappear from view; and we can understand the irritation of the critic L. C. Knights who wrote in 1933: 'It is almost impossible to read a particular comedy without the interference of critical presuppositions derived from one or other of those who have sought to define comedy in the abstract.'[1] This chapter proceeds on the principle that we are indeed likely to derive more critical understanding of the larger aspects of comedy by working out towards them from individual texts than by working inwards from the abstractions of general theory.

Shakespeare: *A Midsummer Night's Dream*

The first problem of comedy, that it seems wholly artificial, wholly frivolous and removed from the serious business of living, can be seen clearly in Shakespeare's first great mature comedy, *A Midsummer Night's Dream*. The play dramatises the mistakes and confusions in the cross-wooing of a group of young Athenians who have none of the individualised particularity of Shakespeare's tragic characters — who seem, indeed, more or less interchangeable; it deals with the farcical efforts of a group of Athenian 'mechanicals', or artisans, to stage a truly dreadful play, 'the most lamentable comedy and most cruel death of Pyramus and Thisbe', for the wedding celebrations of their ruler Duke Theseus; and most of the action of the play takes place in an enchanted wood outside Athens which is populated mainly by fairies. The play has, it is true, a delightful lyric atmosphere achieved mainly by the imagery of moonlight with which Shakespeare drenched his action, but this too, going alongside the magic and the farce of that action, may lead us to think of the work as purely a thing of gauze and gossamer which the rude critic murders to dissect.

Theseus and Love's Irrationality

There is, however, more to *A Midsummer Night's Dream* than lyric escapist fantasy. The play has a strongly delineated moral theme or idea, namely, the irrationality of love, em-

bodied most powerfully in its great central symbolic picture
of the beautiful Queen of the fairies, Titania, waking to dote
on the monstrous Bottom:

> . . . thy fair virtue's force perforce doth move me
> On the first view to say, to swear, I love thee.

Bottom is wearing his ass's head, and he is the play's fool,
but as often with Shakespeare's fools he has wise things to
say, and his reply to Titania's words could be considered an
emphatic statement of the play's 'moral': 'Methinks, mistress,
you should have a little reason for that. And yet, to say the
truth, reason and love keep little company together nowa-
days . . .' (Act 3, scene 1).

The opposition between reason and love is further high-
lighted by Shakespeare's deliberate contrast between the
play's major locations, the city of Athens where it begins and
ends, and the enchanted wood whose presiding powers are
the fairies. Duke Theseus, the ruler of Athens, the most
civilised city of antiquity (itself dedicated to Athene, the
goddess of wisdom), is presented to us as the embodiment or
exemplar of the rational man. His wedding day is at hand,
and by contrast with the young lovers — variously agitated,
confused and even angry in the enchanted wood — Theseus
speaks as a serene master of his emotions. It is significant
that his bride-to-be is Hippolyta, the warlike Queen of the
Amazons. As an Amazon, Hippolyta had abandoned the
traditional role of women for war and adventure, traditional
masculine activities. Thus she had asserted the primacy of
female over male, rather as, in a different context later in the
play, Titania is to assert her primacy over Oberon. This, in
Elizabethan eyes, was to flout the ideas of natural hierarchy
embodied in the notion of the 'Great Chain of Being', where
every created thing had its appropriate place in a scale running
down from the angels to the animal and vegetable worlds. In
subduing Hippolyta to his love, therefore, Theseus has re-
asserted the natural hierarchy and order of things, and brought
concord out of discord. Hippolyta has laid aside her arrows
and her deadly bow of war; instead we find her referring in
her first words to the 'silver bow' of the moon which

New-bent in heaven, shall behold the night
Of our solemnities.

Theseus attaches a social value to love and marriage; for him
marriage is not a private contract between two individuals —
or not only that, but a cause for general rejoicing in society,
since, public man and rational upholder of the law that he is,
he knows that ultimately marriage is the bond which ties
society together and ensures its continuance. This is why he
proclaims public revels — a symbolic outward demonstration
of the social and rational aspect of love that leads to the legal
contract of marriage.

The plot's complications begin with that kind of clash
between parent and child — Egeus's wish to have his daughter
Hermia marry a man she does not love — which occurs so
frequently in dramatic comedy, from Greek and Roman
times down to the present, as to be one of the identifying
marks of the form. Egeus appeals to Theseus as his ruler and
bases his appeal on both the concept of natural hierarchy
which demands that the child obey the parent, and the law of
Athens, which backs up the 'natural' law with dire penalties.
Theseus as the rational ruler and upholder of the law must
accede to Egeus; but in offering Hermia time to reflect, to
pause, and in the stately and dispassionate gravity of his words
(contrasting effectively with the excited and hot-tempered
exchanges among the others in the scene), he seems more
than ever a stable focus of wisdom, a man in command of
himself surrounded by those — especially the young lovers —
who lack self-control and self-knowledge.

Though Theseus does not appear again in the play until the
end of Act 4, we are constantly reminded of the play's theme,
the irrationality of love. Significantly, the young lovers flee
the city of reason for the wood, the place of unreason:
Shakespeare puns on an Elizabethan sense of 'wood', which
could also mean 'mad' when he has Demetrius say that he is

wood within this wood
Because I cannot meet my Hermia.

Their behaviour there is indeed 'wood', and we have already

noticed the symbolic force of the picture at the centre of the action when Queen Titania wakes to dote on an ass. But significantly, when the mistakes and confusions are almost all sorted out, Theseus appears (Act 4, scene 1). Once more he is associated with images of concord produced out of discord (the 'music' produced by his hunting hounds 'matched in mouth like bells,/Each under each'). Further, it is morning — the phantasmal moonlight in which the 'fond pageant' of love was played out has vanished and the light of reason shines again with the sun. He invites the young lovers to return with Hippolyta and himself to Athens and there, 'three and three' they shall be wed. The movement from wood to city is clearly symbolic; the multiple marriages not only help to give the play's ending a joyous festive sense but also indicate that love has now been domesticated, its power and force directed towards the common good of society; the conflict between individual desire and social law (the conflict which originally drove Hermia and Lysander out of Athens) is resolved. The very famous speech of Theseus at the beginning of the last Act discounts the tale of the young lovers about their experiences, passes judgement on the irrationality of love and of the imagination, seeing both as close allies of madness, and asserts the supremacy of 'cool reason':

> I never may believe
> These antique fables, nor these fairy toys.
> Lovers and madmen have such seething brains,
> Such shaping fantasies, that apprehend
> More than cool reason ever comprehends.

The speech is a more eloquent restatement of Bottom's words about the incompatibility of reason and love, and, like those words, can be said to sum up the theme of the play.

Comedy and the Celebration of Love

So far *A Midsummer Night's Dream* has been interpreted in a moralistic way. But it is also clear that — both from the play's language and from something built into the very structure of comedy — we must see the marriage law of Athens, which is in a sense an expression of Theseus's exemplary rationality, as a stupid law. It may be the law, but it is contrary to nature, as this kind of imagery, deliberately and ironically put into the mouth of Theseus himself, makes clear. He asks Hermia

> Whether, if you yield not to your father's choice,
> You can endure the livery of a nun,
> For aye to be in shady cloister mewed,
> To live a barren sister all your life,
> Chanting faint hymns to the cold fruitless moon . . .
> . . . earthlier happy is the rose distilled
> Than that which, withering on the virgin thorn,
> Grows, lives, and dies in single blessedness.
>
> (Act 1, scene 1)

'Mewed', 'barren', 'fruitless' and 'withering' are all words which suggest the restriction and even denial of the natural impulses which the law enforces.

Literary historians tell us that comedy has its origins in primitive fertility rituals and myths in which an old god or king, representing sterility, was in some way vanquished by a young god or hero representing renewal and spring. It is probably for this reason that there is a very ancient and almost unbroken convention in comedy that we tend always to sympathise with the young, and particularly the young lovers. The weight of this convention and the expectations it arouses make it hard for us to sympathise with the social—legalistic arguments of Theseus and Egeus, and add a moving power to the marvellous speech of Lysander in the opening scene which is almost an anthology of all the reasons why, in romance and comedy, we are always on the side of young love:

> Ay me! For aught that I could ever read,
> Could ever hear by tale or history,
> The course of true love never did run smooth . . .

The speech, too long to be quoted in full here, not only arouses sympathy for these particular true lovers, but its generalising formality stresses the typicality of the situation and invokes our understanding of the plight of *all* young lovers in 'tale or history'. Seen from this angle, the rationality of Theseus becomes just another obstacle to a fulfilment we desire.

The flight of the young lovers from Athens to the enchanted wood, then, does not have to be seen as a symbolic plunge into irrationality but rather as a flight from restriction to the freedom of nature. What happens in the wood may not be explicable in rational terms — Theseus simply rejects the lovers' fumbling attempts to put into words what has happened to them — but as Stanley Wells writes, 'the wood is a place of liberation, of reassessment leading through a stage of disorganization to a finally increased stability'.[2] In simpler terms, it is in the wood, not in Athens, that everything is made right in the end for the young lovers; in it, as Puck says, every Jack gets his Jill. The wood is indeed a richly symbolic place offering imaginative insights and truths beyond the reach of 'cool reason', but to understand this we need to understand something of the significance of the fairies who inhabit it.

The Significance of the Fairies

The fairies are for Shakespeare a useful fiction for exploring certain human truths. They are symbolic manifestations of ideas about love and nature, just as we might say that the witches in *Macbeth* and the gods in *King Lear* are symbolic manifestations of ideas about fate and destiny. At the end of the play Puck makes it explicitly clear in a direct address to the audience that we do not have to take the fairies literally:

> If we shadows have offended,
> Think but this, and all is mended:
> That you have but slumbered here
> While these visions did appear.
> And this weak and idle theme,
> No more yielding but a dream,
> Gentles, do not reprehend.
>   (Act 5, scene 1)

But though 'these visions' need not be taken literally, they must be taken seriously as imaginative devices which enable

Shakespeare to formulate some powerful insights into the relationship of love and reason.

The fairies who inhabit the moonlit wood relate to the daylight city of reason rather as the subconscious mind relates to the conscious mind: not easily explicable, but — partly for that reason — much more powerful. What we find is a reversal of the situation which opened the play: the quarrel between Oberon and Titania in all its discordant mutual jealousy contrasts with the harmonious concord of Theseus and Hippolyta. Simultaneously this discord parallels the violent squabbling that lies ahead for the four bewildered young lovers.

The dispute between Hermia and her father over the two young men in the opening scene evidenced discord in society but the dispute between Oberon and Titania is more serious, producing cosmic discord, or a great upheaval in nature herself. This can be seen most clearly in Titania's great speech (in Act 2, scene 1) where the ideas and imagery as well as the poetic expressiveness anticipate the evocations of cosmic discord later developed in tragedies such as *Macbeth* and *King Lear*. She tells us that their dispute has broken up the dance — a potent symbol of harmony not just in this play but a kind of archetypal symbol in the joyous conclusions of comedy — and that it has caused the fertility of nature to go to waste:

> the green corn
> Hath rotted ere his youth attained a beard;
> The fold stands empty in the drowned field,
> And crows are fatted with the murrion flock.

Even more, the seasonal order and rhythm of nature have been disturbed:

> The spring, the summer,
> The chiding autumn, angry winter, change
> Their wonted liveries; and the mazed world
> By their increase now knows not which is which.
> And this same progeny of evils comes
> From our debate, from our dissension.

Throughout the play the imagery and the setting pervasively associate Oberon and Titania with the powers of nature. They are presented as versions of nature or fertility gods. The connections between fairies and fertility are deeply rooted in folklore, and concord between Oberon and Titania as male and female principles seems to be necessary for the proper ordering of the seasons and of nature herself. When, towards the end of the play, this concord is restored, Shakespeare's imaginative conception of them as agents of fertility and procreation emerges even more clearly: their last task — indeed this is the last action of the play and lingers in our minds — is the blessing of the bride-beds of the three newly married human couples. The play does not end with Theseus, but with these creatures from a more primal level of human experience.

The Two Worlds of Shakespearean Comedy

It would be wrong, in reacting against the moralistic view of the play as a comment on the folly and irrationality of love, to go to the other extreme by suggesting that Shakespeare means us to see Duke Theseus and what he represents as wholly ludicrous. The play maintains a fine balance between two views of reality, the rational and the instinctual. In juxtaposing Athens and the enchanted wood Shakespeare creates a genuinely dramatic conflict. The experiences in the wood which the young lovers and Bottom have undergone, and from which Theseus has been excluded, seem to raise the question as to which *is* reality: the reason embodied in the city of Athens or the imaginative impulses and drives located in the wood. The marvellous passage (in Act 4, scene 1) in which the lovers' awakening is enacted brings out brilliantly this uncertainty and the dramatic poise which sustains it:

Demetrius: These things seem small and undistinguishable,
              Like far off mountains turned into clouds.
Hermia: Methinks I see these things with parted eye,
              When everything seems double . . .
Demetrius: Are you sure
              That we are awake? It seems to me
              That yet we sleep, we dream.

The lovers might have been in contact with true reality in the wood: the social ties of the city state, of law and reason and daylight mundanity — *these* might be the dream. In general terms, perhaps it is just a pretence that the powers of reason govern our lives; perhaps we are really governed by the powers of nature. Yet the question is left open, for all the characters do return to Athens and that social world.

Similar concerns and a similar action are to be found in many of Shakespeare's other comedies, perhaps especially clearly in *As You Like It* (1599), *The Merchant of Venice* (1596) and *The Winter's Tale* (1610). As Northrop Frye puts it: 'The action of the comedy begins in a world represented as a normal world, moves into the green world, goes into a metamorphosis there in which the comic resolution is achieved, and returns to the normal world.'[3] This 'green world' — the wood outside Athens, the Forest of Arden, Belmont, Bohemia — is where, in one way or another, love triumphs over hate, hopeful youth over crabbed age, natural impulse over restrictive law. Behind all this lies something of comedy's ancient origins in fertility myths, with their themes of the triumph of life over the waste land, or spring over winter. This is a 'meaning' of comedy in general, and of *A Midsummer Night's Dream* in particular, which is certainly profound and surely at least as 'serious' as the narrower moralistic view examined earlier. Such a perspective clearly helps to explain the major effect of Shakespearean comedy, its sense of festive joyousness and reconciliation, its endings with dances and multiple marriages, its thematic concentration on love.

Good Fortune

The joyous ending of the comedy is not, however, a foregone conclusion. The young Athenians take their squabbling and confusion in the wood to the threshold of violence and potential tragedy. (Incidentally, even the crudely performed play of Pyramus and Thisbe, other young star-crossed lovers, parallels — at a different level — the potential tragedy of the young Athenians.) What brings concord and harmony out of all this dangerous discord is the benign Fortune that rules in comedy, a benevolent Fortune personified, as it were, in this

play by Oberon. For it is quite clear to the audience from
early in the play that Oberon is benevolently disposed, even
to Titania, and that he has the power — despite some errors
and some maliciousness on the part of his servant Puck — to
order human events so that all will end well. He speaks at the
point of maximum confusion:

> When they wake, all this derision
> Shall seem a dream and fruitless vision,
> And back to Athens shall the lovers wend,
> With league whose date till death shall never end . . .
> I'll to my queen and beg her Indian boy
> And then I will her charmed eye release
> From monster's view, and all things shall be peace.
>
> (Act 3, scene 2)

'And all things shall be peace' — the difference between the
love-stories of *Romeo and Juliet* (1594?) and *A Midsummer
Night's Dream* lies in the difference between Romeo's cold
and hostile stars and that providential or benevolent control
exercised by Oberon. What Oberon suggests and enacts is
a sense that there is a powerful principle of good luck or
good fortune at work in the world which is irresistible. Here
is an example of one of the deepest pleasures of comedy, the
convincing if temporary certainty that everything will work
out, that all will end well. Comedy thus, in one of its guises,
gratifies wish-fulfilment fantasies; it offers us a release in its
art from our gloomy habitual awareness of the iron laws of
necessity and mortality. But surely this is escapist? It may be,
but if the sense of release and of wish-fulfilment present in
comedy is escapist, that is not to say it is evidence of triviality.
On the contrary, it is deeply therapeutic: it meets one of the
strongest needs of the human spirit.

The Non-Comic Universe

The optimism and the joy are not, however, credulous, not
naïve. *A Midsummer Night's Dream* contains a minor but
pervasive sense of a different and darker universe. This

emerges in the wrathful spite of Egeus, in the more painful
moments of confusion among the young lovers, and throughout in Puck's malicious and Olympian detachment from
humanity:

> Shall we their fond pageant see?
> Lord, what fools these mortals be.

In the wonderfully modulated conclusion to the play, when
the human lovers have trooped off to enjoy their bride-beds
after the festive mirth provided by Bottom's play, there is a
moment's pause on the darkened stage. Then Puck enters to
remind us in the images of his speech of a very different
world, a world of unglamorous work, of predatory hunger
and cruelty, of toil and penury, of sickness, age and death:

> Now the hungry lion roars
> And the wolf behowls the moon,
> Whilst the heavy plowman snores
> All with weary task foredone.
> Now the wasted brands do glow
> Whilst the screech-owl, screeching loud,
> Puts the wretch that lies in woe
> In remembrance of a shroud.
>   (Act 5, scene 1)

We are the more ready to accept and enjoy Oberon's benevolent manipulations precisely because we are made aware of
this darker world. Shakespeare's great comedies repeat this
effect: we are the more ready to believe in the Forest of Arden
in *As You Like It* because we know that it is not entirely
idyllic, that it contains savage animals and is subject to winter
cold; Feste the jester in *Twelfth Night* reminds us in the midst
of the play's carnival atmosphere that youth's a stuff will not
endure, and that the wind and the rain and the sad cypress
tree exist too. Thus the affirmations of Shakespearean comedy
gain strength from the clear perception of this alternative,
non-comic, universe.

Ben Jonson: Non-Romantic Comedy

Ben Jonson's kind of comedy is very different from Shake-speare's both in method and effect. Jonson (1572–1637) claimed that his comedies were essentially realistic, that we would find in them 'deeds and language such as men do use' as he put it in the prologue to *Every Man in His Humour* (1598). Further, some of Jonson's writing seems to be a thinly veiled attack on Shakespearean comedy because it is 'romantic' — romantic in the sense that it employs strange, wondrous, essentially non-realistic materials. In the induction to *Bartholomew Fair* (1614), for example, Jonson asks ironically: 'If there be never a servant-monster in the Fair, Who can help it? . . . nor a nest of antics? [The author] is loath to make Nature afraid in his plays like those that beget Tales, Tempests and such like drolleries . . .' Again, in the heavily satiric *Every Man Out of His Humour* (1599) one of the foolish characters asks for the kind of comedy where we will find 'a duke to be in love with a countess, and that countess to be in love with the duke's son, and the son to love the lady's waiting maid: some such cross-wooing, with a clown to be their serving man'. This strikes very directly at a play such as *Twelfth Night*. The crushing reply to this naïvety is delivered by Jonson's spokesman in the play and consists of a restatement of the definition of comedy given by the Roman orator Cicero (106–43 BC); it should be: '*Imitatio vitae* [an imitation of life], *speculum consuetudinis* [a mirror of habits], *imago veritatis* [an image of truth]: a thing throughout pleasant and ridiculous and accommodated to the correction of manners.'

The Question of Realism

It is not very easy, however, to call Shakespeare 'romantic' and Jonson 'realistic', despite all this. Jonson's characterisation is fantastic, distorted and extravagant, as can be seen easily by thinking of Corvino, Corbaccio and Voltore (the names meaning crow, raven and vulture) in *Volpone* (1606), or of a figure such as Sir Epicure Mammon in *The Alchemist* (1610).

Jonson's dramatic language, whether verse or prose, is exuberantly free of the canons of normal speech — think of the imaginative excess, the gusto and zest of Volpone's wooing of Celia:

> Thy baths shall be the juice of July-flowers,
> Spirit of roses, and of violets,
> The milk of unicorns, and panther's breath
> Gathered in bags and mixed with Cretan wines.

Finally there is the amazing ingenuity of Jonson's plots, especially in *Volpone* and *The Alchemist*, where complication follows complication with bewildering speed and the action seems to hurtle forwards.

Looking at the problem from another angle, it is possible to argue that Shakespeare is not less but *more* 'realistic' than Jonson. His settings may be remote or idealised, his plots are nearly always drawn from the prose romances of the late medieval or early Renaissance worlds; but his characters are and have been universally acknowledged as fully rounded human portraits, all presented with their complex human burden of loves and fears and envies.

Jonson's Corrective Aim

The crucial distinction between Shakespeare and Jonson lies not in the degrees of relative 'realism', but rather in the fact that Jonson's comedy is satiric, that its aim is to hold folly up to overt ridicule. His work derives its spirit and techniques more from the insistence of the classical writers of antiquity on the corrective function of comedy than from the medieval romance tradition which so influenced Shakespeare. What is crucial in Jonson's restatement of Cicero's views quoted above is the emphasis on the idea that comedy should be 'accommodated to the correction of manners'. This produces an effect very different from that sense of festive celebration and ceremonious reconciliation in Shakespearean comedy; further, some critics feel that many of Jonson's plays, and especially *Volpone*, can hardly be called comic at all.

The Plot of 'Volpone'

The central plot of *Volpone* is like a beautiful and efficient machine driving the manic puppets of Jonson's imagination through a dizzy maze of intrigue. Volpone (the fox) is a magnifico of Venice, at the time of the play's action the commercial capital of Europe. Aided by his parasite Mosca (the fly), he lays an ingenious trap for the wealthy but greedy citizens of Venice. He pretends to be desperately ill and at the point of death, and gives it out that he is looking for an heir to whom he may leave his considerable wealth. In the hope of Volpone's riches, Voltore, a lawyer, Corvino, a merchant, and the old gentleman Corbaccio heap gifts on Volpone to gain his favour. Corbaccio even disinherits his son Bonario and names Volpone as *his* heir in the hope that this ultimate tribute will clinch Volpone's favour; for the same reasons, Corvino, whose jealousy matches his cupidity, tries to prostitute his wife, the virtuous Celia, to Volpone. The plot becomes so dense and so closely woven that no summary can do it justice; but after some hair's-breadth escapes from discovery, dog tries to eat dog as Mosca cheats Volpone, and the two master-rogues, in turning against each other, are found out. The truth about the deceptions comes out in court; the guilty are punished in a severe manner appropriate to their crimes, and the innocent are waved briefly away.

As Jonson's editors have pointed out, he derived the basic idea for his plot, legacy-hunting, from a great mass of ancient literature, especially that of classical Rome (Jonson was an extremely learned man). But *Volpone* is a *universal* satire on man's greed and gullibility. References in the play make clear Jonson's awareness of the greed of imperial Rome; the Venetian setting enables him to mount a devastating attack on the materialism of Renaissance Europe; and the resemblances between the play's world and acquisitive modern society need no stressing or elaboration.

A Vision of Human Depravity?

Many critics view *Volpone* as a dark and sombre play -- certain

emphases in it have led critics through the centuries to puzzle
over its designation as a comedy, and many to find in it what
one called 'an unrelieved sketch of human depravity'.[4]

In the first place, Volpone's opening invocation to his gold,
where the terminology of religion is so vigorously misapplied,
can be taken as an indication of his own personal perversion
of values:

> O thou son of Sol,
> But brighter than thy father, let me kiss
> With adoration, thee, and every relic
> Of sacred treasure in this blessed room . . .

The imagery used by Volpone (or taken up by Mosca) at
many points in the play condemns him out of his own mouth
— one of Jonson's favourite devices for satirical exposure.
This is well illustrated by the imagery (verbal *and* visual) of
sickness and disease in the play. At the heart of Volpone's
scheme is his pretence that he is mortally ill — the central
image of the whole first act is his supposedly diseased body
lying in its great bed, and the grossness of the alleged diseases
is rammed home to us and the dupes with great glee and gusto
by Mosca, especially in the duping of Corvino:

> Would you would once close
> Those filthy eyes of yours that flow with slime
> Like two frogpits . . .

But throughout, it may be felt that the pretended disease of
the body symbolises the real disease of the spirit: that morally,
Volpone *is* corrupt and stinking. The joke is really on him.
Hence the particular appropriateness of his punishment at the
end, where the outer show is at last forced into conformity
with the inner reality:

> And since the most [of Volpone's wealth] was gotten by imposture,
> By feigning lame, gout, palsy and such diseases,
> Thou art to lie in prison, cramped with irons,
> Till thou be'st sick and lame indeed.

The symbolism of disease and sickness is related organically to the spirit and idiom of the inverted beast-fable format which so dominates the conception of character. In the beast-fable animals behave like human beings; here, as the names so justly imply, humans behave like animals — as Volpone says:

> Vulture, kite,
> Raven and gorcrow, all my birds of prey
> That think me turning carcass, now they come.

The moribund carcass is fit food only for particular kinds of carrion-scavenging birds. The consistency and aptness of the animal imagery throughout the play needs no further stressing: Jonson's characters may be two-dimensional, but they are deliberately so and in being so produce an effect of lurid and distorted intensity found only in the world's great caricaturists.

The logic of those who would question the *comic* status of *Volpone* may now seem clearer. A recent critic, S. Musgrove, links *Volpone* with *King Lear* (both plays were written at much the same time): both plays portray, he says, 'a state of affairs in which one passion is dominant over the rest and over reason itself, in which dog eats dog, and a whole group of human beings goes down before its own instinct to cannibalism'; and he points out that Corbaccio's disinheriting of his son is an example of the disruption of the natural bond between parents and children which is such a major motif in *Lear*.[5]

The argument, in short, is that Jonson's play presents us with a monstrous world. It is fitting therefore that Volpone's household should be comprised of a dwarf, a eunuch and a hermaphrodite. These three function throughout as a powerful visual reminder of Volpone's perversity; and indeed in the first act Mosca tells Corvino — whether truthfully or not — that Volpone is their physical father. Those who see the play as sombre would clearly agree that his parenthood is at least symbolic; and agree with each other that *Volpone* is a dark study of human depravity.

The Attractiveness of the Rogues

The evidence for such a view is certainly available in the text; but *Volpone* even more than most plays illustrates the problem of the double-effect of drama: a play is simultaneously something read in the study *and* a performance on a stage before an audience. The interpretation of *Volpone* so far presented is very reliant on imagery and symbol — in other words it is a very literary reading of the play. A stage performance of the play makes quite a different impression, an impression of mirthful exuberance and high spirits. And this in turn sends us back to the text to check initial perhaps overly solemn impressions.

Volpone himself and (in a different sort of way) Mosca actually strike us in the theatre as attractive figures. Why? In the first place in a world absolutely driven by greed for money Volpone, despite his opening salutation of his gold, does not seem particularly interested in it. Indeed he concludes those famous opening words with this:

> Yet, I glory
> More in the cunning purchase of my wealth
> Than in the glad possession, since I gain
> No common way . . .

The play does demonstrate conclusively the truth of that statement: that for Volpone the whole zest and pleasure of his doings is rather in the cleverness and dash and bravura of his trickery than in the merely avaricious counting of the spoils which are the fruit of that trickery. As a Venetian magnifico Volpone would be rich anyway; so that in a sense all his scheming is a form of self-expression. He puts it best himself:

> What should I do
> But cocker up my genius and live free
> To all delights my fortune calls me to?

'Cocker up my genius' — that is, 'encourage my innate talents', express myself: this expansive assertion of freedom and sense

of power in the exercise of that freedom is the defining tone
of much of Volpone's speech and character. In this respect he
is very much a Renaissance man. Certainly he is as far away
from the traditional stage miser as it is possible to be. That
character is too busy worrying about the next penny to enjoy
life at all; not so Volpone — after an easy morning's cheating,
he can't be bothered going on 'working', and orders the doors
shut and the preparation of 'music, dances, banquets, all
delights'. He is prepared to lavish all his wealth on Celia,
admittedly for base purposes, but however the vices rank in
moral theology, somehow on the stage avarice (of the kind
displayed by genuine misers like Corvino and Corbaccio) is less
attractive than lust, especially lust expressed with Volpone's
imaginative eloquence. Further, he decides later in the play
to pretend that he has died, so that he can watch the excru-
ciating torments of the dupes who will flock to the carcass
only to find that Mosca has been named the heir. The point
is that here Volpone decides to kill the goose that lays the
golden eggs, as it were, and all for the mere sardonic pleasure
of seeing the dupes squirm. The motivation is not that of a
miser.

It would be wrong to suggest that there is anything of the
'lovable rogue' about Volpone. The phrase is too condescend-
ing and misses entirely the genuinely sinister elements in him.
But if reasons are sought for finding the play rather less grim
than 'an unrelieved sketch of human depravity' the best place
to begin is by seeing at least something of Volpone's zest and
energy and sheer enjoyment of his cheating.

The Dupes

It is impossible to separate the impression we form of the
cheats from that made on us by the cheated. They have none
of the attractive intelligence and energy of Volpone and Mosca
— though they are brilliant dramatic creations — and given
their intense cupidity and equally marked gullibility, any
audience or reader *wants* to see them roundly cheated. They
cry out to be duped, they need to be duped, they deserve
to be duped, and we come the more to enjoy the wit and
dexterity of those who contrive the duping. They are so well

differentiated considering the exact similarity of their motivation: Voltore sacrifices his profession, Corbaccio his posterity, and Corvino his wife, but each is driven only by greed. Yet we are never in danger of confusing them, so sharp and hardedged is Jonson's delineation of them. Corvino is perhaps the most repellent morally and the supreme satiric butt, Jonson stressing ferociously the fanatic jealousy of his nature to highlight the more the overriding intensity of his greed, especially in the superb scene where he tries to beat his chaste wife into Volpone's bed.

The Moral Function of Volpone and Mosca

The cheating of such moral cretins by Volpone and Mosca seems therefore most enjoyable. We could go further, and approach the heart of Jonson's excellence, by saying 'also most moral', because what makes it easier for even the more scrupulous consciences in an audience to find the two sharks attractive, whatever their wickedness and duplicity, is that they function in the play as moral agents. That is, what they do in the play is to hold up vices like greed and folly to exposure and the laughter of ridicule. This can be seen in the play from the opening scene:

> *Volpone:* What a rare punishment
> Is avarice to itself.
> *Mosca:* Aye, with our help, sir.

The high excellence of Jonson's satire, what keeps it from sliding into snarling didacticism and keeps it within the realms of comedy, consists in this: that it *is* very moral, but hardly ever moralistic. It rests on a simple, but brilliant device: that the exposure of folly and vice, and the explicit commentary on them, are contrived not by lay preachers but by characters who are themselves deeply morally suspect. Their only virtues, if that is the word, are high intelligence and an ability to manipulate the cupidity of others.

A Cruel Art?

It is true that Jonson's art is a cruel art. It must be admitted that his dramatic world consists purely of rogues and fools and that what an audience enjoys is the precision of the cheating techniques of Volpone and Mosca and the satisfying way in which dog turns on dog at the end.

This in itself, however, need not necessarily raise a query over the play's designation as a comedy. The house of comedy has many rooms, and many comic theorists would argue that one function of the genre is to minister to our feelings of superiority: that is, we enjoy feeling superior to the characters in the play and remain scornfully aloof from their tribulations and their moral flaws. On this view, the kind of sympathetic involvement which we find in Shakespeare's comedies would simply be inappropriate. The French philosopher, Henri Bergson (1859—1941), writing at the beginning of this century, believed that comedy depended on our being made to see characters behaving with mechanical rigidity, under the pressure of some fixed idea or obsession; and further that 'to produce the whole of its effect, the comic demands something like a momentary anaesthesia of the heart. Its appeal is to intelligence, pure and simple'.[6] Clearly such a view would not apply to Shakespearean comedy, but it would go some of the way to explaining the appeal of *Volpone* where the energy, zest and intelligence of Volpone and Mosca strikes a responsive chord in the audience.

The Problem of the Ending

There is more than one kind of comedy, and this fact raises difficult critical questions. For instance, Jonson's play ends with Volpone's punishment (penal servitude) and Mosca's slavery in the galleys. This ending will not trouble an audience or reader who has considered the play dark and sombre throughout, 'an unrelieved sketch of human depravity'. It will seem that moral perverts have received their just rewards. But to the audience or reader manoeuvred in the course of the play into some imaginative complicity with Volpone and Mosca, into enjoying the gusto and skill with which these characters have carried out their schemes against those others who thoroughly deserve the indignities heaped on them, this punitive ending presents a large problem of tone and dramatic tact. This is the more marked since the avocatori or judges who hand out the punishments seem to share many of the venal and corrupt attitudes of the very people they punish: for instance, they begin to look on the unmarried Mosca, now apparently himself a magnifico, as a good match for a daughter or a niece, if only he could be caught. This is to behave just like the despised dupes.

Jonson himself was obviously uneasy about the ending of the play — he seems to have felt that it *did* run counter to the prevailing direction of our imaginative sympathies (if that is the right word) in the play as a whole. This strengthens the interpretation of the play offered above, but does not solve the problem of the discordant ending. Jonson wrote in the dedication of the play to the Universities of Oxford and Cambridge that 'my catastrophe may in the strict rigour of comic law meet with censure'. He goes on to say that he constructed it as he did because 'my special aim [was] to put the snaffle in their mouths that cry out: We never punish vice in our interludes'. All he is really saying is that he allowed the rampant Puritan moralism of the time, virulently hostile to the stage and indeed soon to have its victory with the closing of the theatres in 1642, to impose a shape on the ending of *Volpone*, which his own finer aesthetic sense told him was all wrong. Of course the ending as we have it is very wholesome, but it is not right. Yes, Volpone and Mosca must get their come-uppance: it would be too sentimental if they got off scot-free. But they could have been punished in a way which would have enforced a moral without being itself moralistic. Jonson later achieved such an ending in the falling-out of the rogues at the end of *The Alchemist*, his other great comedy.

At a more general level, the question raised by the ending of *Volpone* is whether comedy is compatible with a strong satiric intention. The satirist wishes to change the world by reforming it: he can never be content to accept the world as it is. It might be argued that comedy as a mode is rather more ready than satire to accept the world with all its imperfections, to affirm the positive aspects of human nature, and to find its faults amusing rather than destructive and contemptible. In a play such as *Volpone*, however, what we witness is an *almost* perfect reconciliation of the comic artist with the satiric moralist; and Jonson, as Shakespeare's great contemporary, shows us that comedy is not a genre to be explained by any easy, single formula.

Later Developments in Comedy

Molière

Molière (1622—73) is one of the world's great comic masters. *Tartuffe* (1664) is a devastating exposure of hypocrisy and lust, embodied in the central figure. His entry is delayed for two whole Acts, building up our comic expectations through the various references to him by other characters. These expectations, when he appears, are wonderfully gratified. Dorine, the maid of the household into which Tartuffe has insinuated himself, is on stage. (Her spirit and common-sense, as well as her role in the play, relate her clearly to the witty *servus* or slave of the Roman comedy of Plautus and Terence, and show Molière's instinctive awareness of ancient comic traditions.) Tartuffe speaks to his own servant:

> *Tartuffe:* Laurent, put away my hair shirt and my scourge and continue to pray Heaven to send you grace. If anyone asks for me I'll be with the prisoners distributing alms.
> *Dorine:* The impudent hypocrite!
> *Tartuffe:* What do you want?
> *Dorine:* I'm to tell you . . .
> *Tartuffe:* For Heaven's sake! Before you speak, I pray you take this handkerchief. [*Takes handkerchief from his pocket.*]
> *Dorine:* Whatever do you mean?
> *Tartuffe:* Cover your bosom. I can't bear to see it. Such pernicious sights give rise to sinful thoughts.

Tartuffe is a moral monster, whose ability to impose on the credulous Orgon almost wrecks the whole family, which is saved only by a *deus ex machina* ending: the direct intervention of the King. In its concentration on serious vice, and in the monstrosity of the central figure, the play resembles

Jonson's *Volpone*. Molière's play, however, is at once less extreme than Jonson's and yet more sombre. Jonson exaggerates his types of greed and credulity to fantastic degrees, so that despite the deep moral thrust of *Volpone* we are made to share in the dramatist's enjoyment of and relish for the world he has created. Molière's Tartuffe is closer to real life and therefore felt by the dramatist and his audience as more of a threat. The play is uproariously funny in parts, but is, for Molière, untypically bitter and didactic — the sensible brother-in-law of Orgon, Cléante, is given a lengthy and dramatically static speech in Act 3 on the need to distinguish between hypocrisy and true religion, between artifice and sincerity.

Molière's plays do not often judge from absolute norms of religion or morality, but from more relative social standards. He is more usually concerned with correcting and improving the manners of society, with ridiculing affectations rather than with lashing vice. *Les Précieuses Ridicules* (*The Affected Ladies*, 1659) exposes the hyper-refinement of fashionable Parisians, their over-elaborate manners and grotesquely convoluted 'polite' conversation. *Le Bourgeois Gentilhomme* (*The Bourgeois Gentleman*, 1670) mocks the absurdity of the shopkeeper who decides to make himself a fine gentleman, hires teachers of music, dancing and fencing, as well as a philosopher from whom he discovers that all his life he has been talking prose, and remains to the end blissfully oblivious to the ridiculousness of the figure he cuts. Both the fashionable ladies in the earlier play and the foolish little shopkeeper in the later one are guilty of excess. The pervasive value in Molière's dramas is that of good sense, the pursuit of the golden mean. Cléante expresses it directly in *Tartuffe*:

Men, in the main, are strangely made. They can never strike the happy mean: the bounds of reason seem too narrow for them: they must needs overact whatever part they play and often ruin the noblest things because they will go to extremes and push them too far.

Philinte in *The Misanthrope* (1666) says exactly the same thing: 'True reason lies in shunning all extremes.'

Molière's comedy makes fun of those follies which are a threat to the structure of society as that society might be conceived of by a rational man who did not expect human beings to be perfect. It is thus tolerant and — on the whole — good-humoured. Its valuation of social standards helped to create and give powerful impetus to the comedy of manners in both France and Restoration England. Molière is not, however, a complacent cynic who accepts the way of the world. His masterpiece, *The Misanthrope*, dramatises the conflict between a man's attempt to sustain his individual integrity and the compromises forced on him by the dictates of social living. Should we always tell others exactly what we think of them? If we do not, are we not engaged in constant hypocrisy? If we do, how can the civility of social living be preserved? In *The Misanthrope*, Alceste argues passionately against the tiny daily hypocrisies of social living and for uncompromising honesty. Philinte puts the opposing view:

What is needed in society is an accommodating virtue. It's wrong to be too high principled . . . This rigorous passion for the antique virtues runs counter to the age and customary usage. It demands too much perfection of mere mortals. We need to move with the times and not be too inflexible, and it's the height of folly to take upon oneself the burden of the world's correction.

This is indeed 'sensible'; the dramatic balance of the play is, however, beautifully sustained. There is a dignity and moral passion in Alceste's view, despite the frailties of his own temperament, and a moving grandeur in his final words as he rejects society: 'Betrayed on all sides, injustice heaped upon me, I mean to escape from this abyss of triumphant vice and search the world for some spot so remote that there one may be free to live as honour bids.' Molière's play dramatises with wit and profundity the central issue of comedy, the problems of living in society. It is as fresh today as when it was written.

The Restoration Comedy of Manners

The restoration of Charles II to the throne of England

in 1660 reopened the theatres which had been closed by the Puritan government for eighteen years. The comedies which the Restoration period produced continued to concern themselves, like Molière's, with social manners, but with a crucial narrowing of range and tone. The plays' audiences were comprised mainly, if not exclusively, of gallants, men-about-town, courtiers and people of fashion. They, like the dramatists who wrote for them, were hostile to the values of the bourgeoisie and citizenry, which they saw as unstylish and dominated by a repugnant Puritan earnestness. Restoration comedy takes its tone, accordingly, from its audience. It celebrates elegance of demeanour and of clothes, polished verbal wit and repartee, the sophisticated delights of 'the town' (London) — the country and the provinces are places of near-hellish exile; its plots turn on sexual intrigues, where the winners are those who most relish the delights of the chase and have most skill in disguising their emotions (if any); 'the proceedings are conducted with a maximum of style and a minimum of regard for moral principle, for the delight if not the edification of an aristocratic élite that had nothing better to do with its leisure than study its own dandified image in the flattering mirror of the drama'.[7] Though highly artificial in one sense, Restoration comedy is realistic in a more important way: it reflects a real society, even if that society lacks any depth.

The plays of George Etherege (1635—91) illustrate most of the generalisations above. *The Man of Mode* (1679) concerns the sexual intrigues of Dorimant, a witty gallant with a highly competitive and automatic response to women and to possible sexual rivals. His is a style of masterly cynicism: 'Next to the coming to a good understanding with a new mistress, I love a quarrel with an old one . . . there is no charm so infallibly makes me fall in love with a woman as my knowing a friend loves her.' At one point in the middle of the play, apart from his casual involvement with whores, we see him 'in love' with the moneyed Harriet, pursuing a new mistress (Belinda), and contemplating a return to his former mistress (Mrs Loveit). She has succeeded in stirring his competitive instincts by pretending to a relationship with the ridiculous Sir Fopling Flutter. In the end, he disentangles himself from his many amours to win the hand of Harriet, though there is little sense of romance about this. He remarks to his friend Bellair: 'You wed a woman, I a good estate.' Harriet, as skilled a player in the game of love as Dorimant, turns off his protestations of love with a witty 'Hold — though I wish you devout, I would not have you turn fanatic.' She is well suited to him: she affects contempt for the state of marriage, loves 'the town' and the 'dear pleasure of dissembling', and abhors the country and all its connotations.

Dorimant is not held up to us as a warning against libertinism and the unbridled ego. The striking feature of the play as a whole is its ethical neutrality, even amorality. 'Style' is what Etherege seems to value above all else, a style of polished cynicism. The chief comic butts of the play are Mrs Loveit and Sir Fopling Flutter. He has no style in his clothes, being foppishly overdressed; she has no style in her love for Dorimant, first because she feels intense passion and second because she cannot dissemble or disguise it. Sex and money and marriage are seen as a game, like billiards or snooker: the winners, like Dorimant and Harriet, have steady hands, cool nerves and no irrelevant problems of feeling. The coldness of the play is compensated for by its wit, by the bravura style of its protagonist, and by the broader, Molièresque mockery of the affectations of Sir Fopling.

It is wrong to generalise too sweepingly about Restoration comedy. The plays of William Congreve (1670—1729), though included in anthologies of this kind of comedy, are much later than those of Etherege. In *Love for Love* (1695) and *The Way of the World* (1700), Congreve's characters take marriage more seriously than Dorimant, and in certain emphases in the plays we can see comedy moving away from the sparkling if brittle depiction of manners to the mode of sentimentalism which was to dominate in the eighteenth century. The plot of *The Way of the World* is an over-complicated mess ('How could an audience both be clever enough to understand the story and stupid enough to be interested by it when they did?' as one critic inquired pertinently); but Congreve's dialogue has an impressive suppleness in its wit, whereas other dramatists' dialogue — such as Etherege's — often seems rather studied, over-consciously aphoristic. His characters, too, are more three-dimensional than the sex-besotted or clothes-bedazzled automata of run-of-the-mill Restoration comedy. They too insist on keeping the masks on, they too believe in style, but Congreve manages to suggest the reality of human emotions behind the masks. Dialogue and characterisation combine superbly in the 'proviso scene' at the end of *The Way of the World*:

> *Millamant:* And d'ye hear, I won't be called names after I'm married — positively I won't be called names.
> *Mirabell:* Names!
> *Millamant:* Ay, as wife, spouse, my dear, joy, jewel, love, sweetheart, and the rest of that nauseous cant in which men and their wives are so fulsomely familiar — I shall never bear that. Good Mirabell, don't let us be familiar or fond, nor kiss before folks . . . nor go to Hyde Park together the first Sunday in a new chariot, to provoke eyes and whispers — and then never be seen there together again, as if we were proud of one another the first week and ashamed of one another ever after. Let us never visit together, nor go to a play together, but let us be very strange and well bred. Let us be as strange as if we had been married a great while, and as well bred as if we were not married at all.

This is closer to the love-scenes of Beatrice and Benedick in Shakespeare's *Much Ado About Nothing* (1598?) than to the cynical opportunism of Dorimant and Harriet.

The dramas of William Wycherley (1640—1716), especially *The Country Wife* (1675) and *The Plain Dealer* (1676), reach back to the works of the great masters, the first to Jonson's *Volpone* and Molière's *L'Ecole des Femmes* (*The School of Wives*, 1662), and the latter to Molière's *The Misanthrope*. This does not mean, however, that Wycherley stands outside, or apart from, the general ethos of Restoration comedy. In *The Country Wife*, the aptly named Horner pretends to be impotent in order to carry on his sexual affairs unhindered by the jealousy of husbands, or by wives' fears for their reputation. (This device may have been in Soyinka's mind when he created the character of the cunning Baroka in *The*

Lion and The Jewel.) The outrageousness of the scene has the
bold vigour of Volpone's stratagems, and enables Wycherley
to use Horner as a satiric device for exposure of the hypocrisy
of the women, whose 'virtue' is their greatest affectation.
Lady Fidget, Mrs Dainty Fidget and Mrs Squeamish avail
themselves freely of Horner's 'service' — the farmyard word
is appropriate — and partake of his 'china' in a notorious,
superbly funny scene. The satire on the women's hypocrisy
is undeniably effective. There is, however, something equivocal
in Wycherley's attitude. Sexual ravenousness in the women is
condemned — but celebrated, in a way, in Horner. The tedious
figure of the silly cuckold, further, is close to the heart of the
play's action. Wycherley is almost as outraged by the stupidity
of the males — Sir Jasper, Sparkish and Pinchwife — who do
not see what is going on, as he is by the behaviour of the
women.

The role and fate of the country wife herself — Marjory
Pinchwife — shows that, ultimately, what Restoration comedy
dramatises most confidently is the artifice and conventions of
the society it reflects. Marjory's innocence threatens the
whole sophisticated game: her frank and natural enjoyment
of sex, and her inability to see that honesty is not the best
policy, almost reveal Horner's scheme; and he and the other
ladies quickly close ranks to instruct Marjory in the way of the
world. Marjory learns what most characters in Restoration
comedy already know: in an artificial world, one may only
be artifical. There *is* variety in Restoration comedy, but that
law is not challenged.

Goldsmith and Sheridan

It was inevitable that the cynicism of Restoration comedy,
especially in its earlier phase, should produce a reaction. Even
by the time of Congreve, the beginnings of the movement
from the comedy of manners to sentimental comedy were
under way. Oliver Goldsmith (1728–74) caustically sums up,
in an essay of 1772, the recipe which governed the construction of the sentimental comedy of the eighteenth century:

  deck out the hero with a riband, or give the heroine a title:

then . . . put an insipid dialogue, without character or humour, into their mouths, give them mighty good hearts, very fine clothes, furnish a new set of scenes, make a pathetic scene or two, with a sprinkling of tender melancholy conversation throughout the whole; and there is no doubt but all the ladies will cry and all the gentlemen applaud. (*A Comparison Between Laughing and Sentimental Comedy*)

Goldsmith's own attempt to write a 'laughing comedy' is *She Stoops to Conquer* (1773), always a popular stage play, because it makes such skilful use of basic comic situations and in the character of Tony Lumpkin offers a pleasing reminder of the richness of Shakespearean clowns, stupid and shrewd at the same time. Young Marlow is 'one of the most bashful and reserved young fellows in the world' — except with barmaids and servant-girls. The whole plot turns on the fact that he mistakes the country-house of the Hardcastle family for the village inn. This produces many very funny scenes (so that an audience is willing to forgive the basic implausibility on which the story depends), as in Marlow's cavalier treatment of old Mr Hardcastle as the innkeeper, and his vigorous flirting with Miss Kate Hardcastle, whom he supposes a servant. This contrasts with his appalled inhibitions when he is presented to her in her real character. The very lack of pretentiousness is one of the reasons why *She Stoops to Conquer* is such an engaging comedy.

R. B. Sheridan (1751–1816), even more than Goldsmith, wished to revive the comedy of manners and banish sentimental comedy from the stage. His first play, *The Rivals* (1775) has all the sparkle (and the enormously complicated plot) of Restoration comedy, though the characters are more interested in marriage than in sexual intrigue. Lydia Languish, the heroine, is a walking embodiment of sentimentalism, her head stuffed with stereotypes and affectations derived from her extensive reading in lending library romances (Jane Austen's Catherine Morland in *Northanger Abbey* is a similar type). The play also contains the wonderfully comic Mrs Malaprop, whose aptitude for misapplying long words — 'as headstrong as an allegory on the banks of the Nile' — has caused her name to pass into the language. The vivacity of plot and characterisation, the sheer high-spiritedness of the whole performance, has kept *The Rivals* permanently popular. His other great comedy, *The School for Scandal* (1777), is brilliantly constructed. The 'screen scene' in Joseph Surface's library where everybody is trying to hide from everybody else is as fine as anything in Jonson's *Volpone* or *The Alchemist*; and the depiction of the scandalmongers, Sir Benjamin Backbite, Lady Sneerwell and Mrs Candour, is highly entertaining but makes its moral point, too. As Sir Peter Teazle leaves their company he remarks: 'Your ladyship must excuse me . . . But I leave my character behind me.' The deftness of this is typical of the whole play, and the elegance and verbal felicity of Sheridan's writing anticipates, over the comic wasteland of the next century, the supremely brilliant repartee of Oscar Wilde (1854—1900).

Oscar Wilde

The Importance of Being Earnest (1895) is a comic masterpiece that revels in its own improbability and absurdity, consistently farcical in tone, characterisation and plot. A baby mislaid in a handbag at a London railway station, and the completely arbitrary desires of young ladies to marry men with the name Ernest are the mainsprings of the plot. Wilde thereby, however, makes a serious point about the contrivance and limitations of the 'well-made play' which dominated the stage of his time. The 'well-made play' is just as artificial as Wilde's comedy: it is simply not as honest in frank admission of its contrivance. It is certainly not as funny. Wilde's dialogue cannot be analysed, only quoted. The flavour of the play, the sense of an immensely agile and vivacious mind, and the rapier-like thrusts of a sardonic intelligence sceptical of received Victorian values, are all present in this exchange between Lady Bracknell, the dreadnought dowager, and Jack. She will consider him as an eligible suitor for her daughter's hand if his answers to her questions are satisfactory:

Lady Bracknell: Do you smoke?
Jack: Well, yes, I must admit I smoke.

Lady Bracknell: I am glad to hear it. A man should always have an occupation of some kind. There are far too many idle men in London as it is. How old are you?

Jack: Twenty-nine.

Lady Bracknell: A very good age to be married at. I have always been of the opinion that a man who desires to get married should know either everything or nothing. Which do you know?

Jack [*after some hesitation*]: I know nothing, Lady Bracknell.

Lady Bracknell: I am pleased to hear it. I do not approve of anything that tampers with natural ignorance. Ignorance is like a delicate exotic fruit; touch it and the bloom is gone. The whole theory of modern education is radically unsound. Fortunately in England, at any rate, education produces no effect whatsoever. If it did, it would prove a serious danger to the upper classes, and probably lead to acts of violence in Grosvenor Square.

Criticism always seems heavy-handed in its laborious attempts to extract the 'serious content' from the glancing allusions to the Victorian social scene in a passage like that. Seriousness is there, however — though Wilde's great talent is to make his points so lightly. Comedy here seems to have created a world all of its own; when we look closer, we see our own world, after all, through the irreverent gaiety of an iconoclastic mind. The line from Wilde to Shaw is clear; and after Shaw, perhaps only Tom Stoppard (b. 1937) in contemporary times has come near Wilde's marvellous verbal dexterity.

6 *Ibsen and Miller: The Individual and Society*

Ibsen: Towards Modern Tragedy

The great Italian dramatist, Luigi Pirandello, remarked, 'After Shakespeare, without hesitation, I put Ibsen first.' Many playgoers and critics would agree with this assessment. Ibsen can be regarded as the father of modern drama, and even in his own lifetime, especially in the last quarter of the nineteenth century, his European reputation was assured. But this reputation was based, in part, on a misunderstanding of where Ibsen's true interests lay.

Ibsen's 'Topicality'

Many admirers saw Ibsen as a social realist concerned with specific problems or issues topical to his day and age. Some of his most widely performed plays seemed to invite the view. For instance, in *The Pillars of Society* (1877), the plot turns on the pollution of the water supply in a small town, and on the manoeuvring of the town politicians to cover up the fact. *A Doll's House* (1879) concerns a woman's right to individual freedom and the ways in which marriage, especially marriage in stiflingly conventional provincial Norwegian society, frustrates and thwarts the individuality of the woman. And *Ghosts* (1881) is about the transmission of inherited venereal disease, and the effects of this on a family. From this kind of play, and these kinds of topics, was distilled 'the quintessence of Ibsenism'.[1] Contemporary enthusiasts, that is, saw Ibsen as a sort of expert consultant doctor, standing by the bedside of the sick patient (society), making a series of diagnoses of specific diseases, and doling out the appropriate prescriptions. What seemed to make Ibsen even more strikingly innovatory was the general state of the nineteenth-century stage, laden with romantic historical dramas, or stale melodramas, or automated farces, or pseudo-Shakespearean heroics. By contrast, Ibsen's topics — small-town corruption, women's rights, venereal disease — brought a revolutionary new kind of social reality on to the European stage.

The Mode of Realism

Of almost equal impact was Ibsen's employment of an intensely realistic dramatic method. Most of his work for the stage up to the midpoint of his career, in the early 1870s, had been in verse. The decision to switch to prose (which he never abandoned) was thus made with typical deliberateness. Prose, he felt, was the only appropriate medium for his vision. Verse is the language of kings and princes, of old, remote, unhappy things and battles long ago. Verse has a comforting and con-solatory remoteness and beauty, and is 'the prime divider between the world of high tragedy and that of ordinary existence'.[2] It was precisely that 'ordinary existence' that Ibsen wished to explore, and he knew that only prose would suit his bourgeois world, and 'force home on an unwilling public the immediacy of the questions which he asked.'[3] Writing to an English admirer who regretted that his first major prose play, *Emperor and Galilean* (1873), had not been in verse, Ibsen said:

It was the illusion of reality I wanted to produce . . . We no longer live in Shakespeare's time . . . In general the form of the language must be adapted to the degree of idealization that is given to the account. My new play is no tragedy in the old style; what I wanted to portray was people, and it was precisely for that reason that I did not allow them to speak with 'the tongues of angels'.[4]

And in the same quest for 'the illusion of reality', Ibsen's costumes and settings are scrupulously faithful to contem-porary life outside the world of his plays.

It would, however, be wrong to see Ibsen as interested in

verisimilitude, mere surface realism, for its own sake. In Ibsen, the reproduction of lifelike, probable speech, behaviour and environment is governed by a dramatic idea; a principle of selection is at work which, in its scrupulous choice from the banalities of everyday life, takes only those details which, linked together, permit us to delve beneath the surface realism and witness the unfolding of an intense psychological drama.

The Dramatic Use of Detail

In Act 1 of *Hedda Gabler* (1890), for example, Tesman and Hedda have just returned from their honeymoon. Tesman's Aunt Juliana has paid them a welcome-home morning visit, and just before she leaves, gives her nephew a little package wrapped in newspaper:

> *Tesman* [*opens the package*] : Good heavens! Auntie Juju, you've kept them! Hedda, this is really very touching. What?
> *Hedda* [*by the what-nots on the right*]: What is it, Tesman?
> *Tesman:* My old shoes! My slippers, Hedda!
> *Hedda:* Oh, them. I remember you kept talking about them on our honeymoon.
> *Tesman:* Yes, I missed them dreadfully. [*Goes over to her.*] Here, Hedda, take a look.
> *Hedda* [*goes away towards the stove*]: Thanks, I won't bother.

This tiny incident of the slippers dramatises how intensely Hedda's husband is still a small boy, surrounded by the smothering, adoring love of his two maiden aunts and their elderly maid, Bertha, in which he has been brought up. But perhaps 'small boy' is wrong. Their possessive idolatry has turned him too into a kind of old woman, obsessed by the little rituals of his own comfort. Hedda's lack of interest in the slippers, her curt 'I won't bother', reveals the quiet desperation of her realisation that she has married not only Tesman but Auntie Juju and Auntie Rena and Bertha as well. She has married into a claustrophobic cosiness completely hostile to her conception of herself as a free, proud and aristocratic spirit. As Ibsen himself puts it in the draft notes for the play:

> George Tesman, his old aunts, and the elderly serving-maid Bertha together form a whole and a unity. They have a common way of thinking, common memories, and a common attitude to life. For Hedda they appear as an inimical and alien power directed against her fundamental nature.

The realistic surface details — the slippers, the chintz covers, Auntie Juju's new hat — are convincing at the naturalistic level, then, but are only of *dramatic* importance in so far as Ibsen uses them, as he habitually does, to enable us to penetrate that surface to the hidden truth beneath.

It would be wrong, then, to confuse Ibsen's use of realistic detail, so intimately connected with psychological revelation of character, with the very different, less selective realism of the documentary kind. But even more important, Ibsen's plays are not 'problem plays': they are only superficially 'about' the topical social issues of his day. This is true even of plays like *Ghosts* and *A Doll's House*, and certainly of a play like *Hedda Gabler*. The real inner centre of Ibsen's drama is its powerful portrayal of the fundamental clash between man and society. This is what prevents Ibsen's plays from seeming dated, and what gives some of them what many feel is a tragic intensity.

Individualism Opposed by Social Pressures

Ibsen believed in individualism, that it was part of man's nature to strive to achieve the fullest realisation of his self-hood, to be free in terms of his powers and potentialities. Self-realisation is man's highest value, an absolute value, and Ibsen's belief in this kind of freedom is built into all his great protagonists, from the uncompromising idealist in *Brand* (1866), to the visionary artist Rubek in his last play, *When We Dead Awaken* (1899).

A man is not only an individual — as a man, he is also, by definition, a social animal. And as such he is not free — he feels the myriad constraints, the hampering thread-like pressures of society, so well described in George Eliot's novels. He is trapped inside a web of relationships, to his family, his friends, his community and his past. And as the incident with the slippers in *Hedda Gabler* shows, Ibsen's sense of the constricting pressures of society, which may manifest themselves at any moment in the most mundane contexts, is every bit as powerfully dramatised as are the urges to freedom and self-realisation in his protagonists.

Ibsen is concerned, then, not with advocating superficial changes in the social structure, whether these be the need for divorce or cures for syphilis, but rather with the fundamental opposition between man's individualistic aspirations and his bondage to societal forces. The conflict between the individual and society is, of course, a major and pervasive theme of Western literature of the last two centuries, but before we turn to an examination of how Ibsen embodies this theme, supremely, in *Hedda Gabler*, one further point should be made. What gives his plays intense psychological power is that the conflict is an *internal* one; that is, Ibsen sees that the battle between what we may call the individualist or self-expressive principle, and the societal or repressive principle, is sited within the self. It is not that the heroic individual confronts intransigent society in a somewhat melodramatic way; rather the individual discovers inside himself that even as he wishes for self-realisation, he is also timid, afraid of ridicule, anxious for security, conformist.

Hedda Gabler

The Setting

The opening movement of *Hedda Gabler* sketches with powerful dramatic economy the nature of the painful and stifling trap into which Hedda has stepped with weary wilfulness. Ibsen's meticulous directions for the stage-set are important. The room is decorated and furnished in dark colours; above all, it is crammed fussily full of furniture — chairs, tables, sofas, a piano, what-nots holding ornaments of terra-cotta and majolica. There is something smothering as well as

sombre here: it is a kind of spatial image of the life-in-death
to which she has committed herself. Even the profusion of
flowers lying around has a vaguely sinister effect. They seem
less bouquets to celebrate Hedda's marriage, rather funeral-
wreaths for her hopes. They make the air heavy with their
oppressive perfume — as Hedda says, 'This room needs fresh
air. All these flowers!' One detail of the set is particularly
suggestive: in the little room behind the drawing-room, right
in the centre of the stage when the curtain goes up, broods
the portrait of a handsome old man in general's uniform —
General Gabler. It is as if we get a glimpse here of Hedda's
deeper self. The title of the play is intended to indicate that
as a personality she is to be regarded rather as her father's
daughter than as her husband's wife. And many references in
Act 1 help to make us aware how different Hedda's way of
life and expectations are from that of the Tesmans — her
extravagant amount of luggage, her husband's half-timid, half-
proud (and wholly misplaced) sense that only this expensive
house could please her, her desire for a footman and a bay
mare, her airy decision that, since her old piano doesn't suit
the room, they'll get a second one; and, in general, the hauteur
of her face, figure and bearing:

> *Miss Tesman:* . . . General Gabler's daughter! Think what
> she was accustomed to when the general was alive! You
> remember how we used to see her out riding with her
> father? In that long black skirt? With the feather in her
> hat?
> *Bertha:* Oh yes, miss. As if I could forget! But, Lord! I
> never dreamed I'd live to see a match between her and
> Master Georgie.

Tesman

Hedda married Tesman because her father's death had left
her without money to support her extravagant way of living,
because she had a scared intuition about approaching age and
loneliness (Ibsen unobtrusively works in the detail near the
beginning of the play that it is September, and that the leaves
are golden and withered), and because, unlike her other
admirers, he asked her. We need to be told these things,

because Bertha's surprise at this match is, on the face of it, very much justified. Tesman is portrayed by Ibsen in a way that is perilously close to caricature: he is an unimaginative pedant, who has spent his honeymoon rooting in archives for his research on the domestic industries of Brabant in the Middle Ages, who prefers filing and indexing notes to creative thought, and the summit of his ambition is the possibility of a professorship. He is very reluctant to let go the sheltering petticoats of his adoring Auntie Juju and Bertha.

Hedda's Desperation and Aggressiveness

Hedda feels herself hemmed in on every side, the very baby she is carrying a threat to her independence (throughout the play she angrily rejects any innuendoes, however well-meant, about the patter of tiny feet), and her reaction to her new and constricted situation takes two main avenues. One is a kind of silent scream of torment and desperation. When she is alone on stage for the first time, the direction reads: *'Tesman is heard sending his love to Aunt Rena and thanking Miss Tesman for his slippers. Meanwhile Hedda walks up and down the room, raising her arms and clenching her fists as though in desperation.'*

The other response to the stifling atmosphere of Tesman domesticity is fierce aggression, an assertion of her sense of caste superiority, which produces the wonderful dramatic moment when she deliberately and cruelly 'mistakes' Aunt Tesman's new hat, bought in her honour, for the servant's old one — another excellent illustration of Ibsen's power to reveal psychological tensions and pressures of the most intense kind from brilliant artistic manipulation of 'trivial' details.

Loevborg

Even in the first Act, we have been made aware in oblique ways that Hedda's concealed aspirations, her demands on life and happiness, are somehow focused on Eilert Loevborg, creative scholar and reformed drunkard.

Before her father's death, Hedda has had an intense if rather strange relationship with Loevborg. We are given an insight into the nature of the relationship retrospectively, in the conversation between the two in the second Act, as they pretend to look over the photographs taken during Hedda's honeymoon trip. Clearly, Loevborg was interested sexually in Hedda; but for her it was the style and romantic secrecy of their relationship that appealed, rather than any erotic possibilities in it: indeed she broke off the relationship when it threatened to develop in physical terms. Loevborg's confession to her of his affairs and drinking and general dissipation did more than flatter a young girl's vanity. As she says to him: 'Do you find it so incredible that a young girl, given the chance in secret, should want to be allowed a glimpse into a forbidden world of whose existence she is supposed to be ignorant?' This is less an indication of voyeuristic impulses on her part than an indication that Loevborg and his life represent for her a contrast to the stifling constrictions of society, particularly as these affected a woman of that time. Loevborg stands in Hedda's mind for somebody who just does not care about the conventions of society, and her attitude is only reinforced when she compares him with her timid husband and her admirer, Judge Brack, who for all his surface raciness is presented as a thoroughgoing bourgeois at heart.

Hedda's Romanticism

Loevborg, then, for Hedda more a symbolic type than a potential sexual partner, draws forth from her that powerful aspiration towards individual freedom which is latent in all of Ibsen's major characters. She projects on him the buried poetry of her being. This is the Hedda who sees Eilert Loevborg 'with a crown of vine leaves in his hair, burning and unashamed', bringing into the depressing circumstances of narrow Norwegian life a breath of Grecian expansiveness, a hint — as her images make clear — of Dionysiac or Bacchic energies. This illusion is shattered when she discovers that the vine-leaved Dionysiac of her imagining has in fact spent the night of his re-entry into her life in a thoroughly commonplace and provincial way getting drunk, visiting the local brothel, and finally scuffling with the police. But the thwarted romanticism of Hedda's vision is not destroyed: Loevborg can 'redeem' himself by proving himself capable of the 'beautiful' death. The aesthetic and romantic satisfaction she finds in the contemplation of such a death is expressed very directly in an exchange with Judge Brack in Act 4:

> *Hedda:* Oh, Judge! This act of Eilert Loevborg's — doesn't it give one a sense of release!
>
> *Brack:* Release, Mrs Hedda? Well, it's a release for him, of course —
>
> *Hedda:* Oh, I don't mean him — I mean me! The release of knowing that someone can do something really brave! Something beautiful! . . . Oh, I know what you're going to say. You're a bourgeois at heart, too . . . I only know that Eilert Loevborg has had the courage to live according to his own principles. And now, at last, he's done something big! Something beautiful! To have the courage and the will to rise from the feast of life so early!

This illusion, too, is shattered: she learns that Loevborg has shot himself, in obscure circumstances — possibly even accidentally — in the brothel, and not 'beautifully' through the temple, but in the genitals. She is appalled — 'Why does everything I touch become mean and ludicrous? It's like a curse!' — and, almost inevitably, attempts to expunge this sordid, semi-ludicrous tarnish over her image of the beautiful death by shooting herself.

In seeing, or wanting to see, Eilert Loevborg as a Dionysiac flouter of timid conventions, and as a tragic actor capable of the grand gesture (the beautiful suicide), Hedda is quite clearly living vicariously through him. Elizabeth Robins, the actress who was prominent in introducing Ibsen's work to the London stage, put this well in speaking of Hedda's 'strong need to put some meaning into her life, even at the cost of borrowing it, or stealing the meaning out of someone's else's'.[5] Hedda thus does not see Loevborg as a person in his own right, and this explains her destructive and — by any standards — intolerable interference in, and manipulation of, his life. Rather, to her, he is simply an extension of herself, a romantic and symbolic *alter ego*.

Why does Hedda's desire for self-realisation and self-fulfilment take this deflected, projected, vicarious form? The answer to this question takes us to the heart of Ibsen's vision. It is because of the powerful operation, in Hedda herself, of the force of the very conventionality she professes to despise, because of the power over her of 'the social' which seems always in Ibsen's work to be antagonistic to the individual's development. Hedda is torn internally by the conflict between the demands of the self for assertion and fulfilment, and the demands of the 'societal self', as it were, that the rules be obeyed. Hence she projects on Loevborg an image of romantic freedom by which she attempts to 'live', being too timid to try to live out that freedom in her own life.

Hedda's Conventionality

Timidity is not a quality one would at first sight associate with Hedda. But in fact, Hedda only appears unconventional because of the external conventionality of the people who surround her, the Tesman family. Her fear and dislike of scandal, her orthodoxy in social terms, is dramatised at many points in the play, nowhere more deftly and ironically than in her exchange with Thea in Act 1. Thea, under some pressure, reveals to Hedda that she will never go back to her husband:

Hedda: You mean you've left your home for good?
Thea: Yes. I didn't see what else I could do.
Hedda: But to do it so openly!
Thea: Oh, it's no use trying to keep a thing like that secret.
Hedda: But what do you think people will say?
Thea: They can say what they like. I had to do it.

The irony here is obvious: Hedda despises Thea for her meekness, and is jealous and contemptuous of Thea's moral regeneration of Loevborg (for it is with Thea's help that Loevborg has stopped drinking and written his impressive book); yet it is the timid Thea, whom Hedda had terrorised with her arrogant self-assurance when they were both schoolgirls, who is capable of an act of genuine courage, flouting the conventions of propriety and social decorum in a way which shocks the apparently more emancipated Hedda — 'But what do you think people will say?'

The same inhibition has shaped her relationship with Loevborg. Still unmarried, she was curious about his erotic adventures, but unwilling to offer him love herself. In Act 2, he reproaches her for having broken with him. She replies that she didn't want the friendship to develop into 'something else':

> *Hedda:* Shame on you, Eilert Loevborg! How could you abuse the trust of your dearest friend?
> *Loevborg* [*clenches his fists*] : Oh, why didn't you do it? Why didn't you shoot me dead? As you threatened to!
> *Hedda:* I was afraid. Of the scandal.
> *Loevborg:* Yes, Hedda. You're a coward at heart.
> *Hedda:* A dreadful coward.

This brings out very well Hedda's deflection of her desire for experience into living vicariously through the experience of another. She can only take her rejection of the mean and constricting social pressures so far, because these pressures are so deeply ingrained in her own self that she is, as Loevborg says, a coward when it comes to the moment of decision. Hedda is in fact totally deadlocked, and the deadlock is produced not just by her individuality encountering smothering, outside, social pressures, but by the *inner* conflict between aspiration and the weight of convention, by the impasse in her soul. When Loevborg disappoints her -- as he was bound to, given the amount of romantic capital she had invested in him and given her discovery that one cannot live through another person -- it is too late for her to try to begin to live life purposefully for herself and by herself. And since Loevborg hasn't even been able to kill himself 'beautifully', the only act left open to Hedda is to kill herself, 'beautifully'. Ibsen wants us to see her suicide as inevitable as anything in Greek tragedy -- it is where the deadlock in her spirit has been pointing her since the opening of the play, towards finding in death the fulfilment she has been unable to find in life.

A Tragic Drama?
Ibsen may be seen as a social dramatist in the sense that *Hedda*

Gabler, like many of his greatest plays, is deeply engaged with the problems of the relationship between the individual and society. But he is not a social dramatist in the simpler sense that he is trying to find answers to remediable social 'problems'. Rather, his great dramas, in various ways, deal with the major theme of *Hedda Gabler*, which is simultaneously a characteristic and tragic dilemma of modern man: how to be oneself, yet at the same time how to live in society? Because Ibsen sees no easy answer to this impasse, or perhaps no answer at all, he has created one form of modern tragedy. John Northam's remarks are apposite:

> For a man of Ibsen's generation the great opponent of man was seen to be society — not just society in its 'problem play' aspect, the source of definable, limitable, and often remediable misery, but society as a force working through a myriad of obscure agencies and trivial occasions, but working with a power and mystery comparable to that displayed by the Greek gods or the Elizabethan universe.[6]

Many would object to the view that *Hedda Gabler* could be considered a tragedy. Such objections might be based, for example, on a feeling that prose is an inappropriate medium for the tragic vision, lacking the dignity and loftiness of the verse employed in Greek and Elizabethan tragedy, and incapable of embodying in language the large aspiration and greatness of soul associated with the traditional tragic hero. W. B. Yeats, for example, found in Ibsen only 'the stale odour of spilt poetry'. Closely related is a traditionalist assumption that only certain types of character are suitable for tragic treatment: kings, princes, those in high places. Hedda may seem 'aristocratic' to the mediocre Tesman, but her brand of aristocracy would not be of the kind to give her tragic status in the eyes of the traditionalists. Her fate does not involve the fate of nations, her drama is domestic rather than public and social. However, it can be pointed out to the traditionalists that to tie the essence of tragedy so firmly to a kind of social register seems more and more inappropriate in an egalitarian age, and that much literature of the last two hundred years — in the novel form as well as in the dramatic medium — has powerfully challenged 'the assumption that tragic suffering is the sombre privilege'[7] of the great and high-born, as in Greek and Elizabethan tragedy. It is true that verse can add immeasurably to the tragic effect, intensifying emotion, deepening our sense of character and widening the horizons of a drama to give it a quality of universality. But it would be wrong to believe that Ibsen's deliberate rejection of verse meant that he was not only committing himself to prose, but to the prosaic. *Hedda Gabler* (indeed all of Ibsen's plays from *The Wild Duck* onwards) reveals his ability to imbue his realistic settings, natural and mundane objects, and ordinary speech with a persistent and — to my mind — convincing symbolic resonance. Ultimately it is the power of Ibsen's conception which gives his plays their 'poetic' flavour. The intensity with which *he* sees Hedda's position ensures that we too see not merely a Norwegian housewife walking about in a drawing-room, but a theatrical image of a trapped spirit in a cage; and the famous pistols and the references to the 'vine leaves in the hair' are only extreme examples of a tendency in all the dialogue to move towards deeper and 'symbolic' significances, as Ibsen strives to give dramatic embodiment not to the superficial externals but to the inner core of Hedda's dilemma.

It could still be argued that Hedda is not sufficiently sympathetic to be seen as a tragic heroine. Her contempt for her husband, her meanly destructive treatment of Thea, and her shocking and predatory interference in Loevborg's life — none of these things is likeable. And what do her life and death teach us? Where are the positives in the play? Behind all this there lies the view that insists that the tragic hero must have nobility of spirit, and learn something positive from his suffering. R. P. Draper questions these prescriptions, which, as he says, work well for plays such as *Hamlet* but perhaps not quite so well for another kind of play, such as *Macbeth*:

> Criticism which centres on this kind of tragedy ['heroic tragedy' like *Hamlet*, with its positive emphases] . . . tends to look for triumph in defeat, a tragedy that reassures rather than depresses. The tragedy which comes from

distortion and perversion of the vital forces sustaining humanity, or the tragedy of bleakness deriving from a Schopenhauerian sense of the delusiveness of life itself — these are not catered for, or they are demoted to the level of non-tragedy.[8]

Perhaps, as Draper implies, we need to broaden our notion of the tragic if it is too narrow to admit *Hedda Gabler*; we need to appeal to the theatrical experience. Ibsen's presentation of Hedda, baulked in the very core of her being, surely stirs a compassionate chord in even the most stony-hearted member of the audience.

Miller's *Death of a Salesman*

Arthur Miller (b. 1915), who has been deeply influenced by Ibsen, clearly agrees with the great Norwegian's implied position, that the social status of the protagonist is irrelevant to the tragic effect, and emphasises rather the importance of 'the self-conceived role':

> It matters not at all whether a modern play concerns itself with a grocer or a president if the intensity of the hero's commitment to his course is less than the maximum possible. It matters not at all whether the hero falls from a great height or a small one . . . if the intensity, the human passion to surpass his given bounds, the fanatic insistence upon his self-conceived role — if these are not present there can only be an outline of tragedy but no living thing.[9]

Miller's plays, too, focus on the clash between the individual and society, and on the grip of the past on the present. The latter theme, the notion of the individual caught within the determining fields of force of his own past, is dramatised with special theatrical elegance and strength in Miller's best-known play, *Death of a Salesman* (1949). Miller's original title was *The Inside of His Head*, which suggests something of the expressionist nature of the treatment. The play largely consists of memory sequences which, though not seen specifically from Willy Loman's point of view, are motivated by, and run concurrently with, Willy's state of mind in the present. (Thus, Willy's present momentary sense of pride in his son Biff, for example, causes to 'happen' on the stage an incident of years before, when Biff was a golden football hero with the world at his feet.) It is one of Miller's great achievements in *Death of a Salesman* to find a highly striking means of dramatising the past. This is not, of course, merely a method, but part of the whole vision. As Miller says:

> The *Salesman* image was from the beginning absorbed with the concept that nothing in life comes 'next' but that everything exists together and at the same time within us; that there is no past to be 'brought forward' in a human being, but that he is his past at every moment . . .
>
> The way of telling the tale, in this sense, is as mad as Willy and as abrupt and as suddenly lyrical . . . In the hands of writers who see it as an easy way to elicit anterior information in a play it becomes merely a flashback. There are no flashbacks in this play but only a mobile concurrency of past and present, and this, again, because in his desperation to justify his life Willy Loman has destroyed the boundaries between now and then . . .[10]

The theatrical devices associated with the expressionist or memory sequences of the play — the drenching of the stage in a green pattern of leaves, the use of colour generally to suggest mood, and the similar use of music — have a certain poetic quality which offsets the generally realistic method, as Ibsen's symbols similarly pull against his grainy prose.

The Problem: 'Social Tragedy'

Miller's method of dramatising the past is the most impressive aspect of *Death of a Salesman*. His attempt to reconcile social drama with tragedy is, however, less successful. The play seems to give a double, contradictory message. In its analysis of American society, a powerful condemnatory picture is given of an exploitative and indifferent form of social organisation, which — as in the great scene between Willy and Howard Wagner — prefers to play with its tape-recorders than to listen to the cries of anguish from its own human casualties. Miller's 'message' from this angle is clearly and simply social: change the system. But in its presentation of Willy Loman, the representative victim of this society, the play seems to suggest that his fate is unavoidable, that his is an *inevitable* tragedy. No change is possible. The play moves uneasily between these poles, and for all its power and great emotional impact, never achieves satisfactory artistic or dramatic resolution.

Willy's Values

The problems centre, of course, on Willy himself. Hedda Gabler's aspiration, though cloudily perceived by her, and in the end thwarted, is clearly a desire to break free of society. In that sense, her role is dynamic, she seems active; in other words, she attempts to assert her own values (what Miller calls the 'insistence upon [the] self-conceived role'). Willy Loman's case is a different one. His values *are* the values of his society, and in that sense it may be said he has no values of his own, and is totally determined by the ethos which surrounds him. For clearly he is not at odds with the basic values of the society of which he is a member — the values of cash, competition, status; in short, the success-ethic. His failure and despair stem from his inability to make those values operative (successfully) in his own life: he never questions their rightness. When he confesses, near the end, to Ben that he has spent his life 'ringing up a zero', the metaphor of the cash-register is very appropriate. He knows that he is not good at hitting the keys of the cash-register but he could never conceive of walking away from it, any more than he can take the job offered him by his neighbour Charley, because he knows that the job is being offered out of compassionate friendship. Such values have no place in Willy's model of the American urban jungle, and his great hero is his brother Ben who at seventeen 'walked into the jungle and when I was twenty-one I walked out. And by God I was rich.' Willy sells himself all his life, and in a final savage irony, literally sells himself in suicide, so that the insurance money will enable his beloved Biff to lord it over Charley's son Bernard once again, as in the past. 'When the mail comes, he'll be ahead of Bernard again.' As Miller says, he has 'committed himself so completely to the counterfeits of dignity and the false coinage embodied in his idea of success that he can prove his existence only by bestowing "power" on his posterity, a power deriving from the sale of his last asset, himself, for the price of his insurance policy'.[11]

Willy as Victim

Willy's attitudes and actions are dramatised with undeniable power, but it is difficult to accept Miller's argument that Willy is a genuine tragic hero. For in the pattern sketched out briefly here, the overwhelming emphasis is on Willy's passivity, his inarticulateness, his inability to perceive, his lack of personal, self-generated values. In all these ways, Willy is seen much more as a victim rather than as a hero, and his fate seems pathetic rather than tragic. Society destroys Willy, yet Willy fully endorses the values of his society. He makes love in blindness to that which destroys him, and unlike Oedipus or Othello never comes to see the truth. Absence of awareness, of insight, of consciousness about what is happening to him, makes his position hopelessly determined. It can, of course, be argued that such a spectacle of suffering, pointless because never really understood or comprehended by the sufferer, is far *more* tragic than suffering seen and understood by its conscious and self-aware victim. Clearly determinism, the sense of an inevitable and inescapable fate must and does play a large part in tragic drama. But determinism on its own cannot make tragedy or tragic heroes, since it reduces the protagonist to mere puppet-victim, whose fate will only stir us to pathos. Miller himself, ironically, puts it very well: 'Determinism . . . is a contradiction of the idea of drama itself . . . The idea of the hero, let alone the mere protagonist, is incompatible with a drama whose bounds are set in advance by the concept of an unbreakable trap.'[12] Willy is in an unbreakable trap, precisely because he does not know he is there; and the extremely effective dramatisation of 'the mobile concurrency of past and present' in the play's handling of time suggests a man who could never have changed.

Linda

Miller tries to suggest that things can be changed, that the conditions of society are alterable. But this is paradoxical of him because he has created a current of feeling in the play which runs counter to such a suggestion. While this position on the part of Miller is understandable, indeed honourable, it is not compatible with the tragic experience, and Miller clearly wishes us to see Willy as tragic. In tragedy, there are no temporal remedies, and man's fate can not be 'solved' by the application of social poultices. The strain between Miller's social reformism and his aspirations towards tragedy becomes especially apparent in the character of Linda Loman, Willy's wife, and in one famous — or notorious — speech by her, addressed nominally to her sons, but in reality aimed straight at the audience:

> I don't say he's a great man. Willy Loman never made a lot of money. His name was never in the paper. He's not the finest character that ever lived. But he's a human being, and a terrible thing is happening to him. So attention must be paid. He's not to be allowed to fall into his grave like an old dog. Attention, attention must finally be paid to such a man.

Several things are awry here. First, the impact of Linda's direct appeal is severely limited by the ambiguous and unsatisfactory role she plays throughout: she accepts Willy for what he is (as here), yet constantly encourages him for what he claims to be, and urges her sons to encourage him in his deluded roseate fantasies. Thus there is a curious dislocation between the responsibility she bears for deflecting her husband from finding his own values, and the emotional sympathy and moral authority Miller accords her in contexts like those of the 'attention' speech. Second, there is a damagingly didactic tone in Linda's words, which have in the dramatic context an air of authorial finality, and are awkward and schoolmasterly. It suggests that having failed to portray convincingly an admittedly unremarkable man in terms which will ensure our sympathy, Miller is forced back on a simple appeal to our broad feelings of liberal humanitarianism.

No Solutions in Tragedy

Most seriously, perhaps, Linda's speech reveals with embarrassing clarity Miller's inability to make us see Willy as anything but pathetic victim. The American writer Mary McCarthy puts it like this:

> Linda is really admonishing the audience that Willy is, as she says, a 'human being'. But that is just it; he is just a Human Being without being anyone. He is a sort of Suffering Statistic . . . a subject for the editorial page, which could take note of his working conditions, ask for unemployment benefits and old-age care for him, call 'attention' in short, to the problem of the salesman in the Welfare State.[13]

Death of a Salesman is a powerful social drama, but it does not encompass tragedy; Miller's basic optimism and decent democratic humanism get in the way. The deterministic aspects of the play are rather willed, and Miller's fundamental belief is that society can be changed. The Ibsen note, of tragic impasse or deadlock, is missing, and Miller's play — for all its extremely moving qualities — shows how difficult it is to achieve tragedy in the context of purely 'secular dilemmas which may be resolved by rational innovation'.[14]

Miller's play has had, however, a worldwide success. It is one of the best-known modern dramas. There are similarities in its theme to those of the two most popular Australian dramas. *Summer of the Seventeenth Doll* (1956), by Ray Lawler (b. 1921), deals with middle age and the loss of a hopeful dream among two cane-cutters and their women. *The One Day of the Year* (1960), by Alan Seymour (b. 1927), depicts movingly another failure who relies on his memories in an attempt to assert his sense of worth. The expressionist nature of Miller's representation of 'the inside of Willy's head' is paralleled in the Malaysian dramatist Edward Dorall's *The Hour of the Dog* (1970), where four different projections of the protagonist, Nick, act out a struggle within his conscience, and are under his control. In *The Floating World* (1974), by the Australian John Romeril (b. 1945), the dramatic mode is again expressionistic: the central character's fantasies take over the action, with consequent role-swapping as a Malay waiter becomes a Japanese soldier, the ship's comic an Australian army officer, and so on, in what is a powerful study of Australia's xenophobic attitudes to Asia. The success of Miller's play thus has popularised and made accessible what had once been an 'intellectual' and esoteric dramatic method.

7 Chekhov and the Drama of Social Change: 'The Cherry Orchard'

The Russian dramatist Anton Chekhov, like Ibsen and Miller, is interested in man's relations with society — his last play, which might be regarded as his masterpiece, *The Cherry Orchard*, is a profound drama of social change. He is, however, a more 'open' dramatist than the other two. That is, Ibsen places a perhaps too insistent emphasis on the intractable nature of the opposition between individual aspiration and social constraints. His views are fixed: his protagonists *must* always, *will* always, be broken in their attempts at self-assertion. If there is a criticism of Ibsen's drama, it is that there is a hint of a predetermined thesis lying behind his plays. Miller's *Death of a Salesman* also suffers from its author's adoption of a rigid stance, in this case the desire to assert the possibility of the tragedy of the common man (Willy's very surname is Loman), which is juxtaposed uneasily with Miller's social insights.

Chekhov's Objectivity

The most immediately apparent quality of Chekhov's art (he was a superb writer of short stories as well as of plays) is its dispassionateness or objectivity. This may be due in part to his direct experience and knowledge of a very wide social spectrum. He was a serf's son, but also a doctor, a landowner and an artist, and moved as easily in Russia's backward villages as in the artistic and intellectual circles of her major cities. Being a doctor brought Chekhov into contact with a wide range of life, but 'though it was important to Chekhov as a source of copy, medicine was still more important in a philosophical sense: it reinforced his pragmatical, down-to-earth view of life'.[1] He writes to a friend in a famous letter:

> You confuse two concepts: the solution of a problem and its correct presentation. Only the second is incumbent on the artist . . . In my view it's not the writer's job to solve such problems as God, pessimism and so on. The writer's job is only to show who, how, in what context, spoke or thought about God and pessimism. The artist must not be the judge of his character and of what they say: merely a dispassionate observer . . .[2]

This dispassionateness of outlook has a deep impact on the dramatic form of Chekhov's plays, giving them an 'open-ended' quality which makes considerable demands on the subtlety and responsiveness of actors and producers. Even more than in most authors is it damaging to separate Chekhov's 'form' from his 'content'. 'How he says it' is very much 'what he says'.

'Real Life': Chekhov's Distaste for Theatricality

Chekhov is a master of dramatic anti-climax, going out of his way to avoid what he considered to be falsely 'theatrical' episodes or moments. He remarked with pride of *The Cherry Orchard* that there was not a single pistol-shot in it, but it is not only gross melodrama which he rejects. He cleverly subverts and confounds even more legitimate dramatic expectations raised by the pattern of his action. Thus the climactic action, Lopakhin's announcement that he has bought the orchard, is made almost apologetically, and in the disarmingly digressive context of Gayev's longing for anchovies, Black Sea herrings and a game of billiards, which affects him every bit as much as the loss of his ancestral lands. Again, a persistent motif in the play is the possibility of a marriage between Varya, Mrs Ranevsky's adopted daughter, and Lopakhin. This would unite two single characters, suggest the virtue of work as an antidote to social disintegration (Varya and Lopakhin are the play's hard workers), perhaps even symbolise a stage

in the evolution of the Russian class system which would fit
in with the play's major thematic interests — in short, a 'loose
end' would be very neatly tied. What happens in the last Act,
however, is that Lopakhin has more or less to be driven to a
tête-à-tête with Varya. Chekhov dramatises it thus, in a way
that perfectly illustrates his art of anti-climax and his mastery
of apparently inconsequential dialogue. Lopakhin has been
left on his own:

> Lopakhin [*with a glance at his watch*] : Yes. [*Pause.*]
> [*Suppressed laughter and whispering are heard from
> behind the door. After some time Varya comes in.*]
> Varya [*spends a long time examining the luggage*] : That's
> funny, I can't find it anywhere.
> Lopakhin: What are you looking for?
> Varya: I packed it myself and I still can't remember.
> [*Pause.*]
> Lopakhin: Where are you going now, Varya?
> Varya: Me? To the Ragulins'. I've arranged to look after
> their place, a sort of housekeeper's job.
> Lopakhin: That's in Yashnevo, isn't it? It must be fifty
> odd miles from here. [*Pause.*] So life has ended in this
> house.
> Varya [*examining the luggage*] : Oh, where can it be? Or
> could I have put it in the trunk? Yes, life has gone out
> of this house. And it will never come back.
> Lopakhin: Well, I'm just off to Kharhov. By the next train.
> I have plently to do there. And I'm leaving Yepikhodov
> in charge here, I've taken him on.
> Varya: Oh, have you?
> Lopakhin: This time last year we already had snow,
> remember? But now it's calm and sunny. It's a bit cold
> though. Three degrees of frost, I should say.
> Varya: I haven't looked. [*Pause.*] Besides, our ther-
> mometer's broken. [*Pause.*]
>
> [*A voice at the outer door:* 'Mr Lopakhin!']
>
> Lopakhin: [*as if he had been expecting this summons*] : I'm
> just coming. [*Goes out quickly.*]

[*Varya sits on the floor with her head on a bundle of clothes, quietly sobbing.*]

It is necessary to quote at length to convey something of the fluidity of Chekhov's dramatic art, especially his handling of dialogue, which makes Ibsen (and indeed many other dramatists) seem stiff and wooden in comparison. Chekhov marries perfectly the naturalistic surface level of speech (with its hesitations, pauses and massive non-sequiturs) to a perception of the real emotional currents flowing in any act of human communication. So here, empty chat about a bit of luggage, train-journeys and the weather simultaneously masks and obliquely reveals the truth of the situation — Varya's inability to drop into tenderness from her usual bossy, managing kind of manner, her fear of being thought to be 'on offer', her hope that he will say something; Lopakhin's fear of his own adequacy, the absence of any genuine commitment to her, his overwhelming embarrassment. It is dramatically absorbing but never seems 'theatrical' in the pejorative sense of the word. Chekhov was very clear about this, writing in a letter which sums up his anti-theatrical stance:

The demand is made that the hero and heroine should be dramatically effective. But in life people do not shoot themselves, or hang themselves, or fall in love, or deliver themselves of clever sayings every minute. They spend most of their time eating, drinking, running after women or men, talking nonsense. It is therefore necessary that this should be shown on the stage. A play ought to be written in which the people should come and go, dine, talk of the weather, or play cards, not because the author wants it, but because that is what happens in real life. Life on the stage should be as it really is, and the people, too, should be as they are, and not on stilts.[3]

Chekhov's Sense of Plot

Another way in which Chekhov gives *The Cherry Orchard* the texture of 'life as it really is' is by his careful construction of a plot which does not give the appearance of being a plot.

There is no character in the play who is in any way manipulating events towards any sort of end — Mrs Ranevsky and
her brother, indeed, seem incapable of action, simply standing
aside helplessly doing nothing to prevent the sale of their
estate. Lopakhin, whom it would have been very easy to cast
in the role of the villain--despoiler, not only does nothing to
get the estate into his power, but, far from employing schemes
and stratagems from self-interest, tries hard to ensure that it
stays in the hands of its hereditary owners. He only buys it at
the last moment, on the spur of that moment, and is rather
dazed at what he has done. A large part of any audience's
sense of a dramatic plot comes from the presence of dynamic
characters who manipulate the action — Edmund in *King
Lear*, Volpone and Mosca, even Hedda Gabler. In suppressing
this type of character in *The Cherry Orchard*, Chekhov contrives to give the action of the play the 'open', random feel
of life — things seem to happen, rather than be made to
happen.

Group Scenes

Chekhov characteristically employs a large group of characters,
often on the stage at the one time, in such normal group
contexts as arrivals, parties and departures, and other social
ceremonies. This may be explained as deriving from his attempt
to suggest the large social representativeness of his action
(whereas Ibsen, concerned with the fate of single individuals,
characteristically focuses on one or two characters in intense
dialogue). These group scenes provide even more opportunities
for Chekhov's mastery of random, inconsequential dialogue,
as the characters speak not so much to each other as past
each other, in contexts which permit of juxtapositions and
non-sequiturs which are sometimes hilarious, sometimes
poignant, and where the polyphony of voices does indeed
create at times a musical effect. No one character dominates,
and this in turn enables Chekhov to achieve his brilliantly
subtle modulations of mood, which more than anything else,
perhaps, make his dramatic texture seem so fluid.

Group or 'crowd' scenes work very well in dramas that
attempt social representativeness. The confused history of an

Ireland in the midst of revolution and civil war is captured brilliantly in O'Casey's three 'Dublin' plays, *The Shadow of a Gunman* (1923), *Juno and the Paycock* (1924), and *The Plough and the Stars* (1926), where the tenement or slum settings enable O'Casey to depict many characters with differing political views and loyalties in communal dispute. The same sense of communal integration and fission is illustrated in works such as Soyinka's *A Dance of the Forests* and in Edward Dorall's *A Tiger is Loose in Our Community*, where the crowd scenes depicting antagonisms between the Chinese and Tamil populations are especially vibrant. (Dorall has completed a postgraduate thesis on O'Casey's plays.)

'Theatre-Poetry'

Chekhov's ability to create mood, and to convey his meaning through the suggestiveness of mood rather than through the much more explicit psychological analysis to be found in Ibsen, can be seen most clearly in the opening of Act 2 of *The Cherry Orchard*. Here all the elements in Chekhov's sense of dramatic form coalesce, to create what has been called 'theatre-poetry'. No verse is actually spoken: the 'poetry' comes from the setting, from the grouping of characters, from the dramatic rhythm (or pace of the action), and from the musical counterpoint of Yepikhodov's guitar. It is open country; a tumbledown old chapel and what seem like old tombstones give intimations of mortality and a hint of the decay of old certainties. The cherry orchard can be seen only dimly, and beyond it a row of telegraph poles and the distant outlines of a big town — a clear visual suggestion of the incursion of a newer modern world on an older, possibly outmoded way of life. The four characters converse after a fashion, but each is absorbed in his own separate thoughts. The sense of separation, of individual loneliness, is strong — Yepikhodov is in love with Dunyasha, but she loves Yasha, who loves only himself. Charlotte the governess says that she doesn't know who she is, where she comes from, and that she is 'alone in the world'. But these four are also a group, a group of servants, which lends ironic point to the demonstration of their separateness. The implication might be that they are all servants of a way of life which is disintegrating. The sun is setting, and from this and the other visual details of the setting, it could be argued that Chekhov is creating a kind of tone-poem on the demise of the landed class, and on the loss of everything which that class had contributed, positively, to the culture. Later in this Act comes the first ominous and symbolic sound of a breaking string, a device taken up and used again in effective counterpoint to the sound of Lopakhin's axes biting into the cherry orchard, in the play's conclusion – if anything, an even more powerful example of 'theatre-poetry'.

Tragedy or Comedy?

Chekhov the elegiac writer is certainly popular; he is the dramatist of the melancholy mood, the poet of the gloom and soulfulness of a Russia about to pass away for ever and aware in its bones of the nature of its lingering disease. But Chekhov is not to be so easily pinned down or labelled. The opening of Act 2 could also be played – and seen – in a much more comic way. Here is one detail from Charlotte's opening speech:

> Who my parents were I don't know either, very likely they weren't even married. [*Takes a cucumber out of her pocket and starts eating it.*] I don't know anything.

The cucumber is robustly bizarre, in the manner of some of Dickens's greatly eccentric and greatly comic unnecessary details; and eating a good firm cucumber is not, especially in a theatre, a silent business. Charlotte herself and Yepikhodov can be seen as essentially farcical, and Yasha and Dunyasha as riddled with comic affectations; the whole scene can be regarded as a parody of the melancholy of the 'superfluous man' (or class), a Russian literary type.

Indeed, Chekhov's ability to modulate tone, or to hold opposing moods in a delicate balance means that *The Cherry Orchard* as a whole resists generic classification. Is it a tragedy or a comedy? Stanislavsky (1863–1938), the great director of the Moscow Arts Theatre closely associated with Chekhov, was in no doubt of its tragic qualities — but this intensely irritated Chekhov, who firmly insisted on calling the play a comedy. This might seem to be conclusive, but the play's final moments — the farewell to the home and the orchard, and the bitter-sweet vignette of the abandoned old servant, Firs — can only be described as comic with some considerable strain. Ronald Hingley's view of the problem seems eminently sensible:

> In firmly describing his plays, above all *The Cherry Orchard*, as comedies, Chekhov was perhaps confusing matters by dragging in a traditional theatrical term inapplicable to his new form of drama. What he was really appealing for, we suggest, was a lightness of touch, a throw-away casual style, an abandonment of the traditional over-theatricality of the Russian (and not only the Russian) theatre.[4]

Once again, we are back with the salient point: that Chekhov's stance is that of a dispassionate (though not cynical) observer, and that consequently his dramatic mode embraces great tonal fluidity, an alert anti-theatricality, a subtle obliquity of dialogue, and an ability to suggest through 'theatre-poetry' what another dramatist might hammer home explicitly. Chekhov's own dramatic mastery in these respects has influenced dramatists as different as Shaw, Pinter and Beckett.

This technique, and the attitude which informs it, enable Chekhov to present his drama of social change both fairly and comprehensively. *The Cherry Orchard*, like nearly all of his plays, is about 'the fate of the cultured classes in the modern world'.[5] In many British stage productions, Chekhov's vision is sentimentalised, and *The Cherry Orchard* becomes an elegy for the doomed gentry, attractive and whimsically eccentric, lovable in spite (or because) of their faults. On the other hand, it is also easy to throw a falsifying over-emphasis in the other direction. This has been especially true of Soviet criticism, which tends to see Chekhov as a breezy extrovert, portraying with comic vigour the inadequacies of the decaying upper class, and looking forward by implication and with confidence to the brave new world which was to be ushered in, only thirteen years after his death, by the Bolshevik revolution. Both approaches distort Chekhov's remarkable flexibility, his ability to make a full diagnosis (to use the medical terminology he himself was fond of). To see this clearly requires a brief discussion of Chekhov's portrayal of Lopakhin, however difficult it is to isolate one aspect of a very closely woven work of art.

Lopakhin

The Cherry Orchard describes the dispossession of a family of land-owning gentry by the son of one of its former serfs, Lopakhin, who has become a self-made man, a dynamic member of the new rising business class. The possibilities of slotting Lopakhin into a melodramatic stereotype are sufficiently obvious, but the portrait is much more subtle.

Lopakhin's great moment in the play, and indeed the climax of whatever action there is, comes near the end of Act 3, when he comes back to the pathetic little party which Mrs Ranevsky is throwing, and announces to a shocked room that *he* has bought the cherry orchard:

And now the cherry orchard is mine. Mine! [*Gives a loud laugh.*] Great God in heaven, the cherry orchard's mine! Tell me I'm drunk or crazy, say it's all a dream. [*Stamps his feet.*] Don't laugh at me. If my father and grandfather could only rise from their graves and see what happened, see how their Yermolay — Yermolay who was always being beaten, who could hardly write his name and ran round barefoot in winter — how this same Yermolay bought this estate . . . where my father and grandfather were slaves, where they weren't even allowed inside the kitchen . . . Hey, you in the band, give us a tune, I want to hear you. Come here, all of you, and just watch Yermolay Lopakhin get his axe into that cherry orchard, watch the trees come crashing down. We'll fill the place with cottages. Our grandchildren and our great grandchildren will see a few changes round here.

The words exude the confidence of a once-repressed class coming into its own. It is the turning-point of the play, and implicitly the turning-point for Russia, the death of the old order. In a good production, the audience should almost be able to feel the ground shaking underneath the characters' feet, as if the steamroller of history was already rumbling up the driveway: 'just watch Yermolay Lopakhin get his axe into that cherry orchard, watch the trees come crashing down'.

The Death of the Old Order

Lopakhin's words refer to some of the exploitative aspects of the old order, and in doing so recall a speech of considerable power and social bite given to the student Trofimov in Act 2. He is trying to point out to Mrs Ranevsky's daughter, whom he loves, the realities of the system on which her traditional status rests:

> Owning living souls, that's what has changed you all so completely, those who went before and those alive today, so that your mother, you yourself, your uncle — you don't realise that you're actually living on credit. You're living on other people, the very people you won't even let inside your own front door.

This whole speech so alarmed the State censor that he insisted that Chekhov should rewrite it. It — and Lopakhin's speech in Act 3 which contains obvious verbal echoes of it — suggest that Chekhov might have approved of the demise of a system of feudal exploitation.

Such a supposition rests on the argument that Chekhov created Lopakhin as a representative of the new dynamic order which was to supplant a decadent gentry. The play certainly paints a strong contrast between the utilitarian, practical Lopakhin (and the doctor in Chekhov approved of the practical and the utilitarian) and the almost incredible lassitude and negligence of Mrs Ranevsky and her brother. Lopakhin also comes extremely well out of the comparison with the play's other 'man of the future', Trofimov. Trofimov is very specific about the Russian disease — too much talking and theorising, and not enough work. The irony is that

Trofimov is a spectacular example of the type that he criti-
cises, the eternal student, full of empty theorising. His often
inflated rhetoric about his 'being in the vanguard' as 'mankind
marches towards a higher truth' compares unfavourably with
Lopakhin's plain speech, that of a man more interested in
doing than in *philosophising*:

> I'm always up by five o'clock, you know. I work from
> morning till night, and then — well, I'm always handling
> money, my own and other people's, and I can see what
> sort of men and women I have around me. You only have
> to start a job of work to realise how few decent, honest
> folk there are about.

Lopakhin's role, then, is dynamic, differentiated sharply
from the dithering gentry and from the windy theorising of
the intellectual; and in him we may feel that Chekhov has
embodied his approval of the direction taken by social change
in Russia since the emancipation of the serfs.

Lopakhin and the Orchard

It is possible, however, to take a very different view of
Lopakhin. This could originate in a sense of the beauty of the
cherry orchard itself. The play begins with it, sparkling white
with frost through the windows of the empty nursery, and ends
with the sound of its destruction. In its mute purity it may
be seen as emblematic of a beautiful lost world — not just the
lost world of a more expansive feudal life-style, but the lost
world of childhood innocence and purity, a world outside
time and change, which is locked up somewhere, in different
shapes and forms, in all our imaginations. Mrs Ranevsky and
her brother do not see in the orchard (as Trofimov insensitively
can only see) a symbol of political and social power, once
wielded, now lost. It is rather a living memento of the innocence and happiness of childhood: for Mrs Ranevsky it contains
a *personal* truth which cannot be measured by the application
of moralistic or political standards, as she tries to explain to
Trofimov in Act 3. And in Act 1, as the windows are thrown
open to the orchard, she exclaims:

Oh, my childhood, my innocent childhood! This is the nursery where I slept and I used to look out at the orchard from here. When I woke up every morning happiness awoke with me, and the orchard was just the same in those days. Nothing's changed. [*Laughs happily.*] White! All white! Oh, my orchard! After the damp, dismal autumn and the cold winter here you are, young again and full of happiness. The angels in heaven have not forsaken you. If I could only shake off the heavy burden that weighs me down, if only I could forget my past.

Lopakhin seems cursed by an absolute insensitivity to the personal meaning of the orchard for Mrs Ranevsky. He fails to respond to its beauty, and crassly begins to chop it down before Mrs Ranevsky is even out of the house, a crassness that is underlined by his inappropriate production of celebratory champagne. His axes thud not only into wood, but into people's deeply felt past and present lives. Chekhov's dramatic fluidity and mastery of tonal modulation easily accommodate the playing up of the pathos of Mrs Ranevsky's position, and accordingly as this is done, so does Lopakhin's position take on the tinge and colouring of the utilitarian barbarian, not actively malicious but so insensitive as to be almost as bad; and the play becomes an elegy for the passing of a culture and a way of life symbolised in the orchard itself — beautiful, but unproductive, and since commercially useless, however graceful, to be destroyed by a harsh new type.

Both views of Lopakhin, one friendly, one hostile, are based on the idea that Chekhov must have had one definite attitude to social change. If that attitude could be 'worked out', the character could be 'explained'. But Chekhov's dramatic complexity — and a good deal of his moral significance for our categorising and polarised modern world — insists that a human being cannot be explained in terms of his class role or his social status, that human acts are never just the products of socio-economic factors, but result from a blend of such factors with other, more unpredictable, personal ones. Chekhov makes it very difficult to pigeon-hole Lopakhin as representative of the new dynamic bourgeoisie.

Lopakhin and Mrs Ranevsky

Lopakhin does not see Mrs Ranevksy as the class enemy. Quite the contrary. Many details in the text suggest that he is in love with her, however difficult it might be to define precisely the nature of that love. As he says to her in Act 1, after getting over his agitation at the prospect of her return:

> This brother of yours calls me a lout of a peasant out for what I can get, but that doesn't bother me a bit. Let him talk. You must believe in me as you used to, that's all I ask, and look at me in the old way, with those wonderful, irresistible eyes. Merciful heavens! My father was a serf, belonged to your father and your grandfather before him. But you — you've done so much for me in the past that I've forgotten all that and love you as a brother. Or even more.

Clearly, with his constant efforts to help Mrs Ranevsky out of her financial predicament, which stem from his love for the woman he is to displace, a major and multiple irony of the play is established. Lopakhin may be cast by history as the man of the future, but he is as besotted by the past and by admiration for the gentry's way of life as they themselves are.

The inheritance of serfdom is still powerfully active within him, spiritually and emotionally. He tells Dunyasha very early in the play that he has 'plenty of money, but when you really get down to it I'm just another country bumpkin;' and he goes on to rebuke her for her claims to lady-like 'nerves': 'You're too sensitive altogether, my girl. You dress like a lady and do your hair like one too. We can't have that. Remember your place.' These terms could easily have come from old Firs, the play's most absolute believer in the values of the feudal past. Lopakhin cannot entirely rid himself of feelings of inferiority to the cultured milieu he now dominates financially, and his decisiveness as a business man is undercut by his dithering in the area of personal relationships, where he is just as ineffective as, say, Gayev is when dealing with the practical problems of life. There is, for instance, his curiously abortive relationship with Varya — into which Chekhov also works Lopakhin's emotional dependence on Mrs Ranevsky: 'I don't feel I'll ever propose to her without you here.'

Chekhov's Moral Tolerance

Lopakhin, like all the major characters of the play, is seen in a kind of double perspective, which liberates him from dramatic or political stereotyping. The obviousness of what Chekhov says should not blind us to its moral importance: what we do, how we act, should never be taken as a definition of, or confused with, what we are — and vice versa. Lopakhin is no more a simple representative of the new bourgeoisie than Mrs Ranevsky is a simple representative of an obsolete gentry. Sympathy is aroused for her by the intensity with which she associates the orchard with her childhood happiness and innocence. Yet Chekhov also shows, with his infinitely lively sense of the complexity of human beings, that Mrs Ranevsky does not make any real effort to save the orchard because she knows that she no longer belongs to its world, but to Paris and her lover. In a sense, she even wants to lose it. While she still owns it, its very beauty and its associations can only jab the more at her conscience, exacerbate a depressed consciousness of her now rootless, feckless life. When the orchard is lost, her outer and her inner life come more into harmony again. Thus her brother says near the end:

> It's quite true, everything's all right now. Before the cherry orchard was sold we were all worried and upset, but when things were settled once and for all and we'd burnt our boats, we all calmed down and actually cheered up a bit . . . And you can say what you like, Lyuba, you're looking a lot better, no doubt about it.

She replies:

> Yes, I'm not so much on edge, that's true. And I'm sleeping better . . . I'm going to Paris and I'll live on the money your great-aunt sent from Yaroslavl to buy the estate — good old Aunty! Not that it will last very long.

The Balance of the Conclusion

The indifference and irresponsibility shown in the insouciant attitude to 'Aunty's money' reminds us again, at this crucial point towards the play's close, of the negligence and extravagance of Mrs Ranevsky's life, in the end the main cause of her loss of her family estate. The ending of the play could have easily, in the hands of a lesser dramatist, turned into a sentimental orgy as the charming aristocrat bids farewell to her home. Indeed, Chekhov's depiction of the leave-taking of Mrs Ranevsky and her brother is deeply moving. But the balance is held: the play ends with a superb picture of the old servant Firs, alone, forgotten by the family, lying down to think over the futility of his devoted service to a family whom even he seems to sense is finished. His words, and their context, clearly do more than refer to his own personal situation:

> Life's slipped by just as if I'd never lived at all. I'll lie down a bit. You've got no strength left, got nothing left, nothing at all. You're just a nincompoop. [*Lies motionless. A distant sound is heard. It seems to come from the sky and is the sound of a breaking string. It dies away sadly. Silence follows, broken only by the thud of an axe striking a tree far away in the orchard.*]

This is wryly funny, but also intensely moving — the distinctive Chekhovian emotional balance is held brilliantly right to the end of the play, that kind of double vision which enables him to see the desperate absurdity of his characters and at the same time the human values in their lives, which tempers his irony with compassion. The 'openness' of Chekhov's dramatic mode is the formal expression of the wide tolerance of his vision of men in society.

8 Shaw and Brecht: 'Making Us Think'

Shaw and Brecht, like Ibsen and Chekhov, derive their dramatic ideas and form from a consideration of man's relationship with society. But their concern takes a more committed, even didactic form — Shaw was a socialist, Brecht a Marxist — and they create dramas which in the end are completely different in spirit and texture from those of Ibsen and Chekhov, whom Shaw, especially, greatly admired.

Shaw

Shaw's Attack on Conventional Morality and Received Ideas

Shaw misunderstood in Ibsen, however, Ibsen's tragic stress on the *intractable* nature of the conflict between individual aspiration and social conformism. As Shaw presents Ibsen in *The Quintessence of Ibsenism* (a characteristically vigorous polemic essay of 1890), he is seen as a social reformer whose chief contribution is his exposure of outmoded or repressive codes and attitudes, social, moral, political, sexual. This is very much an Ibsen in Shaw's own image. Much of Shaw's liveliest work consists of iconoclastic assaults on the current morality and ideology of late Victorian Britain. *Arms and the Man* (1894), for example, satirises the blind orthodoxies of current idealisations of military glory and of romantic love. In *Man and Superman* (written between 1901 and 1903), he mocks the endemic cult of 'respectability', which muzzles even those who regard themselves as radicals, by pointing its connection with the sense of shame — 'The more things a man is ashamed of, the more respectable he is.' The hero of this play, Tanner, is also speaking very much for his creator when he tries to explode conventional sexual morality, which sees premarital pregnancy as worse than death, condemns the father as a cad and a bounder, and yet insists that he 'make reparation' by marrying the girl: 'So we are to marry your sister to a damned scoundrel by way of reforming her character? On my soul, I think you are all mad.'

In *Major Barbara* (1905), among many other goads to conventional attitudes, Shaw brilliantly dramatises the falsity of the notion that poverty is in some way connected with moral worth. The sentimental idealisation of poverty produces such figures as Charles Dickens's Stephen Blackpool in *Hard Times*, as well as a good many other preternaturally virtuous artisans in nineteenth-century fiction. In Act 2 of *Major Barbara*, set in a London Salvation Army shelter, Shaw shows his slum-dwellers and unemployed working class as cynical, hypocritical, aggressive, obsequious − in short, Shaw (surely rightly) sees poverty as demoralising. As his protagonist Undershaft says: 'I have been a common man and a poor man; and it has no romance for me. Leave it to the poor to pretend that poverty is a blessing: leave it to the coward to make a religion of his cowardice by preaching humility.'

In these, and in many other instances, Shaw the iconoclast can be plainly seen. The spirited mockery of conventional *mores* is not only very funny, but gives Shaw's plays their tonic quality, a freshness in the dramatic air, and imparts to them much of Shaw's most appealing quality as a playwright, his zestful energy. Again Tanner in *Man and Superman* speaks for Shaw: 'I have become a reformer, and, like all reformers, an iconoclast . . . I shatter creeds and demolish idols . . . Construction cumbers the ground with institutions made by busybodies. Destruction clears it and gives us breathing space and liberty.' Thus the possibility of destruction (in the shape of German bombs) falling on the exhausted and effete world of *Heartbreak House* (1921) is presented by Shaw at the end of that play as exhilarating and potentially liberating.

Art Must Be Useful

Shaw's destructive iconoclasm is intimately connected with

his didacticism. Shaw, as has often been pointed out, resembles Plato in general outlook: both are obsessed with ethical reform, with the salvation of the community, and both tend to slight those who are not similarly occupied with socially useful ideas. Plato was especially distrustful of the artist, whom he saw as a liar to be banished from the ideal republic. Shaw similarly distrusts the artist who is only interested in his art, who lacks Shaw's own sense of prophetic mission, and who reacts fastidiously against the notion of a socially utilitarian function for art.

In Shaw's own work, 'the poet often appears as a Bohemian aesthete who passes the time of day inventing false ideals, composing sonnets to his mistress's eyebrow, or weaving a beautiful veil of "illusion" over "the unbearable face of truth".'[1] Hence the ridiculous poets in *Candida* (1904) and *Man and Superman*. Shaw only differs from Plato in his insistence that art *can* be socially useful — they share the same premise, that it *should be* socially useful.

Shaw and the Comic Mode

His utilitarian aesthetic, combined with temperamental factors, helps to explain Shaw's predilection for the comic mode. Comedy is the art-form which gives most emphasis to the idea of man as a rational being, and a being who must live in society. Shaw's literary reputation has suffered in part because of this.[2] Many influential modern artists and critics have tended to look slightingly on comedy, with its implicit or explicit invocation of social norms, and its appeal to the ideals of rationality and sociability. For rational, social man, many modern thinkers have substituted a sort of 'essential man', the kind of man who appears in, for example, the novels of D. H. Lawrence (1858–1930), the man who lives most intensely in his impulses and his unconscious or subconscious. Beside such types, Shaw's characters may well seem to be, as Lawrence himself described them, 'fleshless, bloodless and cold'. This is unfair to Shaw, and anyway, it might be argued that his plays are still read and performed because of his unfaltering proclamation that man is not just his loins or his aesthetic sensibility or his imagination, but also a citizen, as he was first and foremost for Plato.

Shaw and Ideas

The general accusation against Shaw is that his interest in, and zest for, the exposition of ideas makes his drama over-cerebral. Shaw himself said in the 1902 Preface to *Mrs Warren's Profession* (1894): 'The drama of pure feeling is no longer in the hands of the playwright; it has been conquered by the musician . . . and there is, flatly, no future now, for any drama except the drama of thought.' This does not mean, however, that Shaw's plays are only loosely dramatised debates, where the characters are merely mouthpieces for Shavian ideas. The characters are driven, emotionally and spiritually as well as intellectually, by their 'ideas', and these ideas are rarely simple or one-dimensional. They constitute any given character's general outlook on, or approach to, life; and hence are much more than philosophic abstractions. Shaw in *Man and Superman* explicitly rejects the attempt to drive a wedge between what he calls 'our moral sense' and our passions:

> *Tanner:* I declare that according to my experience moral passion is the only real passion.
> *Ann:* All passions ought to be moral, Jack.
> *Tanner:* Ought! Do you think that anything is strong enough to impose oughts on a passion except a stronger passion still?
> *Ann:* Our moral sense controls passion, Jack.
> *Tanner:* Our moral sense! And is that not a passion? Is the devil to have all the passions as well as all the good tunes? If it were not a passion — if it were not the mightiest of the passions, all the other passions would sweep it away like a leaf before a hurricane. It is the birth of that passion that turns a child into a man.

If Shaw himself, like Tanner, is a preacher, the preaching in his plays is offset both by its 'passion' and by the context of comedy which — often delightfully — modifies it.

Man and Superman

Man and Superman sets out very clearly the general Shavian philosophy of life while simultaneously conveying the typical zest of his comedy. Indeed, the play's sub-title is 'A Comedy and a Philosophy'. The main outline of the comic plot (for, as nearly always in Shaw, there are amusing, digressive side-thrusts) is straightforward. The death of Ann Whitefield's father has made her the ward of two men. One of these is Roebuck Ramsden, a hidebound Victorian who nevertheless prides himself on his advanced thinking. Ann's other guardian is the man she means to marry, John Tanner, a rich socialist whose more genuinely advanced views shock Ramsden to the core, and through whom Shaw is able to cock an irrepressible snook at all sorts of orthodox pieties. Ann is loved infatu-atedly by a vapid young poet, Octavius Robinson, who idealises her to the skies, and whom she seems to encourage to mask her designs on Tanner.

Tanner does not want to be Ann's guardian. Indeed, he wants to keep contact between them to a minimum, because he is, in general, alarmed by what he sees as the unconscious drive of women towards marriage and procreation, a blind vitalism which reduces the male to a mere instrument. He warns Octavius against Ann, on the grounds that a woman will subordinate everything of aspiration and self-fulfilment in a man to her own purposes:

> *Tanner:* Tavy: that's the devilish side of a woman's fasci-nation: she makes you will your own destruction.
> *Octavius:* But it's not destruction: it's fulfilment.
> *Tanner:* Yes, of her purpose; and that purpose is neither her happiness nor yours, but Nature's. Vitality in a woman is a blind fury of creation . . . Because they have a purpose which is not their own purpose, but that of the whole universe, a man is nothing to them but an instrument of that purpose . . . I think Ann loves you that way: she patted your cheek as if it were a nicely underdone chop.

The joke is that while Tanner is shown to be right about Ann's 'vitality' or 'blind fury', he is too slow to spot that he, not

Octavius, is her target, and, despite his flight to the Sierra Nevada mountains in Spain, he is tracked down and enmeshed in her web of marriage.

The theorist is thus shown ironically as helpless, despite his insight, before the realities of experience. The comic antecedents of the action can be located as far back as Benedick in Shakespeare's *Much Ado About Nothing*, the resolute bachelor who finds that he must, in the end, wear the marriage yoke, and submits with a good grace. And in so far as Tanner expresses many Shavian ideas, Shaw can be seen to be, in this play, partly mocking himself, showing in the dramatic action how life is always larger than theory or logic.

Shaw's Theory of the Life Force

Shaw rejected Darwin's emphasis on natural selection — that is, he accepted, as a good rationalist had to, the idea of evolution, but denied that it was a brute, mindless process in which things survive and evolve more or less by accident. In place of Darwinian evolution, Shaw drew up his theory of creative evolution, which he called the Life Force. This asserts the essentially optimistic and meliorist view that the universe is purposeful, that there is working in every man, especially the philosopher, what is called in *Man and Superman* 'life's incessant aspirations to higher organization, wider, deeper, intenser self-consciousness, and clearer self-understanding'. Man, responding to these aspirations, will himself eventually evolve into what Shaw, borrowing the term from Nietzsche, calls the Superman. (The only evidence for all this on which Shaw seemed to rely was his own intelligence and sense of progress.) Woman's role, of course, is to bear the Superman, and indeed, as she is much closer to the source of vitalism than man, to that extent she is superior to him. What seems to be an attack on woman turns out to be a celebration of her — as the play has it, 'I said, with the foolish philosopher, "I think, therefore I am." It was woman who taught me to say, "I am, therefore I think." '

The Dream Sequence in 'Man and Superman'

All this theorising is very characteristically embodied, in the actual play, in a long dream Tanner has in the Sierra Nevada mountains. In this, he becomes Don Juan in Hell, and Mendoza, the courteous bandit with whom he is spending the night, becomes the Devil. By a typical Shavian paradox, Don Juan turns out to be not the amorous libertine of legend, but the contemplative spokesman for the Life Force ideas against the cynical and pessimistic Devil (whom Shaw also portrays as a great aesthete, thereby getting in his dig at those who refuse to see that art's major function is social, utilitarian). Juan anticipates and predicts the coming of the Superman, and at the same time, his rejection of the comfortable happiness of Hell reveals Shaw's own puritan streak, which made him prefer struggle and reform to passive enjoyment of love and beauty.

The dream sequence is artistically integrated in the play, touching at many points on the central themes and ideas in the 'ordinary' Tanner–Ann story. Nor is it a mere exercise in Shaw's propaganda for the Life Force theory — a charge that could justly be brought against the inert philosophising of *Back to Methuselah* (1921), Shaw's 'Metabiological Pentateuch', which he inexplicably regarded as his greatest achievement. In *Man and Superman*, there is a genuinely dramatic debate, where the Devil is literally given his due, and some of the best lines, lines critical of the streak of arrogance in Shaw himself: 'Beware of the pursuit of the Superhuman: it leads to an indiscriminate contempt for the Human.' Nevertheless, the inclusion of the dream sequence shows Shaw's zest in the dramatic pursuit of ideas; and the debate in Hell is so wittily pursued that the total effect is far from heavily didactic — besides, the Shavian theory it contains is cunningly mocked by the emphasis on the unpredictability and intractability of life in the 'waking' plot, and by the reduction of Superman Tanner to a husband. Finally, it indicates a structural pattern to be found in some of Shaw's other plays, notably *Major Barbara*. The action begins in the drawing-room familiar from the well-made play and the orthodox West End comedy; then Shaw, having thus lulled his audience's expectations, unexpectedly and bracingly moves to a symbolic setting and modulates into what Louis Crompton calls 'a full-fledged Platonic dialogue'.[3] *Man and Superman*, whether the action is in London, Spain, or Hell, fairly fizzes with ideas, and perhaps it is this sense of the author's own buoyant energy which is ultimately the reason for Shaw's appeal.

'Major Barbara': The Challenge of Power

In both *Major Barbara* and *Heartbreak House* Shaw conducts a searching examination of the relationship between power and culture. These plays ask 'who — or what — really rules the world?', and explore the uncomfortable gap that has grown up in our epoch between, on the one hand, the intelligentsia or the cultured, the inheritors and bearers of civilized values, and, on the other, the men who actually control business and politics and war. *Major Barbara*, in particular, engages the problem of power in a very direct way. The combative strength of Shaw's intelligence gives an edge to his treatment that is not to be found in *Howards End* (1910), the fine novel by E. M. Forster (1879–1970), which deals with the same problems.

In Forster's novel, there is the world of culture and 'personal relations' embodied in the Schlegel sisters, and there is the business world, the world of 'telegrams and anger' represented in the Wilcoxes (and, in a different way, in Leonard Bast). The problem is the gulf between the 'civilisation cells', as it were, and the 'power cells'. Forster's position is that of the humanitarian liberal, and his 'solution' is contained in the famous phrase 'Only connect the passion and the prose'. The world of symphonies and High Culture and Personal Relations should be 'connected' — in some way that is not made very clear — to the outer world of telegrams and anger.

Shaw is more comprehensive, more blunt, and more uncomfortable. Andrew Undershaft, the millionaire munitions-maker in *Major Barbara*, is engaged in a trade of which official morality disapproves — but hypocritically, since society, and certainly the hereditary governing class, not only permits it, but actually relies on it to preserve the *status quo*. Piquancy is added to the situation because the hereditary ruling class in the play is represented by Undershaft's wife, Lady Britomart, and his priggish son Stephen. Shaw, through Undershaft, relentlessly exposes the empty cant that lies behind their claim to power and stresses the real power of capitalism. Stephen tells his father smugly that his money

> has kept you in circles where you are valued . . . and deferred to for it, instead of in the doubtless very old-fashioned and behind-the-times public school and university where I formed my habits of mind. It is natural for you to think that money governs England; but you must allow me to think that I know better.
>
> *Undershaft:* And what does govern England, pray?
> *Stephen:* Character, father, character.
> *Undershaft:* Whose character? Yours or mine?

What makes Undershaft disconcerting is that he is no conventional stage ogre, but, rather like the devil in *The Marriage of Heaven and Hell* (1791) by Blake (1759—1827), an embodiment of energy and of a power which is not so much immoral as amoral.

Adolphus Cusins, the Professor of Greek, is Shaw's representative of the liberal and humane values, so celebrated by Forster, and the significant conflict in the play is between him and the representative of the brute reality of power, Undershaft.

> *Undershaft:* When you vote, you only change the names of the cabinet. When you shoot, you pull down governments, inaugurate new epochs, abolish old orders and set up new. Is that historically true, Mr Learned Man, or is it not?
> *Cusins:* It is historically true. I loathe having to admit it . . . Still, it is true. But it ought not to be true.
> *Undershaft:* Ought! ought! ought! ought! Are you going to spend the rest of your life saying ought, like the rest of our moralists? Turn your oughts into shalls, man. Come and make explosives with me. Whatever can blow men up can blow society up. The history of the world is the history of those who had courage enough to embrace this truth . . . Plato says, my friend, that society cannot be served until either the Professors of Greek take to making gunpowder, or else the makers of gunpowder become Professors of Greek.

What Cusins is forced by Undershaft's forensic skill to see is that his cultured type cannot simply fastidiously ignore power, but must undertake its responsibility if not only *his* world, but possibly *the* world, is to survive. 'Culture' cannot simply coexist with power 'connected' to it in some woolly way: the professors of Greek cannot condemn the power-mongers of the world for their evil and folly if they are not prepared to take any action beyond abusing them during the intervals of a Beethoven concert. And so Cusins decides to go into Undershaft's arms factory, 'the factory of death'.

The Conclusion of 'Major Barbara': Confused or Provocative?

R. J. Kaufmann lists among the weaknesses of Shaw's plays 'his relentless chaperonage of our responses', and remarks that Shaw 'begs us to think, but refuses to let us do so'.[4] While this may be true of some of Shaw's work, it certainly does not apply to *Major Barbara* and particularly to its teasing conclusion. Cusins has joined Undershaft's arms factory to 'make war on war', to arm the common people. Clearly here Shaw is emphasising the need to move from a purely theoretical idealism to practical action. On the other hand, Undershaft has insisted throughout — and Cusins has reluctantly accepted — that the faith of an armourer is that arms must be supplied to all who will pay for them, and that profit remains the chief — the only — motive for the business. It is difficult, therefore, to see how Cusins will manage to realise his aims. He may become corrupted, or he may simply remain ineffectual. Shaw certainly seems to imply the latter not only about Cusins, but about his beloved Barbara, who has come to share his vision, because in the closing moments of the play their moral status is undercut by a deal of baby-talk. The dramatically impressive Undershaft gets the last commanding word: 'Six o'clock tomorrow morning, Euripides'

Many critics think that the ending of *Major Barbara* is a muddle, a confusion of unresolved paradoxes. It represents, rather, a significant step forward for drama with a political or social message. The true resolution of Shaw's play — as with many of Brecht's plays, which may explain the German dramatist's unstinted admiration for Shaw — belongs not inside the work of art, but outside it, in society. The audience is left to think out the problems Shaw has raised. It is up to us to try to imagine, and ultimately to bring to pass, a world in which power would be in moral hands and directed towards worthy ends. This implied appeal to the audience, the refusal to create a cathartic climax, 'opens up' Shaw's play and directly anticipates the dramatic ideas of Brecht.

Shaw's Optimism

Shaw's plays, then, are highly comic, highly intelligent, and highly purposive, engaged directly with major social issues — as Brecht said of him, 'his literary preoccupation does not separate him from life'.[5] But Shaw has one major fault. He has no sense of human evil. The system, or outmoded ideologies, or some kind of institution is always to blame for the imperfections of life, never the dark heart of man. So Shaw maintains his optimistic belief in the purposeful evolution of the human race to higher and better things, his optimistic belief in man's reason as a faculty which must lead to improvement for all, despite all the evidence to the contrary that his long life afforded him — the First World War, the great depression, the rise of Fascism and Nazism, Belsen and Auschwitz, Hiroshima and Nagasaki, the Gulag Archipelago. In one sense, there is a certain heroism in Shaw's consistent meliorism; but the effect in his plays is of a rather too contrived sunniness.

Brecht

Brecht's Marxism

Bertolt Brecht (1898–1956) became a Marxist in the early 1930s, as Hitler rose to power in Germany. His creed inevitably affected the thrust and direction of his art, and underpins, philosophically, the great mature dramas: *Mother Courage and her Children, The Life of Galileo, The Good Woman of Setzuan* and *The Caucasian Chalk Circle*, all written in exile in Denmark, Sweden and the United States, between 1933 and 1947, when he returned to East Germany to set up the theatrically immensely influential Berliner Ensemble. He said towards the end of his life in words which are themselves adapted from one of Marx's *dicta*: 'I wanted to take the principle that it was not just a matter of interpreting the world but of changing it, and apply that to the theatre.'[6] His plays thus embody a radical extension of Shaw's socialist ideas, but can in no sense be regarded as simplistic propaganda pieces. First, Brecht's theoretical optimism is heavily qualified by his sense — much more vivid than Shaw's ever was — of the cowardice, cruelty and destructiveness of human nature. The figure of Kattrin in *Mother Courage* illustrates the point: she is dumb because a soldier 'stuck something in her mouth when she was little'; she is further disfigured in the play by a brutal assault from a drunken soldier, which reduces to zero whatever little chance she had of finding a husband; and finally she is shot dead by soldiers besieging the town of Halle, as she tries to warn it of their surprise attack.

Secondly, Brecht avoids naïve and facile optimism by concentrating on *why* the world should be changed, rather than on *how* it will be after the change. He uses Marxism as a weapon for criticising society as it is, and is not interested in creating Utopian portraits of an ideal world, based purely on dogma. *The Good Woman of Setzuan* is a case in point. In this 'parable for the theatre', as Brecht called it, three comically ineffectual gods come down to earth to find one good human being. Only Shen Te, a prostitute, offers them shelter for the night. They reward her with money, but when she opens up a little tobacco-shop, a whole army of spongers, debtors and alleged relatives descend on her. To keep her head above water, she has to invent a ruthless *alter ego* for herself, a male 'cousin', Shui Ta. The play concentrates on this contradiction: that in a corrupt world, the good person can only survive by becoming ruthless and predatory. The gods, when they return to find out how Shen Te is getting on, fatuously ignore her very real dilemma, and float off to heaven smugly convinced that goodness can survive in this world, uncontaminated, despite Shen Te's desperate plea that she will continue to need her 'cousin' at least once a week. Brecht's epilogue illustrates his concern for what Chekhov called posing the problem correctly rather than offering easy solutions to it. The job of finding solutions is left up to us. The epilogue is entirely characteristic of Brecht's whole dramatic outlook, simultaneously committed and 'open'. It is spoken by one of the actors:

> You're thinking, aren't you, that this is no right
> Conclusion to the play you've seen tonight?
> After a tale, exotic, fabulous,
> A nasty ending was slipped up on us,
> We feel deflated too. We too are nettled
> To see the curtain down and nothing settled.
> How could a better ending be arranged?
> Could one change people? Can the world be changed?
> Would new gods do the trick? Will atheism?
> Moral rearmament? Materialism?
> It is for you to find a way, my friends,
> To help good men arrive at happy ends.
> *You* write the happy ending to the play!
> There must, there must, there's got to be a way!

Brecht's Rejection of Naturalist Drama

The form and content of Brecht's plays are not shaped solely by Marxist ideology, however — or, at least, that ideology is itself intimately connected with Brecht's critical understanding of naturalist drama. Brecht sees ideological implications in the form of that naturalist drama, which he reacted strongly against, and the reaction is the basis of his own influential theory of drama. This theory needs to be understood, not because Brecht's plays are in any sense aridly schematic, to be 'explained away' in terms of an *a priori* theory, but because Brecht's theatre is itself an essentially critical theatre, vitally concerned with the effects on the world of different ways of 'seeing'.

Illusion, Emotional Identification, and Inevitability

The kind of drama which Brecht rejects is that based on the major conventions of naturalist theatre, and he calls this drama variously 'Aristotelian', or 'dramatic', or 'Ibsenite'.

He objects first of all to its attempt to create a total illusion of reality, to its verisimilitude, that is, its presentation of events and people and settings on the stage in such a way as to persuade the audience to suspend its disbelief and to take the illusion for actuality. Brecht feels that this convention is harmful in two main ways. First, he sees it as being an attempt to deny any alternative way of looking at the events presented so that the audience is compelled to take the dramatic situation as a 'given', unalterable truth. Secondly, the power of theatrical illusion of this kind inevitably works, Brecht feels, to lead the audience to a strong emotional involvement with the situation presented, and even to emotional identification with certain of the characters in the situation.

Brecht thinks that this particular kind of emotional identification dulls the audience's capacity to reflect *critically* on what is being enacted before it. He also objects to the stress on inevitability in 'Ibsenite' drama. Such drama tends to present character, for example, as psychologically determined: a man — or a woman, like Hedda Gabler — behaves the way he or she does because of a psychological predisposition. By contrast, Brecht believes that behaviour is not to be explained so neatly by reference to an individual's psychological 'core', but is often the product of changing circumstances. Thus one person may be *both* the good Shen Te *and* the ruthless Shui Ta, depending on the surrounding social pressures.

Further, the tightly contrived plots of 'Aristotelian' drama, with their marked causal connections of scene to scene, their carefully worked climaxes, their steady linear development towards the cathartic end powerfully enforce the sense of inevitability.

All these common techniques — the stress on verisimilitude, the invitation to emotional identification, the 'psychological' emphasis in the creation of character, the development of linear plot — imply a relationship between play and audience which Brecht does not like. For him, such drama renders the audience helpless and passive, rather than critical.

Brecht's 'Epic' or 'Open' Theatre

Brecht sees social and political implications in the aesthetic

forms of 'Aristotelian' drama; his rejection of these implications has had inevitable consequences in his own work. He
creates in the place of 'Aristotelian' or 'dramatic' theatre,
his own 'epic' theatre. He himself gives a very clear indication
of the different emphasis:

> The spectator of the *dramatic* theatre says: 'Yes, I have
> felt the same. — I am just like this. — This is only natural.
> — It will always be like this. — This human being's suffering
> moves me, because there is no way out for him. — This is
> great art: it bears the mark of the inevitable. — I am weep-
> ing with those who weep on the stage, laughing with those
> who laugh! The spectator of the *epic* theatre says: 'I should
> never have thought so. — That is not the way to do it. —
> This is most surprising, hardly credible. — This will have to
> stop. — This human being's suffering moves me, because
> there would have been a way out for him. — This is great
> art: nothing here seems inevitable. — I am laughing about
> those who weep on the stage, weeping about those who
> laugh![7]

'Epic' theatre might be much better termed 'open' theatre,
because most of the techniques which Brecht invents for
plays like *Mother Courage and her Children* are aimed at
changing the relationship between the play and its audience
in the direction of 'openness'. His techniques combat the
seductive power of illusion and the idea of the inevitability
of the action; they invite the audience to consider critically
possible alternative courses of action to those adopted by the
dramatic characters; and they consciously and humanely
and democratically insist that a theatre is only a theatre, and
that plays are not life (though they may help us to understand
it).

'Verfremdungseffekt'

Brecht, and nearly all of his critics, try to sum up the general
effect of the techniques of 'epic' or 'open' theatre in the
German word *Verfremdung*, which means 'making strange' or
'distancing'. But it should be emphasised that the *Verfrem-*

dungseffekt (or 'alienation effect', as it is sometimes confusingly translated) in Brecht's plays is not a method of grotesque or surrealistic exaggeration, nor — as the words 'alienation' and 'distancing' might suggest — a method of humourless, forensic, clinical dissection of abstract problems. It is mainly an attempt to make us see ordinary life in a fresh way, to purge the film of familiarity from our eyes.

Remote or Historical Settings

It is remarkable that a political man like Brecht, who lived through the traumatic history of modern Germany (and modern Europe), should have given so many of his plays remote or exotic — certainly not contemporaneous — settings. *Mother Courage* and *Galileo* are set well in the historical past, while the parable plays *The Good Woman of Setzuan* and *The Caucasian Chalk Circle* are set in China and feudal Georgia respectively. Some of Brecht's earlier plays were set in an America he had never visited. This represents deliberate artistic intention. First, Brecht is clearly not interested in the distracting and cumbersome fidelity to surface appearance which is such a feature of the naturalist stage. To show what a Chinese town actually looks like is not necessarily to *say* anything profound about it. Brecht understood that 'displacing' our problems may enable us to see them more clearly, and to explore more fully general ideas — like the connections between war and capitalism.

'Narrative', Not Plot

Brecht rejects 'plot' in favour of 'narrative'. The audience is asked to see the action not as a series of enclosed acts building steadily to a climax, as an aesthetic shape in which, as Brecht put it, 'one scene makes another' and the audience has its 'eyes on the finish'.[8] So *Mother Courage* has twelve scenes which are fitted together, montage-fashion. Each scene can be taken by itself, and often long periods of time separate them. The effect is not unlike the panoramic sweep of Shakespeare's history plays. Brecht uses a 'narrative' or 'chronicle' structure, in which we see the action as a continuing process. That is, the outcome of the action is 'open', not predetermined: what happens depends on human decisions, not on some abstract concept like fate or inevitability. At the end of scene 6 of *Mother Courage*, Kattrin has been disfigured, slashed across the eye and forehead, and Mother Courage curses the war. But scene 7 is titled 'Mother Courage at the Height of her Business Career'; she says: 'I won't let you spoil my war for me. Destroys the weak, does it? Well, what does peace do for 'em, huh? War feeds its people better.' Then scene 8 shows her faced with financial ruin owing to the (temporary) peace. Again, her response is contradictory, unpredictable: 'I'm glad about the peace even though I'm ruined. At least I've got two of my children through the war.' This scene ends with her delight that war has broken out again — 'Well, it wasn't such a long peace, we can't grumble.' Attention is thus switched away from Courage's emotional or psychological 'core', on to the *incidents* which she responds to. What is seen is a character interacting with a set of historical circumstances, and there is a powerful and continuous suggestion that neither of these is 'fixed'.

'*Anti-Illusionist' Theatrical Devices*

Brecht insists that there should be no attempt to disguise the stage apparatus, so that, for example, the lights should be visible, and the machinery for working the revolving stage used to such good effect in *Mother Courage* is not concealed. The pink cloud on which the three gods ascend at the end of *The Good Woman of Setzuan* is deliberately ridiculous, and draws attention to its own theatrical artificiality. Other props may be more realistic — Mother Courage's wagon, for example — but they are always clearly props on a stage. There is no effort to create the total effect of a stage environment, whether interior or exterior, in the manner of the rooms — with all their painstakingly assembled furniture — created in the dramas of Ibsen or Sean O'Casey.

Brecht, then, deliberately creates an antidote to theatrical illusion: the audience is always aware that it is sitting in a theatre, and the barriers between the audience and what happens on the stage are lowered. Further methods of ensuring the audience's critical awareness are the employment of narrators (as in *The Caucasian Chalk Circle*) and the use of screens. (The fertilising effects of Brecht's practice in this regard is illustrated by the Malawian dramatist James Ng'ombe, in his *The Beauty of Dawn*, 1976. In this play there is a sequence in which the narrator speaks the thoughts of one of the characters. This is exactly the method that Brecht uses in *The Caucasian Chalk Circle*, which Ng'ombe knew well since he had acted in it in a travelling production in Malawi in 1969.) On to these screens can be projected filmstrips which connect what is happening on stage with other events and also summaries of the action of a scene before it begins. This last technique deliberately operates against the suspense and sense of progression involved in the conventional linear plot, enabling Brecht's audience to focus on 'the course' rather than on 'the finish'; and can be exploited for its own local ironic effects, which force us to think critically. For example, before scene 5 of *Mother Courage* Brecht's summary reads in part: '1631. Tilly's Victory at Magdeburg Costs Mother Courage Four Officers' Shirts'.

'Mother Courage and her Children': Theory in Practice

Courage as Heroine
Mother Courage and her Children is at once an illustration of and a brilliant vindication of Brecht's theories. Some distinguished critics feel, however, that the play succeeds *despite* the theory. Bamber Gascoigne remarks that it is 'by now a commonplace that [Brecht's] techniques failed, fortunately, to eliminate the audience's emotional involvement with the characters':[9] and Robert Brustein remarks:

> Mother Courage's bitter hostility to heroism has made her, paradoxically, a heroic figure to audiences — an image of the 'little people', beleaguered by forces beyond their control, yet resiliently continuing to make their way . . . There is no question that Mother Courage — like Falstaff, who was meant to be a Vice figure (Sloth and Vanity) but who somehow transcended his morality play role — got away from the author.[10]

Brecht is thus accused of permitting emotional identification
with Mother Courage, who becomes the heroine; and from
here it does not require a very big step to see the play as
'Aristotelian' tragedy, one which shows a protagonist asserting
human resilience in the teeth of a war which in some sense
suggests fate or inevitability.

Certainly a lot of Mother Courage's appeal lies in her
resolute expression of an anti-heroic vision:

> When a general or a king is stupid and leads his soldiers
> into a trap, they need the virtue of courage. When he's
> tight-fisted and hasn't enough soldiers, the few he does
> have need the heroism of Hercules — another virtue. And
> if he's a sloven and doesn't give a damn about anything,
> they have to be as wise as serpents or they're finished.
> Loyalty's another virtue and you need plenty of it if the
> king's always asking too much of you. All virtues which a
> well-regulated country with a good king or a good general
> wouldn't need. In a good country virtues wouldn't be
> necessary. Everybody could be quite ordinary, middling,
> and, for all I care, cowards.

The pungency of her expression here is matched by the
consistency of her deflating, iconoclastic attitude throughout
the play. She has no illusions about the motives behind war:

> To hear the big chaps talk, they wage war from fear of
> God and for all things bright and beautiful, but just look
> into it, and you'll see they're not so silly: they want a
> good profit out of it, or else the little chaps like you and
> me wouldn't back them up.

And her hard-headed realism covers also her own self-awareness: she extends her cynicism, that is to say, to herself, and
does not pretend to any higher motivation than self-interest.
Even her name originates in a cynical joke which she herself
tells with an engaging directness:

> They call me Mother Courage 'cause I was afraid I'd be
> ruined. So I drove through the bombardment of Riga like

a madwoman, with fifty loaves of bread in my cart. They were going mouldy. I couldn't please myself.

All of this makes her attractive and sympathetic to audiences in an age which tends to be deeply suspicious of heroic postures, and even of the notion of heroism itself. Perhaps all 'virtues' are suspect? 'In a good country virtues wouldn't be necessary', she says. The cook in scene 9 sings one of those songs which broaden out the action and seem to make a general comment upon it. It very much confirms Mother Courage's philosophy of life, its basic theme being that 'virtues bring no reward', illustrated by 'historical' reference to Solomon's wisdom, Julius Caesar's bravery, Socrates's honesty, and St Martin's unselfishness; their virtues brought each low:

> God's Ten Commandments we have kept
> And acted as we should.
> It has not done us any good.
> O you who sit beside a fire
> Please help us now: our need is dire!
> Strict godliness we've always shown
> But ere night came and day did go
> This fact was clear to everyone:
> It was our godliness that brought us low.
> Better for you if you have none!

And the pattern of the play as a whole might also be cited as evidence of the basic rightness of Mother Courage's scepticism about moral values. Each of her children has a virtue — Eilif is brave, Swiss Cheese is honest, Kattrin is kind; and the death of each one is directly connected with these virtues running up against the war. Each child is executed because no doubt Brecht is asking his audience to consider not so much the *random* destructiveness of war, but its *ordered* purposiveness, which does not permit of virtue. Surely, then, Brecht himself endorses Mother Courage's opportunistic cynicism and disillusion?

The Limitations of Opportunism
In the corrupt ethos of war, which is seen as an extension of

business by other means, no doubt Mother Courage's attitude has its appealing honesty and could be seen as grittily realistic. But Brecht's art is far more complex than is suggested by this sentimental stereotype of the cynic whose tough front just proves that her heart is in the right place. The whole point of 'epic' theatre is to allow for, invite, stimulate, *critical* attitudes to what is presented; and the breadth of perspective which Brecht brings to bear enables the audience to see the validity of the anti-heroic stance, but also its limitations in the particular context.

Mother Courage has not been a helpless victim sucked willy-nilly into the war — to the sergeant in scene 1 who asks her what she's doing in Dalarna, so far from her Bavarian home, she replies, 'I can't wait till the war is good enough to come to Bamberg.' She has chosen to follow the war and the Chaplain's description of her as a 'hyena of the battlefield' is true, though not the whole story. Brecht does not believe in inevitable tragedy, but in human freedom, and Mother Courage had the choice to participate or not to participate in the war. Worse, of course — it is the major ironic structural motif of the play — is that 'she takes her tradesmanship for motherhood, but it destroys her children one after the other'.[11] She 'looks after' her children, that is, by dragging them over the battlefields where her trade will make them all prosperous. But it can't be done. The sergeant says at the end of scene 1:

> When a war gives you all you earn
> One day it may claim something in return.

What it claims from Mother Courage is all her children, and she never sees the deep contradiction in which she is caught. Her responsibility is made obvious — the profiteering or buccaneering spirit which drives the war forward, and to which Mother Courage cynically assents as the only truth, the way of the world, is involved in each case: she haggles while her children die. She is trying to do her best, but she could not do worse for them. So there is a complexity in Brecht's presentation of her situation, which must cause the audience to think hard not just about the morality, but also the mere utility, of Mother Courage's 'gritty realism'.

The Great Capitulation
There is also a complexity in Brecht's presentation of Courage
herself, which is specially forceful in scene 4, titled 'Mother
Courage Sings the Song of the Great Capitulation'. From her
cynical or realistic acknowledgment of the corruptness of the
world and of power, she argues a young soldier out of making
a just protest against his superiors.

> *The Young Soldier:* It's no use your talking. I won't stand
> for injustice!
> *Mother Courage:* You're quite right. But how long? How
> long won't you stand for injustice? One hour? Or two?
> you haven't asked yourself that, have you? And yet it's
> the main thing. It's pure misery to sit in the stocks.
> Especially if you leave it to then to decide you do stand
> for injustice.

Her song gives general significance to the idea of capitulation
as a way of life:

> Long, long ago, a green beginner
> I thought myself a special case.
> (None of your ordinary run of the mill girls, with my
> looks and my talent and my love of the higher things!)
> I picked a hair out of my dinner
> And put the waiter in his place.
> (All or nothing. Anyway, never the second best. I am
> the master of my fate. I'll take orders from no one.)
> Then a little bird whispers!
> The bird says: 'Wait a year or so
> And marching with the band you'll go
> Keeping in step, now fast, now slow
> And piping out your little spiel.
> Then one day the battalions wheel
> And you go down upon your knees
> To God Almighty if you please!'
> My friend, before that year was over
> I'd learned to drink their cup of tea.

The fascinating issue raised here is the extent to which Mother

Courage has self-knowledge. Another way of asking the question is to ask, 'what is the tone of this song?' Is it a triumphant proclamation of cynicism? Is it a bitter, self-critical admission of the shame of her cowardly acquiescence in the denial of idealism? Is it a mixture of boasting and shame? Does Mother Courage fully understand how she got from being 'a special case' to learning 'to drink their cup of tea'? Brecht's 'open' dramatic technique leaves it to us.

A Play That Makes Us Think
The ambiguity, the ambivalence, the *complexity* of the individual's relations with society and with history, which are dramatised so sparely in the 'Song of the Great Capitulation', inform Brecht's vision throughout the play. *Mother Courage and her Children* is much more than an anti-war play, though it is that, too: it is a play that asks us to think about the ways in which we accept the world, and why we do, and why we might not so accept it. Brecht's achievement is not only to expose, through Mother Courage (and other characters), the hypocrisies and platitudes and brutalities of the conventional establishment. He also presents us, in Mother Courage, with the limitations of a cynicism that is really a form of acquiescence in, or accommodation with, those hypocrisies, that brutality. Thus, our admiration of Mother Courage's Falstaffian 'realism' and rejection of heroics is severely qualified by our sense that her self-defeating cynicism commits her to an endless participation in a game she partly sees through but accepts as inevitable though the game costs her her children, one by one.

Brecht's Dramatic Power

There is an enormous dramatic energy in Brecht's play. It should be obvious that, first, the criticism that Brecht wanted somehow or other to eliminate emotion totally from his work is nonsense. Brecht did want to involve the audience emotionally – but in a complex, dissonant way that would force it to examine its responses. So Mother Courage is *both* a heroine *and* a monster, and we can't have one without the other.

At a basic level, Brecht has a brilliantly theatrical imagination. Consider only the scene where Mother Courage is forced to deny her dead son, or the sheer excitement of the scene where dumb Kattrin frenziedly drums to waken the sleeping town, or the hauntingly sombre final vision of Courage pulling the battered wagon, all on her own, on a completely empty stage which revolves — an image of the terrible circularity to which she is committed.

Brecht is 'one of the greatest poets of German literature', 'the greatest modern German poet'.[12] The qualities of Brecht's dramatic language are palpable even in translation. It ranges from a vigorous earthiness — 'Away he's gone like a louse from a scratch', 'you're just a corpse on furlough', 'I could boil your leather belt and make their mouths water with it' — to a great lyric beauty, as in Mother Courage's 'Song of the Fishwife and the Soldier':

> But the soldier lad with his knife at his side
> And his gun in his hand was swept out by the tide:
> And he floats with the ice to the sea.
> And the new moon is shining on shingle roofs white
> But the lad and his laughter are lost in the night:
> And he floats with the ice to the sea.

Brecht is no arid theorist then, but a dramatic poet of the first rank.

9 Beckett and Pinter: Empty Spaces and Closed Rooms

Beckett: Life Is Illusion

Shaw and Brecht represent one kind of dramatic tradition in the twentieth century, concerned in their plays with the social and political realities of the world. But there is another powerful modern dramatic emphasis, which begins in the later plays of August Strindberg (1849–1912), continues through Pirandello, and reaches its fullest statement in the drama of Ionesco (b. 1912) and Beckett. This drama is sceptical about the validity, even the existence, of external reality: everything beyond the subjective consciousness of the individual is illusory, and even consciousness itself may be illusory. It may not be possible to know anything beyond that illusion. The famous lengthy speech of Lucky in Beckett's *Waiting for Godot* (1952) shows the would-be rational mind unable to give a coherent or rational explanation of the universe, and in breakdown because of this — Lucky begins seeking to establish the existence of God, but ends despairingly, reiterating the word that, as well as any other, describes Beckett's dramatic landscape, 'the skull the skull the skull'. When the curtain goes up at the beginning of *Endgame* (1957) we see a room with two high-up curtained windows, in which the furniture is draped with dustcovers. The curtains are drawn, the dustcovers removed. As Hugh Kenner says: 'This is so plainly a metaphor for waking up that we fancy the stage with its high peepholes, to be the inside of an immense skull.'[1] Beckett's characters are trapped inside their own skeletal subjectivity.

Breaking the Dramatic Illusion

In *Waiting for Godot* and *Endgame* Beckett frequently breaks the dramatic illusion. Though he insists on the traditional 'box' stage, with curtain and proscenium arch, he is not attempting to engage his audience in the traditional naturalist illusion. The characters constantly step out of the frame, reminding the audience that it is an audience in a theatre. Thus, Vladimir, in the first act of *Godot*, needs to urinate:

> *Vladimir:* I'll be back. [*He hastens towards the wings.*]
> *Estragon:* End of the corridor, on the left.
> *Vladimir:* Keep my seat. [*Exit.*]

Whereas Brecht similarly insists on keeping the audience alert to the theatrical illusion, he and Beckett have quite different aims. Brecht wishes the audience to approach the real world critically from a critical reaction to his play's ideas; Beckett 'breaks the boundaries' between stage and audience because of his feeling that what is called 'real life' is as much an illusion as anything on his stage.

Absurdism: Beckett and Ionesco

Beckett is commonly referred to as an 'absurd' dramatist. The term has been popularised by Martin Esslin, who wrote the first, full study of the drama of Ionesco, Beckett, Jean Genet (b. 1910), Arthur Adamov (1908–70) and others in the 'Theatre of the Absurd'.[2] Esslin's book is very useful, but in tracing the intellectual and philosophical backgrounds to the drama, he tends (despite himself) to blur the differences between the dramatists. Ionesco, for example, seems very different from Beckett. His plays, such as *The Bald Prima Donna* (1950), are farces, full of a buoyant and inventive zaniness which is at odds with the theoretical gloominess of his outlook. Beckett's work is that of a poet – his images reverberate in the mind: the two shoddy old men, the withered tree, the empty featureless landscape, the immobility as night falls – whereas Ionesco resembles a savagely funny cartoonist. Esslin's book tends to smooth such differences out, and also, in its listing of philosophic sources for absurdism, to give a misleadingly academic and intellectual portrait of the plays. Beckett himself remarked in 1961: 'If the subject of my novels could be expressed in philosophical terms, there would have been no reason for my writing them.'[3] This applies even more strongly to the plays.

'God is Dead'

Not a deliberate literary movement, nor an intellectual argument, lies behind Beckett's plays, but feelings fairly widely diffused in our times. Among these, the notion that 'God is dead' is especially significant. This feeling deprives man of the sense of a transcendental purpose in life, it inculcates a sense of the futility of life whose only object seems to be death, and it hurls man back on his own puny resources to attempt to give significance to the void left by the disappearance of God. The American dramatist Eugene O'Neill (1888–1953) locates the root of the sickness of our time in 'the death of the old god and the incapacity of science and materialism to give a new god to the still living religious instinct'. The implication of his last phrase is that while man has lost his old beliefs, he still hungers to believe, and so he searches in anguish to find, in O'Neill's words, 'a new meaning of life with which to allay man's fear of death'.[4]

'Unaccommodated Man': Waiting for Godot

Such general considerations do not 'explain' Beckett's *Waiting for Godot*, but at least they point us towards the kind of area with which the play deals. It is a play about the human condition, as Beckett sees it. This explains some of the dramatic methods he uses. The play's setting, for instance, is deliberately vague and unlocalised. Vladimir is a Russian name, Estragon is French, Pozzo Italian and Lucky English or American — again Beckett is avoiding the local in favour of the general. By making the two central characters *clochards* or tramps (there is no precise English translation of the French word), Beckett strips them of jobs, a social role, a family, all of the paraphernalia of existence. He forces them — and the spectator — away from the superficial 'meanings' of life, from the surfaces which so bedazzle and entrap Arthur Miller's Willy Loman, up against their essential solitude against the backdrop of the void. He even deprives them of memory. They cannot be sure of their identity, the identity of others, of place or of time. Thus the very notion of reality is called into question. In a sense, Beckett asks us to share Lear's intense moment of vision, where he looks at poor Tom and cries out: 'Thou art the thing itself. Unaccommodated man is no more but such a poor bare forked animal as thou art.'

'Nothing Happens, Twice'

As well as moving away from a realistically depicted social background, Beckett rejects the use of the sequential plot, the idea of 'telling a story' — a critic has remarked wittily (though not entirely accurately) that *Waiting for Godot* is a play in which 'nothing happens, twice'. It tells no story because there is no story to tell, but only a basic condition or situation to be represented, a bleak stasis where temporal notions like beginning, middle and end, inextricably linked with the concept of story, simply have no place. Similarly, though Beckett has a wonderful gift for creating vivid dialogue, he is not interested in Ibsenite subtleties of characterisation and motivation. It is necessary to see Vladimir and Estragon, like Pozzo and Lucky, as a couple: the emphasis is on the need for relationship, rather than on psychological individuation.

The Christian Interpretation

Beckett has constantly warned against over-interpretation of *Waiting for Godot* (the more desperately perhaps for the very reason that it is one of the most written-about plays of the century). He speaks of it as a play which is 'striving all the time to avoid definition'.[5] Clearly it is an overly allegoric approach which simply translates 'Godot' into 'God' — the play was first written in French, in which 'Godot' would have none of the resonances it has in English. Still, the play is laden with Christian imagery — Jean-Jacques Mayoux speaks of 'the terrifying ruins of religious feeling in Beckett'.[6] Certainly the 'ruins' are very visible. There is the discussion of the crucifixion of the two thieves alongside Christ; there is the tree which is associated directly through imagery with the tree of life, but at other times might variously suggest the Cross itself, or the tree from which Judas hung himself; there is — apart from other incidental symbolism — the whole situation of waiting. This matters far more than the question of the identity of Godot in the play, and has orthodox Christian overtones: behind it, and behind the state of mingled hope and fear in which Vladimir and Estragon wait, are the words of St Augustine: 'Do not despair: one of the thieves was saved. Do not presume: one of the thieves was damned.' Then there are Vladimir's words: 'What are we doing here, *that* is the question. And we are blessed in this, that we happen to know the answer. Yes, in this immense confusion one thing alone is clear. We are waiting for Godot to come.' From this kind of evidence it has been argued that '*Waiting for Godot* . . . is a modern morality play, on permanent Christian themes'.[7]

Pozzo and Lucky

A very different reading, however, may be advanced without recourse to evidence other than that supplied by the text itself, namely, that what the play shows is man's helplessness in his delusion that some power outside himself exists that will give meaning to his life, the hopeful, hopeless fiction that ties him to an inauthentic existence.

Each time Pozzo enters, he is temporarily mistaken for Godot himself. This is extremely suggestive. Before the first entry, Vladimir and Estragon discuss their relationship to Godot:

Estragon [*his mouth full, vacuously*] We're not tied?
Vladimir: I don't hear a word you're saying.
Estragon [*chews, swallows*] I'm asking you if we're tied.
Vladimir: Tied?
Estragon: Ti-ed.
Vladimir: How do you mean tied?
Estragon: Down.
Vladimir: But to whom? By whom?
Estragon: To your man.

Vladimir: To Godot? Tied to Godot? What an idea! No
question of it. [*Pause.*] For the moment.

A moment later, with the terrible cry, the burdened Lucky
staggers on stage roped to the cruel and imperious Pozzo, and
the first exchange with the newcomers concerns the question
as to whether Pozzo is Godot. The implications here are clear.
It is not that Godot *is* Pozzo — to say that would be to project
the same sort of unimaginative definiteness which results
from allegoric readings — but rather that Godot might, if he
exists, be very like Pozzo. Vladimir and Estragon are tied to
him metaphorically in a slavish and abject way as Lucky is
tied literally to Pozzo. We must remember that Pozzo has not
enslaved Lucky or at least that that is not the whole truth,
for Lucky may have chosen his enslavement: to the question
why Lucky does not make himself comfortable Pozzo replies:
'Has he not the right to? Certainly he has. It follows that he
doesn't want to. There's reasoning for you. And why doesn't
he want to? [*Pause.*] Gentlemen, the reason is this . . . He
wants to impress me, so that I'll keep him.' The Pozzo–Lucky
relationship may then be seen as a parallel rather than a
contrast to the old men's relationship with the arbitrary (and
illusory?) Godot, and both sets of relationships as indicating
Beckett's idea of the Christian relationship of man with his
arbitrary (and illusory?) God. (It should of course be stressed
that the play presents such ideas in symbolic images or
patterns rather than in any obvious dogmatic argument.) The
role of Lucky then makes for an especially bitter parodic
demonstration. In his total submission to his master, in his
acceptance of humiliation without a murmur, in his bearing
the literal burdens uncomplainingly — 'because he wants to'
— Lucky may be seen in his relationship to Pozzo as an
embodied *reductio ad absurdum* of Christ's words (Matthew,
11:28–9): 'Come unto me, all ye that labour and are heavy
laden, and I will give you rest. Take my yoke upon you, and
learn of me . . . for my yoke is easy and my burden is light.'
Beckett, then, deliberately confuses Pozzo and Godot, suggests
a parallel in the relationship between Pozzo and Lucky on
the one hand and the old men's relationship with Godot on
the other, shows graphically one of the relationships (and

therefore by implication *both*) as barbaric and degrading, and implies by symbolic suggestion that the same is true of the Christian's relationship with 'God', even inverting and mocking specifically biblical imagery.

'We Always Find Something to Give Us the Impression We Exist'

Beckett implies that there is no Godot to give purpose and point to the 'immense confusion', or that if there is, he is as malevolent and cruel and as ultimately futile as Pozzo and has the same amount of transcendental value as Pozzo which is nil. Waiting for Godot, therefore, is an empty and sterile 'activity', the main purpose of which seems to be to disguise from the tramps the void, the nothingness in which their lives are lived out, which is the only true reality.

It is in the various and unceasing strategies that the two old men adopt to hide from themselves the awareness of the encompassing void that that void, paradoxically, makes itself most clearly evident. In a truly memorable sequence in Act 2, for example, they attempt to kill the time by (a) playing at being Pozzo and Lucky; (b) playing at abusing each other; (c) playing at making it up again; (d) playing at doing physical exercises ('I'm tired breathing'); (e) playing at being the tree. Estragon sums up the point of all this as bluntly as possible: 'We always find something, eh Didi, to give us the impression we exist?' To this Vladimir retorts testily, 'Yes yes, we're magicians.' If their games give them the illusion of purpose and activity, their very words serve to blot out the awful silence which is the concomitant of the awful emptiness:

> *Estragon:* In the meantime let us try and converse calmly, since we are incapable of keeping silent.
> *Vladimir:* You're right, we're inexhaustible.
> *Estragon:* It's so we won't think.
> *Vladimir:* We have that excuse.
> *Estragon:* It's so we won't hear.

Speech and actions then become ritualised as the two men try to impose a shape on the nothingness, or to block it out of the consciousness. Waiting for Godot is the main, the most reliable habit the two have, 'most reliable' in the sense that it gives them the illusion they exist better than anything else does. A lot of these ideas and themes are pulled together in Vladimir's revealing soliloquy near the end of the play. Estragon has been asleep, watched by Vladimir, and as Vladimir speaks he starts to doze off again:

> *Vladimir:* Was I sleeping, while the others suffered? Am I sleeping now? Tomorrow, when I wake, or think I do, what shall I say of today? That with Estragon my friend, at this place, until the fall of night, I waited for Godot? That Pozzo passed, with his carrier, and that he spoke to us? Probably. But in all that what truth will there be? [*Estragon, having struggled with his boots in vain, is dozing off again. Vladimir stares at him.*] He'll know nothing. He'll tell me about the blows he received and I'll give him a carrot. [*Pause.*] Astride of a grave and a difficult birth. Down in the hole, lingeringly, the grave-digger puts on the forceps. We have time to grow old. The air is full of our cries. [*He listens.*] But habit is a great deadener. [*He looks again at Estragon.*] At me too someone is looking, of me too someone is saying, he is sleeping, he knows nothing, let him sleep on. [*Pause.*] I can't go on! [*Pause.*] What have I said?

Here Vladimir is staring at the solipsist nightmare, the question of how one can be sure that one even exists. The only answer in the context of the play — and of course it is not for Vladimir a satisfactory one — is that one's existence is validated by the perception of others. Just as Estragon asleep here 'exists' only because Didi sees him, so Vladimir and Estragon will only 'exist' if Godot or his messengers 'see' them. This is the crucial explanation of their need to believe in him, of the frantically earnest appeals to the boy messenger — 'Do you not recognize me? . . . You're sure you saw me, you won't come and tell me tomorrow that you never saw me!' It also explains the need that they have for each other and the need that Pozzo and Lucky have for each other. To approach the kind of insight Vladimir has in the speech quoted is frightening: it brings the void not only near but actually inside, for one can't be sure that one exists at all. Hence Vladimir's agonised 'I can't go on! What have I said?' But he also mentions a kind of makeshift antidote to the terrifying consciousness of non-being: 'habit is a great deadener'. This refers us back to all the little games and rituals and conversational 'canters' with which they both try to fill the void.

Habit and the Void

These ideas, central to understanding *Waiting for Godot*, were put earlier by Beckett in his 1931 essay on Proust:[8]

> ... We are not merely more weary because of yesterday, we are other, no longer what we were before the calamity of yesterday ... The aspirations of yesterday were valid for yesterday's ego, not for today's ... [This is part of] the poisonous ingenuity of Time in the science of affliction...
> Memory and Habit are attributes of the Time cancer ... The laws of memory are subject to the more general laws of habit. Habit is a compromise effected between the individual and his environment, or between the individual and his own organic eccentricities, the guarantee of a dull inviolability, the lightning conductor of his existence ... Breathing is habit. Life is habit ... The periods of transition that separate consecutive adaptations ... represent the perilous zones in the life of the individual, dangerous, precarious, painful, mysterious and fertile, when for a moment the boredom of living is replaced by the suffering of being ...

This passage helps us to understand Vladimir's flattening or foreshortening reference to time: 'Astride of a grave and a difficult birth. Down in the hole, lingeringly, the grave-digger puts on the forceps.' Time conceived of in the traditional linear way in terms of past, present and future Beckett sees as being another stratagem devised by man to give a sense of continuity, a sense of purpose, and to help validate his sense of his personal existence. Conventional Time is almost embodied in the play in Pozzo, whose Act 1 speeches are filled with references to clock time and who constantly consults his half-hunter watch (until he loses it). This lends all the more force to his great passionate (and lyrical) outburst near the end of the play where he has been apparently brought to the realisation that Time itself is just an illusion:

> *Pozzo:* Have you not done tormenting me with your accursed time! It's abominable! When! When! One day, is that not enough for you, one day like any other day, one day he went dumb, one day I went blind, one day we'll go deaf, one day we were born, one day we shall die, the same day, the same second, is that not enough for you? [*Calmer.*] They give birth astride of a grave, the light gleams an instant, then it's night once more. [*He jerks the rope.*] On!

In the excerpt from the essay on Proust, Beckett deals mainly with the central idea and structural principle of *Waiting for Godot*, namely, the relationship between 'habit' and the void. Habit is seen as a sort of shield which protects one from reality (conceived as nothingness); but there are moments in the life of every individual when the protective habits break down and he becomes aware of true reality. In 1931 Beckett clearly implied that such moments should be cherished, sought for, as moments when one may be able to begin living authentically or genuinely ('being') instead of merely existing in the 'boredom of living'. They are 'painful', partly because giving up any habit is painful, but also 'fertile'. But by the time of *Waiting for Godot* Beckett's vision has darkened and all didacticism has been filtered out. The play, unlike the essay, does not give the impression that facing up to nothingness would be 'fertile' in any way at all. The intuition of the void produces only Estragon's anguished 'I'm in hell, I'm accursed' and Vladimir's appalled 'I can't go on. What have I said?' Facing up to nothingness, the play implies in the tone of its every line, does not bring to birth the existential hero but would produce a kind of total obliteration of the personality. The habit of waiting for Godot, the hope that he may come, may well be delusion and the old men may even be dimly conscious that this is the case. But there is no attractive alternative. Whether one is waiting for Godot or waiting for the void, there is always the waiting. What Vladimir and

Estragon do and say is their only defence against being plunged into silence and timelessness. So we come round with horror to the knowledge that the waiting for Godot is *necessary* even at the simultaneous moment when we perceive that it is a delusion. We even have to recognise that there is something admirable in the games and rituals of the old men, something almost heroic in their stubborn clinging on to their sense of identity at the edge of the extremity. Here we are at the heart of Beckett's bleak vision of life, in the teeth of his iron trap. Man cannot believe in that somebody or something outside himself which will validate and give significance to his futile life, but neither can he afford not to go on pretending that that somebody or something, that Godot, exists and will come. The price of rejection of the pretence is too high, being the admission of and immersion in nothingness and an absolute futility. Thus, he is condemned to play out the farce.

Beckett's Theatricality
The play requires explanation, especially for those who see in it only haphazard and random features. But the trouble with explanation is that it makes the play seem too philosophical, and too glumly negative, because it tends to ignore its startling theatricality, its dramatic method, which constantly pulls against the serious abstractions of critical discourse.

Circularity
In one sense, as in any successful work of art, form and content are closely linked in Beckett's play. Thus the empty, repetitive, circular nature of life, expressed thematically, is reflected formally in the close similarity of event and sequence in the two acts. Within this large circle there are many smaller circles — Estragon's fussing with his boots, Vladimir's little game with his hat, and his endless circular song at the beginning of the second Act, not to mention all the repeated phrases, which re-echo through the play like musical motifs: 'Nothing to be done', 'Will night never come', and, of course, 'We're waiting for Godot'.

'Passing the Time in the Dark'
There is also a more general link between what the play says

and how it says it. Kenneth Tynan, reviewing the first English
production in 1955, pointed out how much the play had
dispensed with in terms of traditional dramatic devices, like
plot, climaxes, and so on — it 'frankly jettisons everything by
which we recognize theatre'. But he then had to understand
why it seemed dramatic, and argued that it appealed to a
really fundamental definition of drama. 'A play, it asserts and
proves, is basically a means of spending two hours in the dark
without being bored.' This is not trivial, as Beckett presents
it: 'Passing the time in the dark, he suggests, is not only what
drama is about but also what life is about.'⁹

Tynan's comment is borne out by those frequent moments
in the play when the barrier between stage and audience is
deliberately broken down by Beckett. What Tynan has seen
also is a certain playfulness in Beckett's own attitude, which
needs to be stressed. His insights may be anguished, but he
presents them to us in a comic way. A grim vision of life is
presented humorously, even if the humour is of that especially
Irish kind known as 'gallows humour'. There is, in this sense,
an invigorating *tension* between vision and a form which owes
much to vaudeville and the music-hall comedians; Beckett's
play carries its own devices for puncturing any kinds of
philosophic pomposity or portentousness.

Dialogue

Beckett's mastery of dialogue, its pacing and rhythm, enables
him to exploit wonderfully effects of bathos and anti-climax.
This exploitation can be seen in individual speeches, such as
that of Pozzo in Act 1, on the sky:

> An hour ago [*he looks at his watch, prosaic*] roughly
> [*lyrical*] after having poured forth ever since [*he hesitates,
> prosaic*] say ten o'clock in the morning [*lyrical*] tirelessly
> torrents of red and white light it begins to lose its efful-
> gence, to grow pale [*gesture of the two hands lapsing by
> stages*] pale, ever a little paler, a little paler until [*dramatic
> pause, ample gesture of the two hands flung wide apart*]
> pppfff! finished! it comes to rest. But — [*hand raised in
> admonition*] — but behind this veil of gentleness and peace
> night is charging [*vibrantly*] and will burst upon us [*snaps

his fingers] pop! like that! [*his inspiration leaves him*] just when we least expect it. [*Silence. Gloomily.*] That's how it is on this bitch of an earth.

More frequently, comic anti-climax or comic juxtaposition is achieved in the use of two speakers who are at cross-purposes. The play's opening exemplifies perfectly this recurrent pattern:

> [*Estragon, sitting on a low mound, is trying to take off his boot. He pulls at it with both hands, panting. He gives up exhausted, rests, tries again. As before.*]
> [*Enter Vladimir.*]
> *Estragon* [*giving up again*] : Nothing to be done.
> *Vladimir:* I'm beginning to come round to that opinion. All my life I've tried to put it from me, saying, Vladimir, be reasonable, you haven't yet tried everything. And I resumed the struggle.

Estragon's reference to his boot problem is taken by Vladimir as a philosophic generalisation, and spurs him to his ludicrously misapplied rhetoric ('resumed the struggle'). The earthiness of the language in much of the play also serves to puncture the windy balloons of philosophising.

The Music Hall, the Circus and the Movies
The dialogue is, further, heavily influenced by the cross-talk and patter derived from the vaudeville and music-hall tradition. This passage is typical of many:

> *Estragon* [*anxious*] : And we?
> *Vladimir:* I beg your pardon?
> *Estragon:* I said, And we?
> *Vladimir:* I don't understand.
> *Estragon:* Where do we come in?
> *Vladimir:* Come in?
> *Estragon:* Take your time.
> *Vladimir:* Come in? On our hands and knees.

If a critical explication of *Waiting for Godot* makes it sound too solemn, the quotation of passages like these should redress the balance. Beckett is very fond of the old silent movies of Charlie Chaplin (1889–1977) and Buster Keaton (1895–1966), of vaudeville and of the circus, and has expressed his vision accordingly in his play. Thus there are the repetitious pantomimes with the boots and the hats, even that favourite clown's stand-by, the dropping of the trousers; the constant, semi-farcical, falling down of the characters; Pozzo, with his whip, suggests the circus ringmaster; the relationship between Vladimir and Estragon is not unlike that between Laurel and Hardy (even the way they dress is similar); Vladimir and Lucky in their different ways have funny walks; and there are many more instances of Beckett's use of popular, even 'low', comic art-forms. What is crucial is that this way of seeing is not tacked on, as it were, to a sombre subject-matter, but is totally integrated with it. The characters themselves see life as a kind of grotesque pantomime, and invite the audience to do likewise:

Vladimir: Charming evening we're having.
Estragon: Unforgettable.
Vladimir: And it's not over.
Estragon: Apparently not.
Vladimir: It's only beginning.
Estragon: It's awful.
Vladimir: Worse than the pantomime.
Estragon: The circus.
Vladimir: The music-hall.
Estragon: The circus . . .
Vladimir: I'll be back. [*He hastens towards the wings.*]
Estragon: End of the corridor, on the left.
Vladimir: Keep my seat.

The low-comedy, unashamedly theatrical convention of the music hall and the silent movie impart an enormous energy and sense of fun to Beckett's play.

Drama is eclectic, and absorbs 'vulgar' or popular art conventions easily and unashamedly. The production of *Oh! What a Lovely War* (1963) by Joan Littlewood (1914–82) was a great theatrical success in Britain through its presentation of the horrors of the First World War in terms of the music hall, Hollywood musical and vaudeville farce; it was also heavily indebted to Brechtian techniques of distancing, such as the use of a back-drop screen which indicated the appalling casualty figures from battles such as those of the Somme and Ypres, while in the foreground, jaunty, jingoistic songs were sung. The Australian dramatist Dorothy Hewett (b. 1923) similarly uses a dramatic style, in works such as *The Chapel Perilous* (1971), which mingles pop songs, Hollywood movies and vaudeville with a higher kind of lyricism. Australia's Michael Boddy (b. 1934) and Bob Ellis (b. 1942) have further shown the links between drama and popular art-forms in their highly successful, vaudeville-style *The Legend of King O'Malley* (1970). Beckett's own awareness of the essentially theatrical nature of drama is clearly demonstrated in *Waiting for Godot* – just as Shakespeare's similar awareness is shown by the inclusion of the lamentable broad-farce tragedy of Pyramus and Thisbe in the lyric structure of *A Midsummer Night's Dream*. The gulf between 'high' and 'low' art is far from unbridgeable.

Beckett's Humanism

The play is a unique achievement in its blend of a pessimistic philosophy with comic vitalism. That is perhaps one reason why it is not depressing. There is the curious liberation which we feel at recognising the basic humanity of the two old men, a humanity which bubbles up irrepressibly even in their situation, astride of the grave and at the edge of darkness. There they are, and yet they are still human, they are still capable of their moments of compassion and charity and humour. They do not give up. Their bodies may be broken and battered, subject to the degrading humiliations of fleshly decay – the stinking feet, the stinking breath, the kidney problem – but their minds spin on, unstoppably. The heroism of Vladimir and Estragon is not the romantic heroism of *Hamlet* or *Othello*, but it is heroism of a kind. In the end, the Beckett of *Waiting for Godot* is a most humane writer whose quiet assertion of man's worth is the more impressive given the skeletal regions he explores.

Pinter: 'Stalking Round a Jungle'

Documentary Realist?

Pinter is one of the most powerful and original dramatic
talents to emerge in Britain in the last twenty years. His
originality was initially disguised, and his work misunderstood, because his first plays coincided with the full flood
of a neo-realistic movement on the stage, in the cinema,
and in the novel in Britain, sometimes referred to as 'kitchen
sink' art. The label is sloppily journalistic, but it seemed to
define some sort of common denominator in plays such as
Look Back in Anger (1956) by John Osborne (b. 1929) and
Chips with Everything (1962) by Arnold Wesker (b. 1932),
and in novels such as *Saturday Night and Sunday Morning*
(1958) by Alan Sillitoe (b. 1928) and *This Sporting Life*
(1960) by David Storey (b. 1933) – both of which were
made into successful films. Pinter was seen as one of this
'school' at first. There was the seedy realism of his settings
– the mouldy cornflakes and soggy fried bread of Meg's
slatternly kitchen in *The Birthday Party* (1958), the bucket
to catch the leak from the roof, the sacks over the window,
and all the junk and rubbish piled up in Aston's room in *The
Caretaker* (1960). There were the specific and detailed –
even affectionate – references to London and its environs:
Mick's fantasia on a bus-route theme in *The Caretaker*,
Davies's reverence for the convenience at Shepherd's Bush
and his yearning for Sidcup, in the same play, Stanley Webber's
famous concert in Lower Edmonton in *The Birthday Party*.
And above all, there was the wonderful accuracy of Pinter's
dialogue, his gift for creating with seeming tape-recorder's
fidelity the speech-patterns of working-class or lower-middle-
class English people, whether in the banal, repetitious exchanges of Meg and Petey in *The Birthday Party*, or (in the
same play) in the vigorous patterned earthiness of Goldberg:

Some people don't like the idea of getting up in the
morning. I've heard them. Getting up in the morning,
they say, what is it? Your skin's crabby, you need a shave,
your eyes are full of muck, your mouth is like a boghouse,

the palms of your hands are full of sweat, your nose is clogged up, your feet stink, what are you but a corpse waiting to be washed?

Though Pinter has a sharp eye — and ear — for the realistic detail his drama is not in the least documentary. When asked what his plays were about, he replied succinctly and tellingly 'The weasel under the cocktail cabinet.'[10] It is appropriate that he should have chosen such a highly charged metaphor, because his plays themselves are intensely imagined poetic visions, embodied in an economical, lean, dramatic style, of the guilt, aggression, insecurity and sexual fantasies which lie behind the surfaces of our lives. The 'kitchen sink' label seems even more inappropriate to his later plays like *Old Times* (1971), *No Man's Land* (1975) and *Betrayal* (1978) which deal with the affluent middle classes; though the originality of his talent is to be seen most clearly in his earlier plays.

Absurdist?

A more complicated source of misunderstanding lay in Pinter being seen as of the theatre of the absurd. There is, it must be admitted, more of a case for Pinter the absurdist than for Pinter the kitchen sink realist. One of his great dramatic characters, Davies the tramp in *The Caretaker*, is superficially at any rate a blood relative of Beckett's Vladimir and Estragon. Further, much of the action in the plays is at first sight mysterious and apparently arbitrary — the sudden irruption into the shabby domesticity of a seaside boarding-house of two sinister emissaries of some powerful but vague organisation (*The Birthday Party*); the enigmatic behaviour and words of Mick in *The Caretaker*; the remarkable promptness with which a mother with three sons accedes to her brother-in-law's request that she works for him as a prostitute, while her academic husband stands by in apparent consent (*The Homecoming*, 1965). In Pinter as in Beckett there is a tendency to deal with extreme situations, with men at the end of their tether (especially true of *The Birthday Party* and *The Caretaker*), which is characteristic of absurd drama. As Pinter has said: 'I'm dealing with these characters at the extreme edge of their living, where they are living pretty much alone, at their hearth, their home hearth.'[11]

The Room and the World

At least Pinter's characters have got a room, a home of some kind, a city to live in. The topography of his world is more familiar than Beckett's, less frighteningly abstract and skeletal. One of the lines in *Waiting for Godot* which defines Beckett's universe is Estragon's sombre remark, 'there's no lack of void'. That is, Beckett's characters are menaced by the metaphysical nothingness all around them and the struggle is not so much to exist as to prove that they exist. The feeling of Pinter's characters is quite different. It is not that there is nothing outside the room which is his favourite dramatic image; it is precisely that there is something or somebody outside, and this is a source of threat which may materialise at any moment. Beckett's 'void' is thus filled in Pinter with menacing entities. As Pinter says of his characters:

> Obviously, they are scared of what is outside the room. Outside the room is a world bearing upon them, which is frightening . . . we are all in this, all in a room, and outside is a world, which is most inexplicable and frightening, curious and alarming.[12]

Pinter has even posited historical realities as lying behind his work: defending *The Birthday Party* against charges that it was simply a surrealistic, absurdist fantasy he stated:

> Again this man is hidden away in a seaside boarding house . . . then two people arrive out of nowhere, and I don't consider this an unnatural happening. I don't think it is all that surrealistic and curious because surely this thing, of people arriving at the door, has been happening in Europe in the last twenty years. Not only the last twenty years, the last two to three hundred.[13]

Menace

This does not mean that *The Birthday Party* is an allegory about Nazism — we do not have to see Gestapo officers in Goldberg and McCann. These two do not 'stand for' any one thing; rather, they suggest a number of possibilities. They are figures of menace, but it is precisely the fact that we do not ever know whom they represent, and what crime they accuse Stanley of, that helps to generalise and universalise the fears and tensions the play stirs in its audiences. As J. R. Taylor says: 'The menace is effective almost in inverse proportion to its degree of particularization . . . the more particularized the threat is, the less it is likely to apply to our own case and the less we are able to read our own semi-conscious fears into it.'[14] Yet there is nothing vaguely suggestive or shadowily portentous about Pinter's portrayal of a universal situation, or nightmare, in the play, the fear of arrest and arbitrary punishment on a charge never specified, the sense of being at the mercy of some remote and impersonal system: the settings, the characters, the action are sharply observed, concrete, alarmingly down to earth.

Pinter and Kafka

Although Pinter's voice and idiom is very much his own, the influence on him of Franz Kafka (1883—1924), whose novels he read as a young man, has often been remarked. There are similarities between Kafka's *The Trial* (1925) and *The Birthday Party*. We do not know why Joseph K. is arrested, any more than we know what Stanley Webber has done; both Joseph K. and Stanley suffer from the tension between the desire to proclaim their innocence and their obscure feeling that, somehow, they are guilty of something, somewhere; neither Joseph K. nor Stanley ever find out anything really definite about the organisations which hunt them down and destroy them; and, perhaps most alarmingly, the emissaries of the organisations in *The Trial* and *The Birthday Party* themselves do not seem to know much about each other (McCann does not even know if Goldberg's first name is Nat or Simey), or much about the powers they serve (if those powers exist).

The Problem of Verification

People who are irritated by Kafka will also be irritated by
Pinter. The charge has been brought against Pinter that he
indulges in deliberate mystification, that the famous suspense,
shock effects and feeling of menace are achieved simply by a
kind of cheap trick, simply by keeping the audience in the
dark. Our natural desire for verification — what *is* Stanley's
crime? who employs Goldberg and McCann? — is constantly
thwarted by Pinter. We ask these questions the more urgently
because of the extreme naturalism with which a nightmare
situation is presented. This effect — Pinter's authentic tone —
is both disturbing and grotesquely comic. By contrast, in the
expressionist dramas of the Swedish dramatist Strindberg
(1849–1912), such as *The Dream Play* (1902) and *The Ghost
Sonata* (1907), very strange events take place and very strange
characters manifest themselves — castles turn into giant
chrysanthemums, Buddha's daughter becomes a housewife,
a mummy woman who can only croak like a parrot is kept
behind a screen in the front parlour, and so on. But, though
powerful in its own way, this expressionist dramatic world
is enclosed, self-consciously always dream-like, a fantasia of
the imagination, where we *expect* the illogical and the un-
expected to happen.

Pinter never allows us to feel that the action presented on
his stage is a dream: the authenticity of setting and dialogue
forbids us to do so. Goldberg and McCann thus are frightening
precisely to the extent that we see them as a loquacious,
slightly sentimental Jew and a morose, homesick, drinking
Irishman — as real, in short, in a real boarding house in a real
seaside town in a real England. Once again, Pinter has bene-
fited from his reading of Kafka, in whose works strange —
even monstrous — events are recorded with a flat, dead-pan
fidelity and naturalism, where any sense of shock is carefully
filtered out of the style. Consider, for illustration, the opening
of Kafka's great short story, *Metamorphosis* (1915):

As Gregor Samsa awoke one morning from uneasy dreams
he found himself transformed in his bed into a gigantic
insect. He was lying on his hard, as it were armour-plated,

back and when he lifted his head a little he could see his
dome-like brown belly divided into stiff arched segments
on top of which the bed-quilt could hardly keep in position
and was about to slide off completely. His numerous legs,
which were pitifully thin compared to the rest of his bulk,
waved helplessly before his eyes.[15]

What is characteristic here is the deflection of attention away
from the truly bizarre to the homely detail about the bed-
quilt being about to slip off.

The Ordinary Is Mysterious

People in Pinter's work do not turn into bugs, but there is a
general stylistic analogy. Pinter achieves a similar fusion of
the perfectly ordinary with the perfectly mysterious because
he believes the perfectly ordinary *is* perfectly mysterious. He
has spoken better than most critics about his own work, and
his self-defence against the charge of deliberate and arbitrary
mystification is both philosophical and literary:

. . . the explicit form which is so often taken in twentieth
century drama is . . . cheating. The playwright assumes
that we have a great deal of information about all his
characters, who explain themselves to the audience. In
fact, what they are doing most of the time is conforming
to the author's own ideology. They don't create themselves
as they go along, they are being fixed on the stage for one
purpose, to speak for the author who has a point of view
to put over. When the curtain goes up on one of my plays,
you are faced with a situation, a particular situation two
people sitting in a room which hasn't happened before,
and is just happening at this moment, and we know no
more about them than I know about you, sitting at this
table. The world is full of surprises. A door can open at
any moment and someone will come in. We'd love to know
who it is, we'd love to know exactly what he has on his
mind and why he comes in, but how often do we know
what someone has on his mind or who this somebody is,
and what goes to make him and make him what he is, and
what his relationship is to others?[16]

In dramatists such as Ibsen and Arthur Miller, characters display an enormous self-awareness and ability to analyse their motivation — even if their self-analysis is wrong, as it frequently is, the depth and unrelentingness of the analysis is something found more commonly on the psychoanalysist's couch. Philosophically, Pinter does not believe that we know that much about ourselves, he believes we know even less about others, and that the communication between ourselves and others goes on in a much more subterranean way than most drama shows. In technical terms, this leads logically to Pinter's deliberate suppression of obvious motivation for his characters, which contributes more than anything else to the disconcerting strangeness of his plays, *vis-à-vis* the naturalistic theatre. As he says:

> We all have our function. The visitor will have his. There is no guarantee, however, that he will possess a visiting card with detailed information as to his last place of residence, last job, next job, number of dependants, etc. Nor, for the comfort of all, an identity card, nor a label on his chest. The desire for verification is understandable but cannot always be satisfied. There are no hard distinctions between what is real and what is unreal, nor between what is true and what is false. The thing is not necessarily either true or false; it can be both true and false. The assumption that to verify what has happened and what is happening presents few problems I take to be inaccurate. A character on the stage who can present no convincing argument or information as to his past experience, his present behaviour or his aspirations, nor give a comprehensive analysis of his motives is as legitimate and as worthy of attention as one who, alarmingly, can do all these things. The more acute the experience the less articulate its expression.[17]

Pinter's characters do not know each other, they want to find out about each other, and yet they do not want to give themselves away to others, because to reveal oneself to others is to place oneself in potentially hostile hands (as Aston finds when he reveals his experiences in the psychiatric hospital to Davies in *The Caretaker*), and it is to lose the hold that one's own mysteriousness gives one over others.

Language as a Weapon

This explains Pinter's brilliant, if initially baffling, handling of the dynamics of dialogue in his plays. His characters use language not so much as a direct means of communication, but as a smokescreen to hide behind, or — more commonly — as a weapon of aggression. When Stanley first meets the sinister Goldberg in *The Birthday Party*, this is what he is treated to:

> *Petey:* Oh hullo, Stan. You haven't met Stanley, have you, Mr Goldberg?
> *Goldberg:* I haven't had the pleasure.
> *Petey:* Oh well, this is Mr Goldberg, this is Mr Webber.
> *Goldberg:* Pleased to meet you.
> *Petey:* We were just getting a bit of air in the garden.
> *Goldberg:* I was telling Mr Boles about my old mum. What days. [*He sits at the table, right.*] Yes. When I was a youngster, of a Friday, I used to go for a walk down the canal with a girl who lived down my road. A beautiful girl. What a voice that bird had! A nightingale, my word of honour. Good? Pure? She wasn't a Sunday school teacher for nothing. Anyway, I'd leave her with a little kiss on the cheek — I never took liberties — we weren't like the young men these days in those days. We knew the meaning of respect. So I'd give her a peck and I'd bowl back home. Humming away I'd be, past the children's playground. I'd tip my hat to the toddlers, I'd give a helping hand to a couple of stray dogs, everything came natural. I can see it like yesterday. The sun falling behind the dog stadium. Ah! [*He leans back contentedly.*]

The comic irrelevance of this digression, the circumstantiality ('She wasn't a Sunday school teacher for nothing'), the barely veiled self-parody ('I'd tip my hat to the toddlers, I'd give a helping hand to a couple of stray dogs') — this is language functioning as a smokescreen. Goldberg's contented affability masks his designs on Stanley, and the never-ceasing articulateness of the whole thing is an oblique assertion of power.

The same sort of thing can be observed in nearly all of Mick's lengthy and circumstantial speeches to the hapless Davies in *The Caretaker* — the farrago of nonsense about London districts and bus-routes in Act 1, the interior designer's fantasy of the ideal home in Act 3 — these are not designed to convey information to Davies: this is Mick's way of asserting his superiority and power, manifested in the torrential and wholly spurious eloquence. It is a pervasive pattern in Pinter's plays, seen again in *The Homecoming* in Lenny's two long (and very funny) stories about the lady who made him 'a certain proposal', and the old lady who needed some help with her mangle. These do not at all explain why Ruth should let him hold her hand (the ostensible reason for the stories); they may not even be true. But it is what is being communicated beneath the surface of the words that is significant, Lenny's sense of his own machismo, his contempt for women, and his hostility to Ruth as a female intruder on his territory. Pinter's insight, as evidenced in these and other passages in his plays, into how human beings communicate, not through the conceptual content of their words but through the manner and context of their utterances, is one of his great dramatic strengths. It cannot be separated from his superbly dramatic use of silence and pauses, which is only bettered in the drama of Chekhov and Beckett. Here, for example, is the awful moment of truth for Davies, near the end of *The Caretaker*, when he realises that Mick is not going to protect him:

> *Mick:* I'm not worried about this house. I'm not interested. My brother can worry about it. He can do it up, he can decorate it, he can do what he likes with it. I'm not bothered. I thought I was doing him a favour, letting him live here. He's got his own ideas. Let him have them. I'm going to chuck it in.
> [*Pause.*]
> *Davies:* What about me?
> [*Silence. Mick does not look at him.*]
> [*A door bangs.*]
> [*Silence. They do not move.*]

Pinter's grasp of the fact that language can be used as an offensive weapon or as a form of camouflage, and his awareness that, paradoxically, silence may be a more intimate form of communication, shapes the rhythm of the dialogue in his plays. Once again, he himself describes it best:

> There are two silences. One when no word is spoken. The other when perhaps a torrent of language is employed. This speech is speaking of a language locked beneath it. That is its continual reference. The speech we hear is an indication of that we don't hear. It is a necessary avoidance, a violent, sly, anguished or mocking smokescreen which keeps the other in its place. When true silence falls we are still left with echo but are nearer nakedness. One way of looking at speech is to say it is a constant stratagem to cover nakedness.[18]

'The Weasel under the Cocktail Cabinet'

'The weasel under the cocktail cabinet' — Pinter's plays present vicious struggles for domination and survival, furious see-saws of aggression and submission in various relationships, the fight for territory. Hence 'weasel': human nature is seen as 'red in tooth and claw with ravine', as in the earlier plays of Strindberg such as *The Father* and *Miss Julie*. But Strindberg is very explicit in his treatment of antagonism, particularly sexual antagonism, whereas Pinter understands the ways in which people can use language obliquely, as a smokescreen. Hence the weasel is 'under the cocktail cabinet'. Peter Hall, discussing his successful direction of Pinter's plays, clarifies further this relationship between violence and concealment in the plays: 'My vocabulary is all the time about hostility and battles and weaponry, but that is the way Pinter's characters operate, as if they were all stalking round a jungle, trying to kill each other, but trying to disguise from one another the fact that they are bent on murder.'[19] Obviously not every character in Pinter is 'bent on murder', but the clash of wills and egotisms, the desire for domination, is a major feature of nearly all his work — 'the question of dominance and subservience', Pinter says, 'is possibly a repeated theme in my plays'.[20]

Dominance and Subservience in 'The Caretaker'

This repeated theme can be seen clearly in Pinter's most popular work, *The Caretaker*. Aston picks Davies up and offers him lodging out of charity, or perhaps just because he is in the habit of picking up pieces of junk (and Davies qualifies as a piece of human flotsam). Davies's suspicious yet obsequious, cowardly but aggressive nature prevents him from accepting Aston's proffered friendship (though not his room, his tobacco, and other gifts). Mick resents this intruder imposing on his soft brother, and decides to get rid of him. But he does not want to hurt or offend Aston by doing it too directly: there is some suggestion that Mick has let the room to his brother as a form of rehabilitation for him after his horrifying experiences in the psychiatric hospital; and therefore Mick does not want to interfere with Aston's independence too obviously.

By alternately bemusing and frightening Davies with his torrents of words, Mick gets Davies to feel that he (Mick) is the centre of power in the triangle, and to shift his 'allegiance' — never very strong — away from Aston back to Mick himself. Davies, feeling himself secure in the patronage of the stronger brother, starts asserting himself over the weaker, even cruelly abusing Aston about his time in the 'nut house'. Aston's tolerance, though great, is at last pushed too far and, gently enough, he tells Davies he had better go. Firm in his sense of collusion with Mick, Davies confidently seeks reassertion from Mick of his dominant position over Aston. Mick can now act, can now spring his trap, thanks to his own manoeuvring, and to Davies's hyena-like nature. He pays Davies off, brutally:

> You're violent, you're erratic, you're just completely un-predictable. You're nothing else but a wild animal, when you come down to it. You're a barbarian. And to put the old tin lid on it, you stink from arse-hole to breakfast time . . . It's all most regrettable but it looks as though I'm compelled to pay you off for your caretaking work. Here's half a dollar.

And so Davies loses the power game, and is last seen crawling submissively to the impassive Aston.

Dark Comedy

No critical account, of course, can convey the theatrical power with which this very basic situation — a territorial battle over a junk-filled room — is treated. Pinter's early experiences as an actor have given him an instinctive stage-understanding, everywhere evident in his dramatic rhythms and especially in his skill in manipulating a good strong curtain. But he is also a poetic dramatist in the same sort of way that Beckett is one. Perhaps in the end what is most distinctive in his work is its ability to blend a desperately bleak and unflattering vision of human nature with highly effective and stylish comedy, a comedy based on the elegance and precision of his language.

'Dark comedy' is a phrase which has been used to describe the mixture of moods in much twentieth-century drama. It applies to the work of Beckett; it applies also to the tragi-comic atmosphere of the plays of Sean O'Casey and Brecht. In *The Happening in the Bungalow* (1969), the Malaysian dramatist Lee Joo For (b. 1929) dramatises an explosive situation in which a colonial Englishman attempts to avenge the murder of an ancestor in the nineteenth century by threatening to kill his Malay girl-secretary and his Chinese neighbour. At the crucial moment a bizarre and disarming touch of comedy is introduced when he agrees to let his victims purify themselves for death according to their racial and religious customs. The girl needs to wash; the Chinese man has to invoke his twenty-four dead ancestors now residing in the Seventh Garden of Heaven. All this takes so long that the crassly drunken Englishman decides he needs another whisky, and almost loses control of the situation. It is an authentic modern tone; and that it is found in an Irishman resident in France (Beckett), a Malaysian, and an English Jew (Pinter), among many others, suggests the basic universality and comprehensibility of drama, its power to move and affect us, however wide our cultural divides.

References

Chapter 1

1. G. B. Tennyson, *An Introduction to Drama* (New York: Holt, Rinehart & Winston, 1967), p. 3; E. Bentley, *The Life of the Drama* (London: Methuen, 1965), p. 150; M. Boulton, *The Anatomy of Drama* (London: Routledge & Kegan Paul, 1960), p. 3.
2. Cited by E. T. Owen, 'Drama in Sophocles's *Oedipus Tyrannus*', in M. J. O'Brien (ed.) *Twentieth Century Interpretations of 'Oedipus Rex'* (Englewood Cliffs: Prentice-Hall, 1968), p. 30.
3. M. C. Bradbrook, *Elizabethan Stage Conditions* (Cambridge: Cambridge University Press, 1968), pp. 30, 34.
4. U. M. Ellis-Fermor, *The Frontiers of Drama* (London: Methuen, 1964), p. 77.
5. Maynard Mack, 'The Jacobean Shakespeare', *Stratford-upon-Avon Studies*, I (1960), p. 13.

Chapter 2

1. E. R. Dodds, 'On Misunderstanding the *Oedipus Rex*', in M. J. O'Brien (ed.), *Twentieth Century Interpretations of 'Oedipus Rex'* (Englewood Cliffs: Prentice-Hall, 1968), pp. 17–29.
2. Ibid., p. 19.
3. Ibid., p. 23.
4. A. J. A. Waldock, *Sophocles the Dramatist* (Cambridge: Cambridge University Press, 1966), p. 158.
5. H. D. F. Kitto, *Greek Tragedy: A Literary Study*, 3rd ed. (London: Methuen, 1961), p. 142.
6. Ibid., p. 145.

7. Thomas Gould, 'The Innocence of Oedipus', in O'Brien, op cit., pp. 106–7.
8. E. F. Watling (ed.), *Sophocles: The Theban Plays* (Harmondsworth: Penguin Books, 1947), p. 13.
9. A. Nicoll, *World Drama*, 2nd ed. (London: Harrap, 1976), p. 35.
10. W. B. Yeats, *Essays and Introductions* (London: Macmillan, 1969), p. 274.
11. H. D. F. Kitto, *Form and Meaning in Drama* (London: Methuen, 1960), p. 149.
12. Waldock, op. cit., p. 108.

Chapter 3

1. Helen Gardner, 'The Tragedy of Damnation', in R. J. Kaufmann (ed.), *Elizabethan Drama: Modern Essays in Criticism* (New York: Oxford University Press, 1961), p. 324.
2. W. W. Greg, 'The Damnation of Faustus', in Clifford Leech (ed.), *Marlowe: Twentieth Century Views* (Englewood Cliffs: Prentice-Hall, 1964), p. 96.
3. Samuel Johnson, *Prose and Poetry*, selected by M. Wilson (London: Hart-Davis, 1968), p. 838.
4. Roma Gill (ed.), *Doctor Faustus* (London: Ernest Benn, 1965), p. xxv.
5. R. B. Sewall, *The Vision of Tragedy* (New Haven: Yale University Press, 1959), p. 66.
6. A. Nicoll, *World Drama*, 2nd ed. (London: Harrap, 1976), p. 219.

Chapter 4

1. L. C. Knights, *Explorations* (Harmondsworth: Penguin Books, 1964, p. 30.
2. Fredson Bowers, *Elizabethan Revenge Tragedy 1587–1642* (Princeton: Princeton University Press, 1940), p. 72.
3. Maynard Mack, 'The World of *Hamlet*', in Cleanth Brooks (ed.), *Tragic Themes in Western Literature* (New Haven: Yale University Press, 1955), p. 53.
4. Willard Farnham, 'The Tragic Qualm', in A. Harbage (ed.), *Shakespeare, The Tragedies: Twentieth Century Views* (Englewood Cliffs: Prentice-Hall, 1964), p. 19.

5. A. C. Bradley, *Shakespearean Tragedy* (London: Macmillan, 1960), p. 215.
6. Ibid., p. 276.
7. G. I. Duthie (ed.), *King Lear* (Cambridge: Cambridge University Press, 1968), p. xxxiii.
8. See Luke 2:49: 'And he said unto them, How is it that ye sought me? wist ye not that I must be about my Father's business?' (Authorised Version).
9. Samuel Johnson, *Prose and Poetry*, selected by M. Wilson (London: Hart-Davis, 1968), p. 593.
10. Cited by George Steiner, *Language and Silence* (Harmondsworth: Penguin Books, 1967), p. 90.
11. W. H. Clemen, *The Development of Shakespeare's Imagery* (London: Methuen, 1966), p. 16.
12. Bradley, op. cit., p. 295.
13. C. F. E. Spurgeon, *Shakespeare's Imagery* (Cambridge: Cambridge University Press, 1965), pp. 325–7.

Chapter 5

1. L. C. Knights, 'Notes on Comedy', in P. Lauter (ed.), *Theories of Comedy* (New York: Doubleday, 1964), p. 432.
2. Stanley Wells (ed.), *A Midsummer Night's Dream* (Harmondsworth: Penguin Books, 1967), p. 24.
3. Northrop Frye, 'The Argument of Comedy', in D. A. Robertson, Jr (ed.), *English Institute Essays 1948* (New York: Columbia University Press, 1949), pp. 58–73.
4. G. Gregory Smith in J. A. Barish (ed.), *Jonson's 'Volpone': A Selection of Critical Essays* (London: Macmillan, 1972), p. 54.
5. S. Musgrove, 'Tragical Mirth: *King Lear* and *Volpone*', in Barish, ibid., pp. 118–32.
6. Cited by W. Sypher (ed.), *Comedy* (New York: Doubleday, 1956), pp. 63–4.
7. Gāmini Salgādo, *English Drama: A Critical Introduction* (London: Edward Arnold, 1980), p. 143. Salgādo regards this as a prejudiced, stereotyped view.

Chapter 6

1. The title of an essay on Ibsen by G. B. Shaw, published in 1891.

2. G. Steiner, *The Death of Tragedy* (London: Faber & Faber, paperback edition, 1963), p. 241.
3. John Northam, cited by James McFarlane (ed.), *Henrik Ibsen: A Critical Anthology* (Harmondsworth: Penguin Books, 1970), p. 269.
4. Ibid., pp. 82–3.
5. Ibid., p. 414.
6. Cited by R. Fjelde (ed.), *Ibsen: Twentieth Century Views* (Englewood Cliffs: Prentice-Hall, 1965), p. 93.
7. Steiner, op. cit., p. 274.
8. R. P. Draper (ed.), *Tragedy: Developments in Criticism* (London: Macmillan, 1980), p. 20.
9. Arthur Miller, *Collected Plays with an Introduction* (London: Cresset Press, 1958), p. 33.
10. Ibid., pp. 23, 26.
11. Ibid., p. 34.
12. Ibid., p. 54.
13. Mary McCarthy, cited by D. Welland, *Miller: A Study of his Plays* (London: Eyre Methuen, 1979), pp. 50–1.
14. Steiner, op. cit., p. 291.

Chapter 7
1. R. Hingley, *A New Life of Anton Chekhov* (London: Oxford University Press, 1976), p. 52.
2. M. H. Heim and S. Karlinsky (eds), *Letters of Anton Chekhov* (London: Bodley Head, 1973), p. 117.
3. Cited by R. Brustein, *The Theatre of Revolt* (London: Methuen, 1970), p. 142.
4. Hingley, op. cit., p. 302.
5. Brustein, op. cit., p. 178.

Chapter 8
1. R. Brustein, *The Theatre of Revolt* (London: Methuen, 1970), p. 185.
2. See Bruce R. Park, 'A Mote in the Critic's Eye: Bernard Shaw and Comedy', in R. J. Kaufmann (ed.), *G. B. Shaw: Twentieth Century Views* (Englewood Cliffs: Prentice-Hall, 1965), pp. 42–56.
3. L. Crompton, *Shaw the Dramatist* (Lincoln: Nebraska University Press, 1969), p. 75.

4. Kaufmann, op. cit., 'Introduction', p. 10.
5. Bertolt Brecht, 'Ovation for Shaw', in Kaufmann, op. cit., p. 17.
6. *Brecht on Theatre*, trans. J. Willett (London: Methuen, 1964), p. 248.
7. Cited by M. Esslin, *Brecht: A Choice of Evils* (London: Mercury, 1965), p. 15.
8. *Brecht on Theatre*, op. cit., p. 37.
9. B. Gascoigne, *Twentieth Century Drama* (London: Hutchinson, 1962), p. 123.
10. Brustein, op. cit., p. 271.
11. A. D. White, *Bertolt Brecht's Great Plays* (London: Macmillan, 1978), p. 93.
12. Hanns Eisler and Ronald Bryden, cited by White, ibid., p. 171.

Chapter 9

1. Hugh Kenner, *A Reader's Guide to Samuel Beckett* (London: Thames & Hudson, 1973), p. 155.
2. M. Esslin, *The Theatre of the Absurd*, 2nd ed. (Harmondsworth: Penguin Books, 1968).
3. C. Duckworth (ed.), *En Attendant Godot* (London: Harrap, 1966), p. xxxv.
4. See Eva Metman, 'Reflections on Samuel Beckett's Plays', in M. Esslin (ed.), *Beckett: Twentieth Century Views* (Englewood Cliffs: Prentice-Hall, 1965), p. 117.
5. J. Fletcher and J. Spurling, *Beckett: A Study of his Plays* (London: Eyre Methuen, 1972), p. 72.
6. Jean-Jacques Mayoux, 'Samuel Beckett and Universal Parody', in Esslin, *Twentieth Century Views*, op. cit., p. 77.
7. G. S Fraser in R. Cohn (ed.), *Casebook on 'Waiting for Godot'* (New York: Grove Press, 1967), p. 134.
8. *Proust* (London: Chatto & Windus, 1931; reprinted Calder, 1965), pp. 13, 19.
9. *Tynan on Theatre* (Harmondsworth: Penguin Books, 1964), pp. 36–7.
10. Exchange at a new writers' discussion group, cited by J. R. Taylor, *Anger and After: A Guide to the New British Drama* (Harmondsworth: Penguin Books, 1963), p. 285.

11. Radio interview of 1960, cited by M. Esslin, *Pinter: A Study of his Plays* (London: Eyre Methuen, 1973), p. 34.
12. Ibid., p. 35.
13. Ibid., p. 36.
14. Taylor, op. cit., pp. 288–9.
15. Franz Kafka, *Metamorphosis and Other Stories* (Harmondsworth: Penguin Books, 1961), p. 9.
16. Esslin, *Pinter*, op. cit., p. 39.
17. Pinter's programme note to the 1960 production of *The Room* and *The Dumb Waiter*, cited by Taylor, op. cit., pp. 300–1.
18. Pinter's lecture to a student drama festival in 1962, cited by Esslin, *Pinter*, op. cit., p. 46.
19. Catherine Itzin and Simon Trussler, 'Directing Pinter', *Theatre Quarterly*, XVI (Winter 1975), 4–17.
20. L. M. Bensky, 'Harold Pinter', in *Writers at Work: The Paris Review Interviews* (London: Secker & Warburg, 1968), p. 362.

Select Bibliography

General Works on Drama and the Stage

Bentley, E., *The Life of the Drama* (London: Methuen, 1965).

——, (ed.), *The Theory of the Modern Stage* (Harmondsworth: Penguin Books, 1968).

Boulton, M., *The Anatomy of Drama* (London: Routledge & Kegan Paul, 1960).

Bradbrook, M. C., *Elizabethan Stage Conditions* (Cambridge: Cambridge University Press, 1968).

Brook, P., *The Empty Space* (Harmondsworth: Penguin Books, 1972).

Brustein, R., *The Theatre of Revolt* (London: Methuen, 1970).

Dawson, S. W., *Drama and the Dramatic* (London: Methuen, 1970).

Draper, R. P. (ed.), *Tragedy: Developments in Criticism* (London: Macmillan, 1980).

Ellis-Fermor, U. M., *The Frontiers of Drama* (London: Methuen, 1964).

Gascoigne, B., *Twentieth Century Drama* (London: Hutchinson, 1962).

Hartnoll, P. (ed.), *The Oxford Companion to the Theatre*, 3rd ed. (London: Oxford University Press, 1967).

Hinchliffe, A. P. (ed.), *Drama Criticism: Developments since Ibsen* (London: Macmillan, 1979).

Lauter, P. (ed.), *Theories of Comedy* (New York: Doubleday, 1964).

Leech, C., *Tragedy* (London: Methuen, 1969).

Magarshack, D. (ed.), *Stanislavsky on the Art of the Stage* (London: Faber & Faber, 1950).

Merchant, W. M., *Comedy* (London: Methuen, 1972).

Nicoll, A., *The Development of the Theatre*, 2nd ed. (New York: Harcourt Brace Jovanovich, 1946).

———, *World Drama*, 2nd ed. (London: Harrap, 1976).

Nkosi, L., *Tasks and Masks: Themes and Styles of African Literature* (London: Longman, 1981).

Salgādo, G., *English Drama: A Critical Introduction* (London: Edward Arnold, 1980).

Sewall, R. B., *The Vision of Tragedy* (New Haven: Yale University Press, 1959).

Steiner, G., *The Death of Tragedy* (London: Faber & Faber, 1961).

Styan, J. L., *Drama, Stage and Audience* (Cambridge: Cambridge University Press, 1975).

———, *The Elements of Drama* (Cambridge: Cambridge University Press, 1960).

Sypher, W. (ed.), *Comedy* (New York: Doubleday, 1956).

Tennyson, G. B., *An Introduction to Drama* (New York: Holt, Rinehart & Winston, 1967).

Tynan, K., *Tynan on Theatre* (Harmondsworth: Penguin Books 1964).

Williams, R., *Drama in Performance* (Harmondsworth: Penguin Books, 1972).

———, *Drama from Ibsen to Brecht* (London: Chatto & Windus, 1968).

———, *Modern Tragedy* (London: Chatto & Windus, 1966).

Willett, J. (ed.), *Brecht on Theatre* (London: Methuen, 1964).

Individual Dramatists

The major works of each dramatist are given, followed by the text(s) used in this book, and a selection of critical studies.

Samuel Beckett (1906–); born in Dublin.

Major Works
Waiting for Godot (1952); *Endgame* (1957); *Krapp's Last Tape* (1958); *Happy Days* (1961).

Texts Used
Waiting for Godot (London: Faber & Faber, 1965).

Critical Studies
Alvarez, A., *Beckett* (London: Fontana/Collins, 1973).
Doherty, F., *Samuel Beckett* (London: Hutchinson, 1971).
Duckworth, C. (ed.), *En Attendant Godot* (London: Harrap, 1966).
———, *Dramatic Effect in Beckett and Ionesco* (London: Allen & Unwin, 1970).
Esslin, M., *The Theatre of the Absurd*, 2nd ed. (Harmondsworth: Penguin Books, 1968).
———, (ed.), *Beckett: Twentieth Century Views* (Englewood Cliffs: Prentice-Hall, 1965).
Fletcher, J., and Spurling, S., *Beckett: A Study of his Plays* (London: Eyre Methuen, 1972).
Hinchliffe, A. P., *The Absurd* (London: Methuen, 1969).

Bertolt Brecht (1898—1956); born at Augsburg in Germany.

Major Works
The Threepenny Opera (1928); *Mother Courage and her Children* (1941); *The Life of Galileo* (1943); *The Good Woman of Setzuan* (1943); *The Caucasian Chalk Circle* (1949). (The dates are approximate, due to Brecht's constant revisions.)

Texts Used
Mother Courage and her Children, ed. E. Bentley (London: Methuen, 1962); *Parables for the Theatre: 'The Good Woman of Setzuan' and 'The Caucasian Chalk Circle'*, ed. E. Bentley (Harmondsworth: Penguin Books, 1966).

Critical Studies
Demetz, P. (ed.), *Brecht: Twentieth Century Views* (Englewood Cliffs: Prentice-Hall, 1962).
Esslin, M., *Brecht: A Choice of Evils* (London: Mercury, 1965).
White A. D., *Bertolt Brecht's Great Plays* (London: Macmillan, 1978).
Willett, J. (ed.), *The Messingkauf Dialogues* (London: Methuen, 1965).

_____ , (ed.), *Bertolt Brecht on Theatre* (London: Methuen, 1964).

Anton Chekhov (1860–1904); born near Moscow.

Major Works
The Seagull (1896); *Uncle Vanya* (1899); *Three Sisters* (1901); *The Cherry Orchard* (1904).

Text Used
Chekhov: *'Uncle Vanya', 'The Cherry Orchard' and 'The Wood Demon'*, ed. R. Hingley (London: Oxford University Press, 1965).

Critical Studies
Hahn, B., *Chekhov: A Study of the Major Stories and Plays* (Cambridge: Cambridge University Press, 1977).
Hingley, R., *A New Life of Anton Chekhov* (London: Oxford University Press, 1976).
Jackson, R. L. (ed.), *Chekhov: Twentieth Century Views* (Englewood Cliffs: Prentice-Hall, 1967).
Pitcher, H., *The Chekhov Play: A New Interpretation* (London: Chatto & Windus, 1973).
Styan, J. L., *Chekhov in Performance* (Cambridge: Cambridge University Press, 1971).
Valency, M., *The Breaking String* (London: Oxford University Press, 1966).

Athol Fugard (1932–); born in Middelburg, South Africa.

Major Works
The Blood Knot (1961); *Hello and Goodbye* (1965); *Boesman and Lena* (1969); *Sizwe Bansi is Dead* (1972); *The Island* (1974).

Texts Used
'Boesman and Lena' and Other Plays (London: Oxford University Press, 1978); *Statements: Three Plays* (London: Oxford University Press, 1974).

Critical Studies
Green, R. J., 'South Africa's Plague: One View of *The Blood Knot'*, *Modern Drama* (February 1970), 331—45.
———, 'Athol Fugard's *Hello and Goodbye*', *Modern Drama* (September 1970), 139—55.
Heywood, C. (ed.), *Aspects of South African Literature* (London: Heinemann, 1976).
Woodrow, M., 'South African Drama in English', *English Studies in Africa*, XIII, 2 (Autumn 1970), 391—410.

Henrik Ibsen (1828—1906), born at Skien, in Norway.

Major Works
Brand (1866); *Peer Gynt* (1867); *A Doll's House* (1879); *Ghosts* (1881); *The Wild Duck* (1884); *Rosmersholm* (1886); *Hedda Gabler* (1890); *The Master Builder* (1892).

Text Used
Hedda Gabler, ed. M. Meyer (London: Eyre Methuen, 1974).

Critical Studies
Downs, B., *A Study of Six Plays by Ibsen* (Cambridge: Cambridge University Press, 1950).
Fjelde, R. (ed.), *Ibsen: Twentieth Century Views* (Englewood Cliffs: Prentice-Hall, 1965).
McFarlane, J. (ed.), *Henrik Ibsen: A Critical Anthology* (Harmondsworth: Penguin Books, 1970).
Northam, J., *Ibsen's Dramatic Method* (London: Faber & Faber, 1953).

Ben Jonson (1572—1637); born in London.

Major Works
Every Man in His Humour (1598); *Every Man Out of His Humour* (1599); *Volpone* (1606); *Epicoene, or The Silent Woman* (1609); *The Alchemist* (1610); *Bartholomew Fair* (1614).

Text Used
Ben Jonson, *Three Comedies: 'Volpone', 'The Alchemist',
'Bartholomew Fair'*, ed. M. Jamieson (Harmondsworth:
Penguin Books, 1966).

Critical Studies
Bamborough, J. B., *Ben Jonson* (London: Hutchinson, 1970).
Barish, J. A. (ed.), *Jonson's 'Volpone': A Selection of Critical
Essays* (London: Macmillan, 1972).
──── (ed.), *Jonson: Twentieth Century Views* (Englewood
Cliffs: Prentice-Hall, 1963).
Enck, J. J., *Jonson and the Comic Truth* (Madison: Wisconsin
University Press, 1957).
Knights, L. C., *Drama and Society in the Age of Jonson*
(London: Chatto & Windus, 1937).

*Christopher Marlowe (1564–93); born at Canterbury in
England.*

Major Works
Tamburlaine (1587); *The Jew of Malta* (1589); *Dr Faustus*
(1592); *Edward II* (1592). (The dates of Marlowe's plays are
much disputed.)

Text Used
Dr Faustus, ed. Roma Gill (London: Ernest Benn, 1965).

Critical Studies
Leech, C. (ed.), *Marlowe: Twentieth Century Views* (Engle-
wood Cliffs: Prentice-Hall, 1964).
Levin, H., *The Overreacher: A Study of Christopher Marlowe*
(London: Faber & Faber, 1954).
Mahood, M. M., 'Marlowe's Heroes', in *Poetry and Humanism*
(New Haven: Yale University Press, 1950).
Sanders, W., *The Dramatist and the Received Idea* (Cambridge:
Cambridge University Press, 1968).
Steane, J. B., *Marlowe: A Critical Study* (Cambridge:
Cambridge University Press, 1964).

Arthur Miller (1915–); born in New York.

Major Works
All My Sons (1947); Death of a Salesman (1949); The Crucible (1952); A View from the Bridge (1955); The Price (1968).

Text Used
Death of a Salesman (Harmondsworth: Penguin Books, 1961).

Critical Studies
Corrigan, R. W. (ed.), *Arthur Miller: Twentieth Century Views* (Englewood Cliffs: Prentice-Hall, 1969).
Welland, D., *Miller: A Study of his Plays* (London: Eyre Methuen, 1979).

Harold Pinter (1930–); born in London.

Major Works
The Birthday Party (1958); The Caretaker (1960); The Homecoming (1965); Old Times (1971); No Man's Land (1975).

Texts Used
The Birthday Party (London: Methuen, 1960); *The Caretaker* (London: Methuen, 1962); *The Homecoming* (London: Methuen, 1965).

Critical Studies
Esslin, M., *Pinter: A Study of his Plays* (London: Eyre Methuen, 1973).
Hayman, R., *Harold Pinter* (London: Heinemann, 1968).
Taylor, J. R., *Anger and After: A Guide to the New British Drama* (Harmondsworth: Penguin Books, 1963).
Trussler, S., *The Plays of Harold Pinter: An Assessment* (London: Gollancz, 1973).

William Shakespeare (1564–1616); born in Stratford-upon-Avon.

Major Works
Richard II (1595); *A Midsummer Night's Dream* (1595?);
Henry IV, parts 1 and 2 (1597—8); *Much Ado About Nothing*
(1598?); *Julius Caesar* (1599); *As You Like It* (1599); *Twelfth
Night* (1600?); *Hamlet* (1601); *Othello* (1604?); *King Lear*
(1606?); *Macbeth* (1606?); *Antony and Cleopatra* (1607);
The Tempest (1612).

Text Used
William Shakespeare: The Complete Works, ed. P. Alexander
(London: Collins, 1951).

Critical Studies
There is such a large number of books on Shakespeare that
the student is referred to four convenient anthologies of
critical essays, each of which contains extensive bibliographies.
Also listed are two useful books on Shakespeare and the stage.

Harbage, A. (ed.), *Shakespeare, The Tragedies: Twentieth
Century Views* (Englewood Cliffs: Prentice-Hall, 1964).
Lerner, L. (ed.), *Shakespeare's Comedies: An Anthology of
Modern Criticism* (Harmondsworth: Penguin Books, 1967).
_____ (ed.), *Shakespeare's Tragedies: An Anthology of Modern
Criticism* (Harmondsworth: Pelican, 1963).
Muir, K. (ed.), *Shakespeare, the Comedies: Twentieth Century
Views* (Englewood Cliffs: Prentice-Hall, 1965).
Brown, J. R., *Shakespeare's Plays in Performance* (Harmonds-
worth: Penguin Books, 1966).
Styan, J. L., *Shakespeare's Stagecraft* (Cambridge: Cambridge
University Press, 1967).

George Bernard Shaw (1856—1950); born in Dublin.

Major Works
Arms and the Man (1894); *Mrs. Warren's Profession* (1894);
Man and Superman (1903); *Major Barbara* (1905); *Pygmalion*
(1912); *Heartbreak House* (1921); *Saint Joan* (1923).

Texts Used
Man and Superman (Harmondsworth: Penguin Books, 1946);
Major Barbara (Harmondsworth: Penguin Books, 1960); *Mrs.
Warren's Profession* (Harmondsworth: Penguin Books, 1970).

Critical Studies
Bentley, E., *Bernard Shaw*, 2nd ed. (London: Methuen, 1967).
Crompton, L., *Shaw the Dramatist* (Lincoln: Nebraska University Press, 1969).
Gibbs, A. M., *Shaw* (Edinburgh: Oliver & Boyd, 1969).
Kaufmann, R. J. (ed.), *G. B. Shaw: Twentieth Century Views* (Englewood Cliffs: Prentice-Hall, 1965).

Sophocles (c. 496–406 BC); born at Colonus in Greece.

Major Works
Ajax (*c.* 440 BC); *Antigone* (*c.* 442 BC); *Oedipus the King* (*c.* 427 BC); *Electra* (*c.* 418 BC); *Philoctetes* (409 BC); *Oedipus at Colonus* (presented posthumously, 401 BC).

Text Used
Sophocles: The Theban Plays ed. E. F. Watling (Harmondsworth: Penguin Books, 1947).

Critical Studies
Bowra, C. M., *Sophoclean Tragedy* (London: Oxford University Press, 1944).
Kitto, H. D. F., *Form and Meaning in Drama* (London: Methuen, 1960).
——, *Greek Tragedy: A Literary Study*, 3rd ed. (London: Methuen, 1961).
Knox, B. M. W., *Oedipus at Thebes* (New Haven: Yale University Press, 1957).
O'Brien, M. J. (ed.), *Twentieth Century Interpretations of 'Oedipus Rex'* (Englewood Cliffs: Prentice-Hall, 1968).
Waldock, A. J. A., *Sophocles the Dramatist* (Cambridge: Cambridge University Press, 1966).

Wole Soyinka (1934–); born at Abeokuta in Nigeria.

Major Works
The Lion and the Jewel (1958); *A Dance of the Forests* (1960); *The Road* (1965); *Kongi's Harvest* (1967); *Madmen and Specialists* (1970).

Text Used
Wole Soyinka, *Collected Plays*, vols I and II (London: Oxford University Press, 1973—4).

Critical Studies
Dathorne, O. R., *African Literature in the Twentieth Century* (London: Heinemann, 1974).
Jones, E. D., *The Writings of Wole Soyinka* (London: Heinemann, 1973).
King, B., *A Celebration of Black and African Writing* (London: Oxford University Press, 1976).
———, *Introduction to Nigerian Literature* (New York: Evans, Holmes & Meier, 1972).
———, *The New English Literature* (London: Macmillan, 1980).
Laurence, M., *Long Drums and Cannons: Nigerian Dramatists and Novelists, 1952—66* (London: Macmillan, 1968).
Soyinka, W., *Myth, Literature and the African World* Cambridge: Cambridge University Press, 1976).

Other Dramatic Texts Used

Bateson, F. W. (ed.), R. B. Sheridan, *The School for Scandal* (London: Ernest Benn, 1979).

Clark, J. P., *The Ozidi Saga* (Ibadan: Ibadan University Press, 1977).

Cook, D., and Lee, M. (eds.), *Short East African Plays in English* (Nairobi: Heinemann, 1968).

Davis, T. (ed.), Oliver Goldsmith, *She Stoops to Conquer* (London: Ernest Benn, 1979).

Duthie, E. (ed.), R. B. Sheridan, *The Rivals* (London: Ernest Benn, 1979).

Fernando, L. (ed.), K. Das, Edward Dorall, Lee Joo For and Patrick Yeoh in *New Drama*, 2 vols., Oxford in Asia Modern Authors Series (Kuala Lumpur: Oxford University Press, 1972).

Gibbs, J. (ed.), *Nine Malawian Plays* (Lilongwe: Likuni Press, 1975).

Molière, *'The Misanthrope' and Other Plays*, translated with an introduction by John Wood (Harmondsworth: Penguin Books, 1959).

―――, *'The Miser' and Other Plays*, translated with an introduction by John Wood (Harmondsworth: Penguin Books, 1953).

O'Casey, Sean, *Three Plays* (London: Macmillan, 1966).

Salgādo, G. (ed.), *Three Restoration Comedies* (Harmondsworth: Penguin Books, 1968).

Wilde, Oscar, *Plays* (Harmondsworth: Penguin Books, 1954).

Index

Major discussions of authors or
plays are printed in **bold**.

Adamov, Arthur   172
Arden, John   9
  Sergeant Musgrave's Dance
    9–10
Aristotle   12, 22–3, 159–61,
  165
  The Poetics   12, 22
Augustine   175
Austen, Jane   109
  Northanger Abbey   109

Barish, J. A.   200
Beckett, Samuel   6, 8, 12–13,
  67, 139, **171–85**, 187–8,
  194, 197, 202
  Endgame   171–2, 202
  Waiting for Godot   12–13,
    171–85, 187–8, 202
Bensky, L. M.   203
Bentley, E.   1, 198
Bergson, Henri   100
Blake, William   155
  *The Marriage of Heaven and
    Hell*   155
Boddy, Michael   185
  The Legend of King O'Malley
    185
Boulton, M.   1, 198
Bowers, F.   57, 199
Bradbrook, M. C.   5, 198
Bradley, A. C.   64, 66, 73, 200
Brecht, Bertolt   6, 8, 12, 147,
  156–70, 171–2, 185,
  197, 202

The Caucasian Chalk Circle
  157, 162, 164
The Good Woman of Setzuan
  12, **157–60**, 162–3
The Life of Galileo   157, 162
*Mother Courage and Her
  Children*   8, 157–8,
    161–3, **164–70**
Brooks, C.   199
Brustein, R.   139, 149, 164,
  201–2
Bryden, R.   170, 202
Buso, Alexander   14
  The Front-Room Boys   14
  *Coralie Lansdowne Says
    'No'*   14

Chaplin, Charlie   184
Chekhov, Anton   5, 9, 13, 33,
  132–46, 147, 158,
  194, 201
  The Cherry Orchard   9, 13,
    132–46
Cicero   92–3
Clark, John P.   2
  The Ozidi Saga   2
Clemen, W. H.   72, 200
Cohn, R.   202
Coleridge, Samuel Taylor   40
Congreve, William   106–8
  Love for Love   106
  The Way of the World
    106–7
Crompton, L.   153, 201

Darwin, Charles   152
Das, K.   3
  Lela Mayang   3

Dickens, Charles   11, 138, 148
   Hard Times   148
Dodds, E. R.   23, 25, 28, 198
Dorall, Edward   64, 130, 137
   The Hour of the Dog   130
   A Tiger is Loose in Our
     Community   64, 137
Draper, R. P.   124–5, 201
Duckworth, C.   202
Duthie, G. I.   66, 200

Easmon, Sarif   7
   The New Patriots   7
Eisler, Hanns   170, 202
Eliot, George   116
Eliot, T. S.   16, 50
   The Waste Land   50
Ellis, Bob   185
   The Legend of King O'Malley
     185
Ellis-Fermor, U. M.   16, 198
Esslin, M.   172, 202–3
Etherege, George   105–6
   The Man of Mode   105–7

Farnham, W.   62, 199
Fielding, Henry   11
Fjelde, R.   201
Fletcher, J.   202
For, Lee Joo   197
   The Happening in the
     Bungalow   197
Forster, E. M.   154–5
   Howards End   154
Fraser, G. S.   175, 202
Frye, N.   89, 200
Fugard, Athol   6, 14, 30
   The Blood Knot   6
   Boesman and Lena   6–7
   The Island   30
   Sizwe Bansi Is Dead   14

Gardner, H.   42, 199
Gascoigne, B.   164, 202
Genet, Jean   172
Gill, R.   44–5, 199
Goldsmith, Oliver   108–9
   She Stoops to Conquer   109

Gould, T.   30, 199
Graft, J. C. de   7
   Sons and Daughters   7
Greg, W. W.   42, 199

Hall, P.   195, 203
Hampton, Christopher   3
   Savages   3
Harbage, A.   199
Hardy, Oliver   184
Hardy, Thomas   11
Hegel, G. W. F.   31–2
Heim, M. H.   201
Hewett, Dorothy   185
   The Chapel Perilous   185
Hibberd, Jack   14
   A Stretch of the Imagination
     14
Hingley, R.   132–3, 139, 201
Hitler, Adolf   157

Ibsen, Henrik   5–7, 12, 32–3,
   50, **112–25**, 132, 135–6,
   147, 159–60, 163, 174,
   192, 200–1
   Brand   115
   A Doll's House   50, 112, 115
   Emperor and Galilean   113
   Ghosts   112, 115
   Hedda Gabler   6, 32, **114–25**,
     127, 136, 160
   Pillars of the Community
     112
   When We Dead Awake   115
   The Wild Duck   12, 124
Ionesco, Eugene   171–2
   The Bald Prima Donna   172
Itzin, C.   203

James, Henry   11
Johnson, Samuel   43, 58, 70,
   199–200
Jonson, Ben   5, **92–102**, 200
   The Alchemist   92–3, 101,
     110
   Bartholomew Fair   92
   Every Man in His Humour
     92

Every Man Out of His Humour 92
Volpone 92—102, 103, 108, 110, 136, 200

Kafka, Franz 67, 71, 189—90, 203
Metamorphosis 190—1, 203
The Trial 189
Kamlongera, C. F. 2
Karlinsky, S. 201
Kaufmann, R. J. 156, 199, 201—2
Keaton, Buster 184
Kenner, Hugh 171, 202
Kironde, Erisa 3
The Trick 3
Kitto, H. D. F. 28, 35, 198—9
Knight, G. Wilson 50
Knights, L. C. 50, 81, 199—200
Kyd, Thomas 57, 60
The Spanish Tragedy 57, 60

Laurel, Stan 184
Lauter, P. 200
Lawler, Ray 130
Summer of the Seventeenth Doll 130
Lawrence, D. H. 149
Leech, C. 199
Littlewood, Joan 184
Oh! What a Lovely War! 184—5

McCarthy, Mary 130, 201
McFarlane, J. 201
Mack, M. 62, 198—9
Marlowe, Christopher 5, 12, 15, 40—8, 49, 199
Dr Faustus 12, 15, 40—8, 49, 199
Tamburlaine 40—1
Marx, Karl 147, 157—9
Mayoux, Jean-Jacques 174, 202
Metman, E. 202
Miller, Arthur 125—31, 132, 174, 192, 201
Death of a Salesman 125—30, 132, 174

Milton, John 43, 71
Paradise Lost 43
Samson Agonistes 71
Molière 102—7
Le Bourgeois Gentilhomme 103
L'Ecole des Femmes 107
Les Précieuses Ridicules 103
Tartuffe 102—3
The Misanthrope 103—4, 107
Morality Plays 41, 164
Everyman 41
Mosiwa, J. 2
Musgrove, S. 96, 200

Ng'ombe, James 2, 164
The Beauty of Dawn 164
Nicoll, A. 32, 48, 199
Nietzsche, Friedrich 152
Northam, J. 113, 123, 201

O'Brien, M. J. 198
O'Casey, Sean 3, 5, 10, 137, 163, 197
Juno and the Paycock 10, 137
The Plough and the Stars 10—11, 137
The Shadow of a Gunman 137
The Silver Tassie 3
Omara, Tom 3
The Exodus 3
O'Neill, Eugene 173
Osborne, John 186
Look Back in Anger 186
Owen, E. T. 1, 198

Park, B. R. 201
Pinter, Harold 8, 13, 139, 186—97, 202—3
Betrayal 187
The Birthday Party 186—90, 193
The Caretaker 13—14, 186, 192, 194, 196
The Dumb Waiter 203

The Homecoming   187, 194
No Man's Land   187
Old Times   187
The Room   203
Pirandello, Luigi   6, 112, 171
Plato   149—50, 153
Proust, Marcel   179—80, 202

Restoration Comedy   9, 14,
    104—8
Robertson Jr, D. A.   200
Robins, E.   120
Romeril, John   130
    The Floating World   130—1

Salgãdo, G.   105, 200, 205
Schopenhauer, Arthur   125
Serumaga, Robert   2
    Renga Moi   2
Sewall, R. B.   47, 199
Seymour, Alan   130
    The One Day of the Year
    130
Shaffer, Peter   3
    Equus   3
    The Royal Hunt of the Sun   3
Shakespeare, William   3, 5,
    8—9, 11, 18, 24—5, 33,
    40, 45, 47—8, 49—91,
    92—3, 100, 102, 107,
    109, 112—13, 152, 162,
    185, 198—200
    Antony and Cleopatra   5, 16
    As you Like It   3, 89, 91
    Hamlet   9, 11, 25, 40, 49,
    50—62, 63, 67, 71, 76,
    124, 185, 199
    Henry IV (Falstaff)   164,
    169
    King Lear   5, 8, 16, 24—5,
    49, 62—71, 76, 86—7, 96,
    136, 174, 200
    Macbeth   12, 16, 18, 24—5,
    47, 49—50, 52, 71, 72—9,
    86—7, 124
    Merchant of Venice   89

A Midsummer Night's Dream
    3, 11, **81—91**, 185, 200
Much Ado About Nothing
    107, 152
Othello   8, 11—12, 16—17,
    128, 185
Romeo and Juliet   90
Twelfth Night   9, 21, 91—2
A Winter's Tale   89
Shaw, George Bernard   6,
    111—12, 138, 147—57,
    158, 171, 200—2
    Arms and the Man   147
    Back to Methuselah   153
    Candida   149
    Heartbreak House   148, 154
    Major Barbara   148, 153,
    154—7
    Man and Superman   147—50,
    151—4
    Mrs Warren's Profession   150
    *The Quintessence of
    Ibsenism*   147, 200
Sheridan, R. B.   108—10
    The Rivals   109—10
    The School for Scandal   110
Sillitoe, Alan   186
    *Saturday Night and Sunday
    Morning*   186
Smith, G. Gregory   95, 200
Sophocles   4—5, 9, 17,
    19—38, 39, 198—9
    Antigone   5, 9, 30—8, 39
    Oedipus   17, 19—30, 38—9,
    51, 63, 67, 128, 198—9
Soyinka, Wole   2—3, 7, 15,
    17, 63, 107, 137
    A Dance of the Forests   3,
    15, 137
    Kongi's Harvest   7—8, 15—16
    The Lion and the Jewel
    17—18, 107—8
    Madmen and Specialists   63
    The Road   2
    The Strong Breed   63
Spurgeon, C.   78, 200
Spurling, J.   202
Stanislavsky, K.   138—9

Steiner, G.   113, 124, 200–1
Stoppard, Tom   111
Storey, David   186
   This Sporting Life   186
Strindberg, August   171, 190,
   195
   Dream Play   190
   The Father   195
   The Ghost Sonata   190
   Miss Julie   195
Synge, J. M.   3, 15
   *The Playboy of the Western
    World*   15
   Riders to the Sea   3
   The Shadow of the Glen   3
Sypher, W.   200

Taylor, J. R.   189, 202–3
Tennyson, G. B.   1, 198
Thackeray, W. M.   11
Thiong'o, Ngugi wa   8
   The Black Hermit   8
Tourneur, Cyril   60
   The Revenger's Tragedy   60

Trussler, S.   203
Tynan, K.   182, 202

Waldock, A. J. A.   28, 37,
   198–9
Watling, E. F.   31, 199
Welland, D.   201
Wells, S.   86, 200
Wesker, Arnold   186
   Chips with Everything   186
White, A. D.   167, 202
Wilde, Oscar   14, 110–11
   *The Importance of Being
    Earnest*   14, 110–11
Willett, J.   202
Wilson, M.   199–200
Wycherley, William   107–8
   The Country Wife   107–8
   The Plain Dealer   107

Yeats, W. B.   3, 33, 63, 123,
   199
Yeoh, Patrick   7
   The Need to Be   7